NTC's
Dictionary
of
COMMON
MISTAKES
in
SPANISH

John Pride

NTC Publishing Group

Library of Congress Cataloging-in-Publication Data
is available from the United States Library of Congress

Published by NTC Publishing Group
A division of NTC/Contemporary Publishing Group, Inc.
4255 West Touhy Avenue, Lincolnwood (Chicago), Illinois 60646-1975 U.S.A.
Copyright © 1995 by NTC/Contemporary Publishing Group, Inc.
Printed in the United States of America
Library of Congress Catalog Number: 95-175688
International Standard Book Number: 0-8442-7255-8 (cloth)
                                                                    0-8442-7252-3 (paper)
18   17   16   15   14   13   12   11   10   9   8   7   6   5   4   3   2   1

Introduction

The Purpose of the Book

The purpose of *NTC's Dictionary of Common Mistakes in Spanish* is to provide English-speaking learners of Spanish with a reference guide to those words and phrases which can so easily cause difficulties and confusion. It is quick and easy to use, and will enable learners to select the appropriate Spanish terms for the situations they find themselves in.

For ease of use and access, the entries in the book are presented in alphabetical order in English, just like a dictionary. But the words and phrases chosen for inclusion are those that are most likely to cause learners problems in everyday situations. The examples are carefully selected to alert learners to common errors, anglicisms, and false cognates. Personal, social, and business terms are all included so that the basic needs of learners of all kinds are met. Idioms are difficult to contend with in another language, and there is a wide range of idiomatic Spanish included to help learners cope with English concepts which are difficult to translate into another language. There are also some brief notes to draw attention to essential grammar rules. It should be noted that examples involving the word "you" are rendered by the *tú* form in Spanish, except where the phrase would normally be used to a stranger, or is of a very formal nature; in such cases the *usted* form is used.

NTC's Dictionary of Common Mistakes in Spanish can be used for individual study or in the classroom. It will be useful for learners at all levels of proficiency and in particular for those who are planning a trip to a Spanish-speaking country.

Latin American Spanish

Just as there are differences between the English of the USA, Canada, Britain, Australia, and the other English-speaking countries, there are also differences in the Spanish spoken in Spain and the various countries of North, Central, and South America. This has been taken fully into account in this book. The abbreviation *[LA]* following an entry indicates that the word is used throughout most or all of Spanish America, but not in Spain. Terms which are country-specific are likewise indicated.
(See the list of abbreviations on page vi.)

How to Use This Book

For browsing

Pick out the words and phrases you particularly want or need to use. Mark them in some suitable way so that you can find them easily.

You will probably find as you go through the book that you have been using expressions that are not authentically Spanish. You should pay special attention to these. After some entries there is a line or two introduced by the warning symbol Ø. This symbol indicates words that look very similar in both English and Spanish but have quite different meanings. They are the real *amigos falsos* (false friends). As an example, *el suceso* means "happening" and not "success;" "success" is *el éxito* which does not mean "exit."

For practice

As an English speaker, it is much easier for you to read or understand Spanish than to express yourself clearly in that language. There are words you recognize when you see or hear them, but are not part of your working, spoken vocabulary. It is often possible to guess unknown words from the context. However, when you want to speak Spanish, there is no substitute for knowledge; guessing won't do. By using the wrong word or phrase, not only might you be totally misunderstood, but you might even insult the person you are talking to!

A regular study plan will help you make excellent use of this text. Start with the entries you have marked for special attention, or pick a section you particularly want to learn. Repeat the Spanish aloud until you master it. A few days later, return to it, cover the Spanish side and see if you can recall the key phrases. You will find your fluency will improve with practice. The more regular and systematic your practice, the more successful the results.

For quick reference

If you are looking for a common word or expression, turn to this book before going to a standard bilingual dictionary. There is a good chance you will find what you need here. All the entries are presented in context, in both Spanish and English, to help you make the right choice and steer you away from errors. When you need to look up an English word in an English-Spanish dictionary, make sure you check the options available. If you are unsure about your choice, check in the Spanish-English section to make certain you pick the right word. In this way you can avoid major blunders such as: *Compró un tapón para la lámpara.* The word for an "electrical plug" is *un enchufe; tapón* refers to the plug you use in the bathtub or wash basin.

If you consult a Spanish dictionary or alphabetical vocabulary published before 1994, you will find that *ch* and *ll* are listed as separate letters of the alphabet, coming between *c* and *d*, and *l* and *m* respectively. This is now no longer the case.

For choosing the right word

Quite often the same English word may be translated into Spanish in a number of different ways, depending on context. In this book you will find a range of possibilities and clear examples to illustrate the various uses. For example, under the entry for the word *time*, you will find seven subheadings that will guide you to the correct choice. Examples of usage include:

"Have a good time!" *(¡Que lo pases bien!);* "What time is it?" *(¿Qué hora es?);* "from time to time" *(de vez en cuando);* "a long time ago" *(hace mucho tiempo);* "at the time of the Incas" *(en la época de los incas);* "at this time of the year" *(en esta estación del año).*

For identifying the part of speech

When you look up a word it is useful to know what part of speech it is. Be aware of English words that may be two different parts of speech.

Some examples:

help (verb) "to help somebody" *ayudar a alguien*
help (noun) "I need your help." *Necesito tu ayuda.*
half (adjective) "half a dozen eggs" *media docena de huevos*
half (noun) "I paid half of the cost." *Pagué la mitad del coste.*
hard (adjective) "This bread is hard." *Este pan es duro.*
hard (adverb) "She works hard." *Trabaja mucho.*
long (adjective) "It's a long trip." *Es un viaje largo.*
long (verb) "I long to go back to Chicago." *Anhelo volver a Chicago.*

When you look up a verb it is sometimes necessary to know if it is transitive (can take an object) or intransitive (cannot take an object). Examples:

move *(verb trans)* "They moved the piano." *Movieron el piano.*
move *(verb intrans)* "He moved to Lima." *Se trasladó a Lima.*

A note about prepositions

Prepositions are often used very differently in English and Spanish. For example, depending on context, "for" could be translated as *para, por,* or *de.* If you are not sure, pause for a moment to check your choice. Every preposition entry in this dictionary gives a broad selection of phrases illustrating Spanish usage, for example: "at home" *(en casa);* "at two o'clock" *(a las dos);* "at night" *(de noche);* "by hand" *(a mano);* "by airmail" *(por avión).*

Take it everywhere you go!

Take *NTC's Dictionary of Common Mistakes in Spanish* with you wherever you go — to class, the beach, the office. Consult it often to review phrases that you want to remember when speaking or writing. And of course, make sure you have it with you when you visit a Spanish-speaking country. Don't pack it! Keep it in your hand luggage!

Abbreviations

adj	adjective	masc	masculine
adv	adverb	masc pl	masculine plural
art	article	masc sing	masculine singular
conj	conjunction	n	noun
dem	demonstrative	pl	plural
excl	exclamation	prep	preposition
fam	familiar	pron	pronoun
fem	feminine	sing	singular
fem pl	feminine plural	v	verb
fem sing	feminine singular	v intrans	verb intransitive
fig	figurative	v trans	verb transitive
inter	interrogative		

Parts of speech

Please note that the part of speech indicated for each entry is for the English word. The Spanish equivalent will not necessarily be the same part of speech as the English.

Abbreviations used in the examples

sb   somebody
sth   something

Ø   warning symbol

Abbreviations used for the Spanish-speaking countries and areas

Arg	Argentina	Gua	Guatemala
Bol	Bolivia	LA	Latin America
Car	Caribbean	Mex	Mexico
Chi	Chile	Per	Peru
Col	Colombia	Sp	Spain
Ecu	Ecuador	Uru	Uruguay
ES	El Salvador	Ven	Venezuela

A

a *n*
[the letter a]

la a [Note: all letters take the feminine article]

a/an *art*
a(n)
a pencil/a house
a housewife/an axe

un [masculine] una [feminine]
un lápiz/una casa
un ama de casa/un hacha [Note: **Un** is used in place of **una** before feminine nouns beginning with a stressed **a** or **ha**.]

rate
The car was traveling at 80 kilometers an hour.
Gas costs one dollar a gallon here.
How much a kilo are the oranges?
It will cost five dollars a meter.
He visits his mother twice a week.
She used to earn 1000 pesos a week.

El carro iba a 80 kilómetros por hora.
Aquí la gasolina cuesta un dólar por galón.
¿Cuánto cuestan por kilo las naranjas?
Costará cinco dólares por metro.
Visita a su madre dos veces a la/por semana.
Ganaba mil pesos por semana.

with nationality, profession, religion
Are you an American?
His wife is Canadian.

¿Eres norteamericano(a)?
Su esposa es canadiense. [Note: no article]

She is a lawyer.
She is a brilliant lawyer.

Es abogada. [Note: no article]
Es una abogada brillante. [Note:use of article when noun is modified.]

Are they Christians or Jews?
Is he a Catholic or a Protestant?

¿Son cristianos o judíos?
¿Es católico o protestante? [Note:no article]

omitted
Does he have a car?
They don't have a house.
I'll wait half an hour.

¿Tiene carro?
No tienen casa.
Esperaré media hora.

ability *n*
[skill]
He doesn't have the ability to do it.
[general ability]
My son has a lot of ability.
to the best of one's ability
I did it to the best of my ability.
to have the ability to do sth

la habilidad/la capacidad
No tiene la habilidad de hacerlo.
el talento
Mi hijo tiene mucho talento.
lo mejor que se pueda/sepa
Lo hice lo mejor que pudiera/supiera.
ser capaz de hacer algo

able *adj*
[capable]

capaz

1

about

She is a very able person.	Tiene mucho talento./Es una persona de mucho talento./Es muy capaz.
[skillful]	hábil
He's an able worker.	Es un obrero hábil.
to be able to (do sth)	poder/saber/ser capaz de
My uncle is unable to walk; he has broken his leg.	Mi tío no puede caminar; se ha roto la pierna. *[Note: **Poder** is used to denote physical ability.]*
Are you able to speak Russian?	¿Sabes hablar ruso? *[Note: **Saber** is used to denote having the 'know-how' to do something.]*
Is he able to do that alone?	¿Es capaz de hacer eso solo?

about *prep*
relating to

	de/acerca de/sobre/con respecto a
They informed me about the accident.	Me informaron sobre el accidente.
Can you tell me something about the Incas?	¿Puedes decirme algo acerca de los incas?
I have a book about Mexican history.	Tengo un libro sobre la historia de México.
What's that film about?	¿De qué trata esa película?
It's about a shipwreck.	Trata de un naufragio.
What about your bill?	¿Y tu cuenta?/¿Con respecto a tu cuenta?
What's it all about?	¿De qué se trata?/¿Qué pasa?

verb + about

to ask about	hacer preguntas sobre/pedir informes sobre
They asked about your father.	Preguntaron sobre tu padre.
We asked about the war.	Hicimos preguntas sobre la guerra.
to hear about	oír hablar de
I've heard a lot about your horses.	He oído hablar mucho de tus caballos.
to talk about	hablar de
We were talking about music.	Hablábamos de la música.
to walk about	pasearse por/andar por
They walked about the town.	Se pasearon por la ciudad.

on the point of

I am about to write to him.	Estoy a punto de escribirle.
We were just about to leave.	Estábamos para salir.

approximately *[see around]*

above *adv*

above	arriba/encima/por encima
the apartment above	el apartamento de arriba
above all *[especially]*	sobre todo
see above *[in text]*	véase más arriba

above *prep*

above	encima de/sobre
The bathroom is above the kitchen.	El cuarto de baño está encima de la cocina.
We are 500 meters above sea level.	Estamos a quinientos metros sobre el nivel del mar.

It's above me. *[fig.]*   No lo entiendo.

academic *adj*
the academic year   el año escolar *[school]*/el año académico
                                 [University]

That's an academic question.   Es una cuestión puramente teórica.

accent *n*
He speaks Spanish with a   Habla castellano con acento
  Mexican accent.   mexicano.
You don't have an accent.   No tienes acento./Hablas sin acento.
a written accent   un acento gráfico

accidentally *adv*
[by chance]   por casualidad
We met by chance at the café.   Nos encontramos por casualidad en
                                   el café.

[unintentionally]   sin querer
She broke it accidentally.   Lo rompió sin querer.

account *n*
a bank account   una cuenta bancaria/de banco
[bill/invoice]   una cuenta/factura
[report]   una cuenta/un relato/un informe
to take sth into account   tener algo en cuenta
to be of no account   ser de poca importancia
on account of   por/a causa de/por motivo de
on that account   por eso
on no account   de ninguna manera

Ø **el cuento** means "story."

ache *n & v*
I have a headache.   Tengo dolor de cabeza.
I have a stomachache.   Tengo dolor de estómago.
I have a toothache.   Tengo dolor de muelas.
I ache all over.   Tengo dolores por todas partes.
My head/stomach aches.   Me duele la cabeza/el estómago.
That noise makes my head ache.   Ese ruido me da dolor de cabeza.
*[see also **hurt**]*

acknowledge *v*
[to admit, recognize]   admitir/reconocer
I acknowledge you are right.   Admito que tienes razón.
[to greet sb]   saludar a alguien
She acknowledged us in the street Nos saludó en la calle.
[correspondence]   acusar
I acknowledge receipt of your   Acuso recibo de su carta. *[Note: formal
  letter.   usage hence the **usted** form of the
                                    adjective]*

Ø **acusar** also means "to accuse."

across *prep*
[from one side to another]   a través de/al través de
They went across the bridge.   Fueron a través del puente.
to go across the street   cruzar/atravesar la calle
They ran across the street.   Cruzaron la calle corriendo.

She walked across the square.	Cruzó la plaza a pie.
We drove across the bridge.	Cruzamos el puente en carro.
[on the other side]	al otro lado de/del otro lado de
The park is across the street.	El parque está enfrente.
right across (the street) from her apartment	en el otro lado de la calle/ enfrente de su apartamento
the café across the street	el café del otro lado de la calle

act *n*

[action, deed]	un acto
[in the theater]	un acto
a play in three acts	una comedia en tres actos
[legal act, law]	una acta

actually *adv*

[the fact is]	es que
Actually, she's away.	Es que está fuera.
[really, in fact]	realmente/en realidad/en efecto
Actually they are nurses.	En realidad son enfermeras.
What I actually said was...	Lo que dije concretamente fue...
Did you actually hit him?	¿Lo pegaste realmente?

Ø **actualmente** means "at present."

add *v*

to add [in general]	añadir
You must add water.	Debes añadir agua.
Value Added Tax (VAT)	Impuesto de Valor Añadido (IVA)
to add up	sumar
He added up the bill.	Sumó la cuenta.
It doesn't add up to much.	Es poca cosa.

addict *n*/ addicted *adj*

an addict (fanatic)	un(a) partidario(a)/un(a) entusiasta
a tennis addict	un(a) entusiasta del tenis
a drug addict	un(a) toxicómano(a)
to be addicted to drugs	ser toxicómano(a)
to be addicted to gambling	ser aficionado(a) al juego

addition *n*

in addition	además
In addition, they're strangers.	Además, son forasteros.
In addition to the apartment he has a house in the country	Además del apartamento tiene una casa en el campo.

Ø **en adición** is not Spanish.

additional *adj*

They need additional workers.	Necesitan más obreros.
an additional [extra] week	una semana suplementaria
an additional charge	un suplemento

admire *v*

to admire	admirar

Ø **admirar** more often means "to amaze."

admission n

Free admission	Entrada gratis
No admission	Se prohíbe la entrada.
There's a charge for admission.	Hay que pagar la entrada.
[to a school/a club]	el ingreso
[acknowledgment]	una confesión
It's an admission of guilt.	Es una confesión de culpabilidad.

admit v

to own up to — reconocer, confesar

to admit a mistake	confesar un error
I must admit that I'm guilty.	Debo confesar que soy culpable.
He admitted the robbery.	Se confesó culpable del robo.

to let in

to let in	dejar entrar
Let them in!	¡Déjalos entrar!
to be admitted to a university/ a club	ingresar(se) en una universidad/ una sociedad

advantage n

advantage [general & in tennis]	una ventaja
to take advantage of sb	abusar de alguien
to take advantage of the conditions to ...	aprovecharse de las condiciones para...

advertise v

to advertise a product	anunciar/dar publicidad a un producto
to advertise in the paper	poner un anuncio en el periódico
to advertise for	buscar por medio de anuncios

Ø **advertir** means "to advise," "to inform."

advertisement n

an advertisement	un anuncio
classified ads	los anuncios
a TV ad [a commercial]	una emisión publicitaria

Ø **una advertencia** means "a warning."

advice n

advice	el consejo
a piece of advice	un consejo
to ask sb for advice	pedir consejos a alguien
to take sb's advice	seguir los consejos de alguien
to take legal/medical advice	consultar a un abogado/médico
[report, information]	un informe/una noticia/un aviso

Ø **aviso** means "warning," "announcement."

advise v

to advise sb to do sth	aconsejar a uno hacer algo
[to inform]	avisar/informar
to advise/warn	advertir
Keep me advised!	¡Tenme al corriente/al tanto!

affair n

a love affair	una aventura amorosa
one's affairs	sus asuntos personales

I explained the Nicaragua affair to them.	Les expliqué lo de Nicaragua.

affluent adj

We live in an affluent society.	Vivimos en una sociedad opulenta.
an affluent family	una familia acaudalada

Ø **un afluente** means "a tributary."

afford v

[money]	tener bastante dinero/con que
I can't afford it/that.	No tengo bastante dinero.
	No puedo permitírmelo.
She can afford to buy it.	Tiene bastante dinero para comprarlo.
We can't afford a new car.	No tenemos con que comprar un carro nuevo.
I can't afford to go.	No me puedo permitir el lujo de ir.
Can you afford to wait?	¿Puedes esperar?
You cannot afford to miss this chance.	No puedes desperdiciar esta oportunidad.

afraid adj

to be afraid of

to be afraid of sb	tener miedo a alguien
He is afraid of his father.	Tiene miedo a su padre.
to be afraid of sth	tener miedo de algo
My daughter is afraid of lightning.	Mi hija tiene miedo de los relámpagos.
Don't be afraid!	¡No tengas miedo!/¡No temas!

to be afraid to

to be afraid to do sth	temer/tener miedo de
She is afraid to go in.	Teme entrar./Tiene miedo de entrar.
to be afraid that ...	temer que [+ subjunctive]
I'm afraid (that) you'll get hurt	Temo que vayas a hacerte daño.
I'm afraid of getting hurt.	Temo hacerme daño. [Note: The infinitive is used if both verbs have the same subject.]

to regret

I'm afraid the manager is out.	Lo siento, pero el gerente no está.
I'm afraid I cannot go.	Lo siento, no puedo ir.

after adv

after(wards)	después/más tarde
Afterwards they went home.	Después volvieron a casa.
I'll do it afterwards.	Lo haré más tarde.
soon after	poco después

after prep & conj

after	después de [prep]/después de que [conj]
I saw her after the game.	La vi después del partido.
I read the paper after my wife had gone to bed.	Leí el diario después de que mi esposa se había acostado.
They arrived at the station after the train had left.	Llegaron a la estación después de que había salido el tren/después de la salida del tren. [Note: The noun form is preferred.]

I'll do it after he's paid me.

Lo haré después de que me haya pagado. *[Note: **Después de que** takes the present subjunctive when future time is involved.]*

She loaned me the magazine after reading it/she had read it.

Me prestó la revista después de leerla. *[Note: The infinitive is used when the subject of both verbs is the same.]*

afternoon *n*
Good afternoon
*[see also **evening**]*

Buenas tardes

again *adv*
once more
Do it again.
I've lost my gloves again.
He's absent again.

una vez más/otra vez/de nuevo
Hazlo una vez más.
He perdido mis guantes otra vez.
Está ausente de nuevo.

in a negative
He won't do it again.
never again

no... más
No lo hará más.
nunca más

verb + again
to do sth again
to go out again
to go up/down again
She went in again.

volver a hacer algo
volver a salir
volver a subir/bajar
Volvió a entrar.

agenda *n*
[things to do]
[for a meeting]

el programa
el orden del día

Ø **la agenda** means "appointment book" or "diary."

aggravated *adj*
to be aggravated at sb/sth

estar irritado(a) con alguien/por algo

Ø **agravar** means "to make worse;" **agraviar** "to wrong."

ago *adv*
a long time ago
a short time ago
many years ago
a few minutes ago
He was born two days ago.
How long ago did she die?

hace mucho tiempo
hace poco tiempo
hace muchos años
hace unos minutos
Nació hace dos días.
¿Hace cuánto tiempo murió?

agree *v*
to be in agreement
Do you agree?

estar de acuerdo/estar conforme
¿Estás de acuerdo?/¿De acuerdo?/
¿Conforme?

No, I don't agree (with you).
I agree with the others.
He doesn't agree.

No, no estoy de acuerdo (contigo).
Estoy de acuerdo con los otros.
No está de acuerdo.

to come to an agreement
They have agreed on the price.

ponerse de acuerdo/convenirse
Se han puesto de acuerdo sobre el precio.

Did he agree on the details? | ¿Se convino en los detalles?

to consent
He agreed to sell the house.
Did they agree to come with us?

consentir en/quedar en
Consintió en vender la casa.
¿Quedaron en acompañarnos?

in grammar
In Spanish, the adjective
  agrees with the noun.

En castellano, el adjetivo
  concuerda con el sustantivo.

of food
Garlic doesn't agree with me.

El ajo no me sienta bien.

ahead adv
Go ahead!
Go straight ahead!
to get ahead of sb
to get ahead
to be ahead [sport]
The USA are ahead by 2-1.

¡Adelante!
¡Va todo seguido(a)/derecho(a)!
adelantarse a alguien
adelantar/progresar
ir ganando/llevar ventaja
Los Estados Unidos van ganando por
  2 a 1.

all adj

todo/toda/todos/todas
He does it all the time.
All the people attended.
She read all (of) the books.

Lo hace todo el tiempo.
Toda la gente asistió.
Leyó todos los libros. [Note: "Of" is not
  translated.]

I've seen all (of) the films.

He visto todas las películas.

all pron

todo/toda/todos/todas
That's all.
They are all awake.
All of you must take part.

Es todo.
Todos están despiertos.
Todos deben participar. [Note: "Of"
  is not translated.]

We must all help.
Repeat all together.

Todos debemos ayudar.
Repitan todos juntos.

all (that)
All that he brought is on the table.
Do all (that) you can.

todo lo que
Todo lo que trajo está en la mesa.
Haz todo lo que puedas. [Note: Subjunctive
  used after **todo lo que** when what is
  referred to is indefinite.]

all right [see okay]

allow v
to permit
to allow sb to do sth
I cannot allow you to go in.
Allow me!

permitir/dejar a alguien hacer algo
No puedo permitirte entrar.
¡Permite que te ayude! [Note: The
  subjunctive is used.]

Parking is not allowed.
Bicycles not allowed.
Is smoking allowed here?

Prohibido aparcar./Se prohíbe aparcar.
Bicicletas prohibidas.
¿Se puede fumar por aquí?

to allocate
I must allow an hour to reach
  the airport.

Debo dejar una hora para llegar al
  aeropuerto.

8

How much shall I allow per person?   ¿Cuánto dejo por persona?

almost *adv*
Lunch is almost ready.   La comida está casi preparada.
She almost died/fell.   Por poco se muere/se cae.

alone *adj*
[on one's own]   solo(a)
Are you alone?   ¿Estás solo(a)?
[the only one]   el único/la única
I'm not alone in thinking so.   No soy el único/la única en pensarlo.
We stand alone.   Somos únicos(as).

along *prep*
along   por/a lo largo de
along the river   a lo largo del río
The road runs along the river.   La carretera sigue el río/va a lo largo del río.
all along the beach/the street   todo lo largo de la playa/la calle
Let's walk along the beach.   Vamos por la playa.

also *adv*
He also went to the concert.   Él también fue al concierto.
I bought shirts and also shoes.   Compré camisas y zapatos también.

in addition   además
Also, I have a meeting.   Además, tengo una reunión.

although *conj*
although   aunque
She went out, although it was snowing.   Salió aunque estaba nevando.
I'll buy it although it will cost me a lot of money.   Lo compraré aunque me cueste mucho.
    *[Note: **Aunque** is followed by the subjunctive when the English meaning is "even if" or "even though," or when the statement is contrary to fact.]*

alumni/alumnae *n*
[graduates of a school]   los graduados/las graduadas

A.M.
It's/At five A.M.   Son las/A las cinco de la mañana.

amaze *v*
to amaze   admirar/asombrar
Their enthusiasm amazed me.   Su entusiasmo me asombró./Me admiró su entusiasmo.

to be amazed at sth   estar/quedarse asombrado(a) de/con algo/admirarse de algo
I was amazed at her wealth.   Me quedé asombrado(a) de/con su riqueza/Me admiré de su riqueza.

America *n*
[general]   América

9

America *[USA]* · (los) Estados Unidos (de América)

American n & adj
[general] · americano(a)
American *[from the USA]* · norteamericano(a), estadounidense
[Note: Latin Americans are sensitive to the use of "America" and "American" to refer just to the USA.]

and conj
and · y/e
bread and butter · pan y mantequilla
you and I · tú y yo
father and son · padre e hijo
Teresa and Isabel · Teresa e Isabel *[Note:The **e** form is used before a word beginning with **i** or **hi** except where the next letter is a vowel, e.g., **nieve y hielo** "snow and ice."]*

angry adj
to be angry · estar enojado(a)/enfadado(a)
to be angry about sth · estar enojado(a)/enfadado(a) por algo
I am angry about the decision. · Estoy enojado(a) por la decisión.
to be angry at/with sb/sth · estar enojado(a)/enfadado(a) con alguien/algo

They are angry with you. · Están enfadados contigo.
to get angry · enojarse *[LA]*/enfadarse/ponerse furioso(a)

Don't get angry! · ¡No te enojes!/¡No te enfades!/No te pongas furioso(a)/enojado(a)/ enfadado(a)

announcer n
radio/TV announcer · el locutor/la locutora
el anunciador/la anunciadora *[Mex]*

another adj
additional
I would like another cup of coffee. · otro(a)/más
We need another two players. · Quisiera otra taza de café.
without another word · Necesitamos dos jugadores más.
sin decir palabra

different · otro(a)/distinto(a)
They want another car; they · Quieren otro carro; no les gusta
don't like this one. · éste.

*[Note **otro** and **otra** are never used with **un** and **una**.]*

another (one) pron
additional · otro(a)/uno(a) más
She's lost her map; she needs · Ha perdido su mapa; necesita otro.
another (one).

different · otro(a)
I don't like this film. I'm · No me gusta esta película. Voy a
going to watch another one. · mirar otra.

answer v
to answer sb · contestar/responder a alguien
to answer a letter · contestar/responder a una carta

to answer to the description — corresponder a la descripción
to answer a charge — defenderse a una acusación
to answer for sth — responder de algo
You will answer for his behavior. — Responderás de su conducta.
to answer for sb — responder por alguien
I'll answer for my grandson. — Responderé por mi nieto.
to answer s.o. back — replicarle a alguien
Don't answer me back! — ¡No me repliques!/¡No seas respondón(ona)!

antique *n*
[an object] — una antigüedad
[a piece of furniture] — un mueble de época
an antique shop — un anticuario/una tienda de antigüedades

[old relic] — una antigualla
Their TV set is an antique. — Su televisor es una antigualla.
an antique dealer — un anticuario/un comerciante en antigüedades

Ø **una antigüedad** also means "antiquity."
Ø **antiguo(a)** means "ancient," "old."

anxious *adj*
worried — inquieto(a)/preocupado(a)
Is he anxious about the exam? — ¿Se inquieta por el examen?

eager — deseoso(a)
anxious to help — deseoso(a) de ayudar
They're anxious to see you. — Tienen ganas de verte.

any *adj*
whatever, whichever — cualquier
You can take any train. — Puedes tomar cualquier tren.
Any taxi driver will take you. — Te llevará cualquier taxista.
Buy any hat you like. — Compra cualquier sombrero que te guste. *[Note: subjunctive after **cualquier** when the reference is to any object or person, no matter who or what.]*

in a question
Is there any fruit? — ¿Hay fruta?
Are there any cookies? — ¿Hay galletas? *[Note: Spanish rarely uses a word for "any" in such questions.]*

after a negative — ningún/ninguna
He doesn't have any money. — No tiene dinero. *[Note: "Any" is often not translated in such sentences.]*

I don't have any brothers. — No tengo ningún hermano. *[Note: singular]*
No tengo hermanos.

any *pron*
any (one) at all — cualquiera
What brand of coffee do you want? - Any one will do. — ¿Qué marca de café quieres? - Me bastará cualquiera.
You can have any one you like. — Puedes tener cualquiera que te guste. *[Note: subjunctive after*

anybody/anyone

cualquiera when the reference is to any object no matter which one.]

any (some)

Do you want ice-cream? - No, I don't want any.

We have no more stamps. Do you have any?

alguno(a)/algunos(as)
ninguno(a)/ninguno(s)
¿Quieres helado? - No, no quiero ninguno. *[Note: the **ninguno** forms are used after the negative **no**.]*
No nos quedan estampillas. ¿Tienes algunas?

anybody/anyone *pron*
anyone you like
Anybody will tell you.
Anybody else would have helped.
Tell anyone you meet.

cualquiera
Cualquiera te lo dirá.
Cualquier otro hubiera ayudado.
Díselo a cualquiera con quien encuentres. *[Note: subjunctive after **cualquiera** when the reference is to any person, no matter who.]*

in the negative
I didn't speak to anybody.
Don't tell anybody!

nadie
No hablé con nadie.
¡No se lo digas a nadie!

in a question
Is there anyone there?
Did you see anyone?
Do you know anybody who speaks Portuguese?

alguien
¿Hay alguien?
¿Viste a alguien?
¿Conoces a alguien que hable portugués? *[Note: subjunctive after **alguien** when the reference is to any person, no matter who.]*

anyhow/anyway *adv*
at any rate

[in spite of everything]
They are coming anyway.
It was raining but I played golf anyway.
[haphazardly]
He keeps his accounts anyway.

de todos modos/de todas formas/con todo
sin embargo/a pesar de todo
Vienen a pesar de todo.
Estaba lloviendo, sin embargo jugué al golf.
de cualquier modo
Lleva las cuentas de cualquier modo.

anyone *[see anybody]*

anything *pron*
anything you like
You can buy anything.
They give her anything she wants.

cualquier cosa/todo lo que
Puedes comprar cualquier cosa.
Le dan todo lo que quiera. *[Note: subjunctive after **todo lo que** when the reference is something indefinite or non-specific.]*

something
She is going to buy something for her children.
I have something to do.

algo/alguna cosa
Va a comprar algo para sus hijos.

Tengo algo que hacer.

in the negative

nada

12

We couldn't find anything.
Marta hasn't anything to read.

in a question
Did they find anything?
Anything else? *[in a store, restaurant, etc.]*

any time *adv*
[whenever]
You can phone me any time.

anyway *[see anyhow]*

anywhere *adv*
wherever

We can go anywhere.
You can buy them anywhere.

in a question
Did you go anywhere?
Did you see them anywhere?

in a negative
They didn't go anywhere.
I couldn't find it anywhere.

apartment *n*

apologize *v*
to apologize for
They apologized for the noise.

I apologize for not writing sooner.
to apologize to sb

I apologized to the clients.

[for absence]
He apologized for his absence.

apology *n*
an apology
to make an apology

Ø **la apología** means "apologia."

apparent *adj*
apparent

Ø **aparente** means "suitable."

appear *v*
to seem, look
She appeared tired.
It appears that...

to come into view

No encontramos nada.
Marta no tiene nada que leer.

algo
¿Encontraron algo?
¿Algo más?

cuandoquiera/en cualquier momento
Puedes llamarme cuando quieras/
en cualquier momento.

a cualquier parte/en cualquier
parte/dondequiera/en todas partes
Podemos ir a cualquier parte.
Puedes comprarlos dondequiera.

a/en alguna parte
¿Fuiste a alguna parte?
¿Los viste en alguna parte?

a/en ninguna parte
No fueron a ninguna parte.
No lo encontré en ninguna parte.

el apartamento/el departamento
[Mex, Chl], el piso *[Sp]*

disculparse de/pedir perdón por
Se disculparon del ruido./Pidieron
perdón por el ruido.
Me disculpo de no haber escrito antes.
disculparse con alguien/pedir
perdón a alguien
Me disculpé con los clientes./Pedí
perdón a los clientes.
presentar sus excusas
Presentó sus excusas.

una disculpa/una excusa
disculparse/presentar sus excusas

evidente

parecer
Pareció cansada.
Resulta/Parece que...

aparecer/presentarse

13

He appeared in the distance.	Apareció a lo lejos.
She appeared on the balcony.	Se presentó en el balcón.

Ø **aparear** means "to pair, match, mate."

appearance n
[looks]	la apariencia/el aspecto
to have a/be of good appearance	tener buen aspecto
His appearance amazed me.	Su aspecto me admiró.
[act of appearing]	la aparición
The appearance of the horses startled her.	La aparición de los caballos la sobresaltó.
to make an appearance	aparecer/presentarse/dejarse ver
to make a personal appearance	aparecer en persona
to keep up appearances	guardar/salvar las apariencias

appetizers n
[snacks served before a meal with drinks	los aperitivos/las botanas [Mex]/ los bocadillos [Per]/los pasapalos [Ven]/las bocas[ES]/ las tapas [Sp]
[first course of a meal]	los entremeses

application n
[most senses]	la aplicación
for external application (use) only [medical]	solamente para uso externo
a job application	una solicitud para un puesto
to make an application for	solicitar
I'm going to put in an application.	Voy a presentarme.
to fill out an application	rellenar un formulario de solicitud.

apply v
to apply for a job	solicitar un puesto/presentarse a un puesto
to apply for a passport	solicitar un pasaporte
to apply to a university	presentarse a una universidad
to apply to sb for sth	dirigirse a alguien para algo
He applied to the secretary for the details.	Se dirigió al secretario para los detalles.
[to concern]	tener que ver con/ser aplicable a/ referirse a
This does not apply to me.	Esto no tiene nada que ver conmigo.

appoint v
to appoint [to a position/an office]	nombrar
She was appointed president.	La nombraron a ella presidenta.
I appointed him to the position.	Lo nombré a él para el puesto.
at the appointed time	a la hora fijada/señalada

Ø **apuntar** means "to write down," "to make notes," and also "to aim/point at."

appointment n
[date, engagement]	una cita/un compromiso
We made an appointment.	Nos dimos una cita.
to make an appointment with sb	citarse con alguien
Do you have an appointment?	¿Tiene usted hora?
I have an appointment with the doctor at five.	El médico me dio hora para las cinco.

by appointment (only)   sólo por hora citada
[position, job]   un puesto/un empleo

Ø **el apunte** means "note" (taken in class).

appreciate υ
to be grateful for   agradecer
I appreciate your help.   Te agradezco tu ayuda.

in a business letter
We would appreciate a prompt   Les estaríamos muy agradecidos
  reply.   por una respuesta inmediata.

to like sth   entender/saber apreciar
She doesn't appreciate poetry.   No entiende de poesía./
    No sabe apreciar la poesía.

to understand   comprender
We appreciate your problems.   Comprendemos tus problemas.

Ø **apreciar** also means "to esteem, estimate."

ardor n
ardor   el fervor/el entusiasmo/la pasión
to cool sb's ardor   enfriar la pasión de alguien

Ø **ardor** means "heat" or "burning sensation," e.g., **un ardor de estómago** "a burning sensation in the stomach."

area n
[surface extent]   la superficie (en metros cuadrados)
It has an area of 50 square   Tiene una superficie de 80
  miles.   kilómetros cuadrados.
[of a country]   una región
[of a town]   un barrio
[place, spot]   el área [masc]
a depressed/prohibited area   una zona deprimida/prohibida
postal area   el distrito postal
area of expertise   el campo
[see also field]

argument n
debate   una discusión/una disputa
to have an argument with sb   tener una discusión con alguien
I had a heated argument with   Tuve una discusión acalorada con
  the boss.   el jefe.
We had an argument.   Nos disputamos.

reason   el argumento
an argument for/against sth   un argumento en pro de/en contra de
    algo

Ø **el argumento** also means "plot" (of book/film).

arm n
[part of body]   un brazo
[sleeve]   una manga
[of record player]   un brazo
weapon   un arma [fem]
arms race   la carrera de armamentos
arms [heraldry]   las armas

coat of arms	un escudo de armas

armored *adj*

armored	blindado(a)
an armored car	un vehículo blindado

around *adv & prep*

approximately

I have around a hundred books.	Tengo más o menos cien libros.
Around 10,000 people attended.	Asisitieron unas diez mil personas.
around fifty	unos cincuenta

más o menos/unos(as)

time

a eso de

They came back around five.	Volvieron a eso de las cinco.

position

[movement within a place]	por
to walk around the garden	pasearse por el jardín
to walk around the house	andar por la casa
[surrounding]	alrededor de
the gardens around the hotel	los jardines alrededor del hotel
There were gardens all around the palace.	Había jardines alrededor del palacio.
[alongside]	al lado de
They were sitting around the swimming pool.	Estaban sentados al lado de la alberca.
[everywhere]	por todas partes
There were people all around.	Había gente por todas partes.
[around the corner]	a la vuelta de la esquina
It's around the corner.	Está a la vuelta de la esquina.

other expressions

to go around the world	dar la vuelta al mundo
Is Manuel around?	¿Está Manuel?
Are they are around?	¿Están por aquí?
When she's around her friends ...	Cuando está con sus amigas...

arrangements *n*

He made all the arrangements.	Lo arregló todo./Lo preparó todo./ Hizo todos los preparativos.
to make one's own arrangements	obrar por cuenta propia

musical arrangement

una adaptación

arrest *n & v*

They arrested him at home.	Lo detuvieron en casa.
They were arrested by the police.	Fueron detenidos(as) por la policía.
to be under arrest	estar detenido(a)
You're under arrest.	Queda usted detenido(a).

art *n*

art	el arte *[Note: masculine in the singular]*
fine arts	las bellas artes *[Note: feminine in the plural]*
an art museum	un museo de bellas artes
an art school	una escuela de arte
a work of art	una obra de arte

academic subjects	las Letras
Faculty of Arts	la Facultad de Filosofía y Letras
a Bachelor of Arts	un(a) Licenciado(a) en Filosofía y Letras
arts and crafts	artes y oficios

as *conj & prep*
in comparisons

as ... as	tan... como
as big as	tan grande como
as quickly as	tan rápidamente como
as soon as	lo más pronto posible
as long as *[see long]*	
as much as *[see much]*	
as many as *[see many]*	
as if/as though	como si *[+ subjunctive]*
She looked as if she were ill.	Parecía como si estuviera enferma.

time	como
She left as they were arriving.	Salió como llegaban.

because, since	como/ya que
As I don't speak Greek I can't read the sign.	Ya que no hablo griego no sé leer el letrero.

manner	como/según
As often happens in New York.	Como ocurre a menudo en Nueva York.
As I was saying ...	Como/Según decía yo...

concerning	en cuanto a/por lo que se refiere a
As for me, I don't like it.	En cuanto a mí, no me gusta.

in the capacity of	como
As a lawyer, I do not agree.	Como abogado, no estoy de acuerdo.
He is working as a teacher.	Trabaja como profesor. *[Note: no article]*

disguised as/dressed as	disfrazado(a)/de/vestido(a) de
I was dressed as a cowboy.	Iba vestido de vaquero. *[Note: no article]*

ask *v*

to ask for sth	pedir algo *[Note: "For" is not translated.]*
to ask sb for sth	pedir algo a alguien
They asked him for money.	Le pidieron dinero.
to ask sb to do sth	pedir/rogar a alguien que haga algo *[Note: subjunctive]*
I asked her to open the door.	Le pedí/rogué que abriera la puerta.
to ask a question	preguntar/hacer una pregunta

asleep *[see sleep]*

assist *v*

to assist sb	ayudar a alguien
Can I assist you?	¿Puedo ayudarte?

Ø **asistir a** means "to be present at" or "to attend."

assume *v*

to assume responsibility	asumir la responsabilidad/hacerse responsable
to assume *[suppose]*	suponer
I assume she's going.	Supongo que vaya. *[Note: subjunctive]*

at *prep*

position

at the office	en la oficina
at school	en el colegio *[Note: use of article]*
at the hairdresser's	en la peluquería
at the theater	en el teatro
at home	en casa
at Carmen's (house)	en casa de Carmen
at his uncle's (house)	en casa de su tío
at my/your house	en mi/tu casa
	en casa mía/tuya
at sea	en el mar
to be (sitting) at the table	estar sentado(a) a la mesa
to be (standing) at the door/window	estar en la puerta/ventana
to be at peace/at war	estar en paz/en guerra

time

at two o'clock	a las dos
at noon/midnight	a mediodía/a medianoche
at that time	en ese momento/en esa época
at the moment	en este momento
at times	de vez en cuando
two at a time	de dos en dos
at night	de noche/por la noche

with verbs

to be at work/at home	estar en el trabajo/en casa
to be angry at sb	estar enojado(a) con alguien
to be astonished at sb/sth	asombrarse de alguien/algo
to be good at (history)	ser hábil/fuerte en (la historia)
to be surprised at sb/sth	sorprenderse de alguien/algo
to laugh at sb/sth	reírse de alguien/algo
to look at sb/sth	mirar a alguien/mirar algo
He looked at the doctor.	Miró al médico.
We looked at the photos.	Miramos las fotos.
to rush at sb/sth	arremeter contra alguien/algo
to stare at sb/sth	mirar fijamente a alguien/mirar fijamente algo

attend *v*

to be present at, go to regularly

	asistir
I attended the concert.	Asistí al concierto.
We have to attend a meeting.	Tenemos que asistir a una reunión.
She attends a history class on Thursdays.	Asiste a una clase de historia los jueves.
to attend a school/university/ church	ir a un colegio/una universidad/ una iglesia

to attend to

	atender
I must attend to the customer.	Tengo que atender al cliente.

attentive adj
[heedful] — atento(a)
[polite] — cortés(esa)/obsequioso(a)

attractive adj
[in general] — atractivo(a)
[interesting] — atrayente/interesante/sugestivo(a)
an interesting offer — una oferta interesante
[person] — atractivo(a)/mono(a)/guapo(a)
His sister is very attractive. — Su hermana es muy atractiva/mona/guapa.

What an attractive guy! — ¡Qué chico bien parecido/guapo!

audience n
[gathering] — el público
There was a large audience. — Hubo mucho público.
[in a theater] — el público/el auditorio
[at a sports event] — los espectadores
[on the radio] — los radioyentes
[on television] — los telespectadores

Ø **la audiencia** means "the audience" one has with a Head of State or the Pope.

available adj
people
I am not available tomorrow. — No estoy libre/Tengo compromiso mañana.
Is the senator available? — ¿Está libre el senador?

goods
Are these boots available in other colors/sizes? — ¿Estas botas existen en otros colores/otras tallas?
That model is no longer available. — Ese modelo ya no está disponible.
Coffee was not available in the village. — No se podía conseguir café en el pueblecito.
The swimming pool is available to everyone. — La alberca está a la disposición de todos.

average adj & n
average — medio(a)
the average price — el precio medio
The thief is of average height. — El ladrón es de regular estatura/de estatura mediana.

on the average — por término medio
the average *[numerical]* — el promedio
The average age of the players is ... — El promedio de edad de los jugadores es...
[typical] — típico
the average Mexican — el mexicano típico

avocado n
avocado — el aguacate/la palta *[Arg, Chi, Uru]*

away adv
They're away. — No están./Están fuera./Están ausentes.
She's away for a month. — Pasa un mes fuera.
The stadium is five kilometers away. — El estadio está a cinco kilómetros (de aquí).

19

away

Our house is ten miles away
  from the border.

Nuestra casa está a diez millas de la
  frontera/dista diez millas de la
  frontera.

far away
The mountains are far away.
to go away
Go away!
to go away from
to get away [to leave]
to get away [to escape]

lejos
Las montañas están lejos.
irse/marcharse
¡Vete!/¡Váyase/¡Váyanse!
alejarse de
salir/irse/marcharse
escaparse

B

baby *n & adj*
[human]   un bebé/un nene/una nena
[animal]   una cría
[adjective]   infantil

bachelor *n*
[unmarried man]   un soltero
[university graduate]   un(a) licenciado(a)
to have a bachelor's degree   ser licenciado(a) en letras/
  in arts/law/science   derecho/ciencias

Ø **un bachiller** would be somebody holding a high school diploma.

back *n*
[part of human body]   la(s) espalda(s)
back to back   espalda con espalda
back to front   al revés
with one's back to   de espaldas a
She was sitting with her back   Estaba sentada de espaldas a la
  to the door.   puerta.
He turned his back on my son.   Volvió las espaldas a mi hijo.
[of an animal]   el lomo
[of a chair]   el respaldo
[of a check]   el dorso
[of a house]   la parte de atrás
The back is a ruin.   La parte de atrás es una ruina.
The garage is in back of the house.   El garaje está detrás de la casa.
I was in the back of the hall.   Estaba en el fondo de la sala.
back-up   el apoyo

back *adj*
back   trasero(a)/de atrás
the back seat [of a car]   el asiento de atrás/el asiento trasero
the back tires   las llantas de atrás
Sit in the back row!   ¡Siéntate en la última fila!
back tooth   una muela

back *adv*
verb + back
to answer back   replicar
to be back   estar de vuelta
to come back/go back (home)   volver/regresar (a casa)
to fly back   volver en avión
to get back (home)   regresar/volver a casa
to get sth back   recuperar/recobrar algo
to give back   devolver
to pay back   reembolsar
to phone back   volver a telefonear
to run back   volver corriendo
to walk back   volver a pie

21

background *n*

in the background	en el fondo
background music/noise	la música/el ruido de fondo
[training, experience]	la formación (profesional)
What is his background?	¿Cuál es su formación?/¿Qué formación tiene?
[social class]	el origen/los antecedentes
They are of Cuban background.	Son de origen cubano.
She comes from a working-class /middle-class background.	Sus antecedentes son de la clase obrera/de la clase media.
[information]	los antecedentes/la información previa
Do you have the background to the problem?	¿Tienes los antecedentes del problema?

bad *adj*

The weather is bad.	Hace mal tiempo. *[Note: **Malo** shortens to **mal** before masculine singular noun.]*
[wicked]	malo(a)
a bad man	un hombre malo
a bad accident/mistake	un accidente/error grave
a bad cold	un resfriado fuerte
He's bad at Spanish.	Es malo en castellano.
[sick]	malo(a)/enfermo(a)
I feel bad *[sick]*.	Me siento mal.
I feel bad about it.	Lo siento/lamento.
*[see also **feel**]*	
to be bad tempered	estar de mal humor
It's going from bad to worse.	Va de mal en peor.

badly *adv*

to dress badly	vestirse mal
badly written	mal escrito(a)
badly injured	gravemente herido(a)
I need/want it badly.	Lo necesito/deseo muchísimo.

bag *n*

[purse/handbag]	una cartera *[LA]*/una bolsa *[LA]*/un bolso
paper bag	una bolsa de papel
shopping bag	una bolsa de la compra
[sack]	un saco

Ø **La Bolsa** *[note the capital]* means "stock exchange;" **el bolsillo** means "pocket."

bake *v*

[bread/cake, etc.]	cocer al horno/hornear
She bakes her own bread/cakes.	Hornea su propio pan/sus propios pasteles.
[meat/fish]	asar
baked chicken	pollo asado
baked potatoes	papas al horno *[LA]*/patatas al horno *[Sp]*
baked beans	judías en salsa de tomate

balance n

[state]	el equilibrio
to lose one's balance	perder el equilibrio
[scales]	una balanza
[commerce]	el balance
a balance sheet	un balance
[statement of an account]	el balance/el estado de cuentas
[remainder]	el resto/el saldo
the balance of payments	el balance de pagos

balance v

to balance	mantener el equilibrio
to balance the budget	nivelar el presupuesto
to balance the books	hacer balance/cerrar los libros

Ø **balancearse** means "to swing."

ball n

[small, e.g., golf, tennis]	una pelota
[large, e.g., football]	un balón/una bola *[LA]*
snowball	una bola de nieve
[globe, sphere]	un globo/una esfera
[a dance]	un baile (de etiqueta)
to have a ball *[enjoy oneself]*	pasarlo en grande
ball game	un partido de béisbol
It's a whole new ball game.	Todo ha cambiado.

band n

[music]	una orquesta/banda
dance/jazz band	una orquesta de baile/de jazz
brass band	una banda/una charanga
military band	una banda/música militar
town band	una banda/música municipal
[a combo]	un conjunto/un grupo (de jazz)
[gang of people]	una gavilla/una pandilla/una cuadrilla
[strip of material]	una banda

bath n

bath *[bathtub]*	un baño/una bañera/una bañadera *[LA]*/una tina *[Mex]*
to have/take a bath	bañarse/tomar un baño

bathroom n

bathroom	un cuarto de baño
*[see also **toilet**]*	

battery n

[dry for radios, etc.]	una pila
I need a battery for my clock.	Necesito una pila para mi reloj.
[wet for cars, etc.]	una batería
The battery is dead.	La batería está descargada.

Ø **la batería** also means "a set of drums," "a hit/stroke" (in baseball) and, in Colombia, "a round of drinks."

be *v*   ser/estar

Ser is used to denote permanent
characteristics such as identity,
nationality:

They are Peruvians.	Son peruanos.
She is a very intelligent girl.	Es una chica muy inteligente.
It's a very beautiful house.	Es una casa muy hermosa.
I'm an engineer.	Soy ingeniero.
These shirts are (made of) silk.	Estas camisas son de seda.
My friends are from New York.	Mis amigos son de Nueva York.

Ser is also used with a past
participle to form the passive voice:

He was run over by a car.	Fue atropellado por un carro.

Estar indicates position(permanent
and temporary),temporary states,
and with a past participle a state
resulting from an action:

My parents are in Chile.	Mis padres están en Chile.
Bogotá is in Colombia.	Bogotá está en Colombia.
Where is the police station?	¿Dónde está la comisaría?
Her husband is not very well.	Su esposo no está muy bien.
Their grandmother is ill.	Su abuela está enferma.
The doors were open.	Las puertas estaban abiertas.
He's sitting in the garden.	Está sentado en el jardín.

Estar is also used with a gerund
to form the continuous present
tense:

It's raining.	Está lloviendo.

Ø You can say **Soy casado(a)** or **Estoy casado(a)** for "I am married."

because *conj & prep*
introducing clause   porque
because he's ill   porque está enfermo

because of + noun   a causa de/debido a
because of the snow   a causa de la nieve

become *v*

to become	llegar a ser
He became very famous.	Llegó a ser muy famoso.
[by one's own efforts]	hacerse
She became an accountant.	Se hizo contable.
[by promotion]	llegar a ser
I became a colonel.	Llegué a ser coronel.
[of emotions]	ponerse
They became violent.	Se pusieron violentos.
She's becoming pale.	Se pone pálida.
He became mad.	Se volvió loco.
[to be changed/transformed]	transformarse
The palace has become a hotel.	El palacio se ha transformado en hotel.

to become of   ser de

What has become of his son?	¿Qué es de su hijo?
What will become of them?	¿Qué será de ellos?

bed n
[for sleeping in] — una cama
to go to bed — acostarse
to put a child to bed — acostar a un niño
[of river] — un cauce/un lecho

bedroom n
la recámara *[LA]*/el dormitorio/la alcoba/la habitación/ el cuarto de dormir

before adv
[time] — antes
a moment before — un momento antes
I saw him the day/night before. — Lo vi el día/la noche anterior.
the week/year before — la semana/el año anterior
Have you seen that film before? — ¿Has visto esa película alguna vez?
No, I've never seen it before. — No, no la he visto nunca.
Have you been to Mexico before? — ¿Has estado en México alguna vez?

before conj
before — antes de *[+ infinitive]*
antes de que *[+ subjunctive]*

I'll do it before I go home. — Lo haré antes de volver a casa.
Do it before the boss gets back. — Hazlo antes de que vuelva el jefe.
*[Note: **Antes de** is used when the subject of both verbs is the same; **antes de que** is followed by the subjunctive when the subject of the verbs is different.]*

before prep
time — antes de
before Christmas — antes de la Navidad
before midday — antes del mediodía

in front of
[place] — delante de
He was standing before the altar. — Estaba delante del altar.
[in the face of] — ante
before the enemy — ante el enemigo

begin v
to begin — comenzar/empezar
to begin to do sth — comenzar a/empezar a hacer algo
We began to sing. — Comenzamos a/Empezamos a cantar.
I began painting. — Comencé a/Empecé a pintar.
to begin by doing sth — comenzar/empezar + present participle
She began by saying that ... — Comenzó/Empezó diciendo que...
To begin with, I would like to say ... — Para empezar quisiera decir...

behind adv & prep
[adverb] — detrás/por detrás/atrás
[preposition] — detrás de
*[see **back**]*

believe v
[to think]
I believe he's sick.
I believe so./I don't believe so
[to have faith in]
Do you believe in God?
I don't believe in ghosts.

creer
Creo que está enfermo.
Creo que sí./Creo que no.
creer en
¿Crees en Dios?
No creo en los fantasmas.

belong v
possession
Who does this belong to?

It belongs to me/José.
Does this bag belong to you?
The house belongs to my uncle.

ser (de)/pertenecer
¿De quién es esto?/¿A quién pertenece esto?
Es mío/de José.
¿Este saco es tuyo?
La casa pertenece a mi tío.

membership
I belong to the Rotary Club.
We belong to the Liberal party.

Soy socio de la Sociedad Rotaria.
Somos miembros del partido Liberal.

below adv
below
Who lives in the apartment below?
See below. [in a text]

abajo/(por) debajo
¿Quién vive en el apartamento de abajo?
Véase más abajo.

below prep
[under]
The damage is below the waterline.
below average
The temperature was below normal.

bajo/debajo de
El daño está debajo de la línea de flotación.
por debajo de la media
La temperatura estaba inferior a la normal.

beside prep
[next to]
There was a table beside the bed.

al lado de/junto a
Había una mesita al lado de la cama.

besides adv & prep
[additionally/in addition to]
Besides, the train was late.
Besides his money he lost his credit cards.
[with a negative]
Nobody was hurt besides the driver.

además/además de
Además, el tren llegó con retraso.
Además de su dinero, perdió sus tarjetas de crédito.
excepto/fuera de
No fue herido nadie excepto el conductor.

best n
the best thing
to do one's best
[see also better/best]

lo mejor [invariable]
hacerlo lo mejor posible

bet v
to bet on a horse
I bet you 50 dollars I'll win.
You bet!

apostar a un caballo
Te apuesto 50 dólares a que gano.
¡Ya lo creo!

better/best *adj*

better	mejor/mejores
best	el/la mejor
	los/las mejores
the better camera	la mejor cámara (de las dos)
the best camera	la mejor cámara (de todas)
	[Note: *La mejor cámara* can mean "the better camera" or "the best camera."]
These are the better/best ones.	Éstas son las mejores.
Buy the best camera in the shop.	Compra la mejor cámara de la tienda. [Note: *After a superlative* **de** *is used to translate "in."*]

better/best *adv*

better	mejor
best	(lo) mejor
He speaks Spanish better than I.	Habla castellano mejor que yo.
His wife speaks Spanish the best.	Su mujer es la que habla mejor castellano.
much better than	mucho mejor que
better and better	cada vez mejor
It would be better not to say anything.	Más valdría no decir nada.
You had better/best wait for her.	Más vale que la esperes. [Note: *subjunctive after* **más vale que**.]
The best thing you can do is to leave.	Lo mejor que puedas hacer es irte. [Note: *subjunctive after* **lo mejor**.]

big *adj*

big	grande
My father is a big man.	Mi padre es un hombre grande.
They lived in a big house.	Vivían en una casa grande.
my big brother	mi hermano mayor
to get big	crecer

Ø **grande** can also mean "great;" in such cases it precedes the noun it describes and also shortens to **gran**: e.g., **El Presidente es un gran hombre.** "The President is a great man."

bill *n*

[invoice]	una factura
electricity bill	una factura/una cuenta de la electricidad
[restaurant, hotel, shops]	una cuenta
[banknote]	un billete
a thousand peso bill	un billete de cien pesos
bill [on billboard]	un cartel
Post no bills!	¡Prohibido fijar carteles!

billboard *n*

billboard	la cartelera

billion *n*

one billion	mil millones
1,000,000,000	1.000.000.000 [Note Spanish punctuation]

Ø **un billón** is US trillion.

birthday n
a birthday · un cumpleaños
birthday party · una fiesta de cumpleaños
*[see also **saint's day**]*

blame v
to blame · culpar/echar la culpa
to blame sb for sth · echar la culpa a alguien de algo
They blamed me for the mistake. · Me culparon del error.
to be to blame for sth · tener la culpa de algo
I am not to blame. · No tengo la culpa.
He is to blame for the row. · Tiene la culpa de la bronca.
Who is to blame? · ¿Quién tiene la culpa?
I'm not to blame; you are. · La culpa no es mía; es tuya.
And I don't blame them! · ¡Y los comprendo perfectamente!

blanket n
blanket · la cobija *[LA]*/la frazada
[Arg, Chi, Uru]/la manta *[Sp]*

block n
[of stone] · un bloque
[of buildings] · una cuadra/una manzana *[Mex & Sp]*
It's two blocks away. · Queda a dos cuadras de aquí.

Ø **la manzana** also means "apple."

boil v
[liquid] · hervir
The water is boiling. · El agua está hirviendo.
[to cook] · cocer
to boil an egg · pasar un huevo por agua
boiled potatoes · papas *[LA]*/patatas cocidas al agua

bored adj
to be bored · estar aburrido(a)
to get bored · aburrirse
I'm bored with all this. · Estoy harto(a) de todo esto.
I was bored to death. · Me aburrí como una ostra.
You look bored. · Pareces aburrido(a).

boring adj
boring · aburrido(a)/pesado(a)
It was a very boring film · Fue una película muy aburrida.

Ø Note that **aburrido** means "bored" and "boring."

born v
to be born · nacer
Where were you born? · ¿Dónde naciste?
I was born in Quito. · Nací en Quito.

borrow v
to borrow sth from sb · pedir prestado algo a alguien
I borrowed a thousand dollars from my father. · Pedí prestado mil dólares a mi padre.
May I borrow your pen? · ¿Me prestas tu pluma?

boss *n*
[general]   el jefe
[owner]   el amo/el patrón; el ama [fem]/la
   patrona
[manager]   el gerente

both *adj*
both   ambos(as)/los dos/las dos
He broke both legs.   Se rompió ambas piernas.
from both sides   por ambos lados
I had to fill out both forms.   Tuve que rellenar los dos formularios.

both *pron*
both   los dos/las dos/ambos(as)
Both of us are going to the game.   Los dos vamos al partido.
I intend to buy both of them.   Pienso comprar los dos.
They both arrived late.   Llegaron tarde las dos.

both ... and *conj*
I like both tea and coffee.   Me gusta tanto el té como el café.
Both my cousin and his wife are
   going to the meeting.   Tanto mi primo y su esposa
   van a la reunión.
She likes both swimming and riding.   Le gusta tanto nadar como
   montar.

bother *v*
to bother sb   molestar a alguien
I'm sorry to bother you.   Siento molestarte.
[to be a nuisance]   fastidiar
The noise of the traffic
   bothers us every day.   El ruido del tráfico nos fastidia
   todos los días.
[worry]   preocuparse
Don't bother about that.   No te preocupes por eso.

bottom *n*
at the bottom of [box, cup,
   garden, river, sea]   en el fondo de
at the bottom of the sea   en el fondo del mar
at the bottom of [hill, page,
   stairs]   al pie de
at the bottom of the stairs   al pie de la escalera

boyfriend *n*
her boyfriend   su novio
[a man friend]   un amigo

brain *n*
[mind, intelligence]   el cerebro
[anatomy]   el seso
brains [cooked]   los sesos
brain dead   clínicamente muerto(a)

break *n*
a break [rest]   un descanso
to take a break   descansar
the class break   el recreo

break away

[interruption]	una interrupción
without a break	sin descansar/interrupción

break away v
[to withdraw]	separarse
[to escape]	escaparse

break down v/breakdown n
to break down [machinery]	descomponerse [LA]/estropearse
to break down [vehicles]	descomponerse [LA]/quedarse parado/ averiarse
They have had a breakdown.	Se han quedado parados.
a breakdown	una pana [LA]/una descompostura [Mex]/una avería [Sp]

emotions
to break down [person]	perder el control
to break down [in tears]	romper a llorar
to have a nervous breakdown	sufrir un colapso nervioso

break off v
to break off an engagement	romper un compromiso
to break off a branch	cortar una rama
[to interrupt]	interrumpirse
They've broken off the talks.	Se interrumpieron las conferencias.

bright adj
I like bright colors.	Me gustan los colores vivos.
a bright light	una luz clara
bright sunshine	un sol brillante
[clever, intelligent]	listo(a)/inteligente
His son is not very bright.	Su hijo no es muy listo/inteligente.
[cheerful]	alegre/animado(a)/optimista
It's a very bright room.	Es una habitación bien iluminada.

bring v
to bring	traer
Bring the children.	Trae a los niños.
I'll bring the glasses.	Traigo los vasos.

brown adj
brown	marrón/castaño(a)/pardo(a)/café (color café)
My hair is brown./I have brown hair.	Tengo pelo castaño.
He always wore brown shoes.	Siempre llevaba zapatos marrones.
Do you like brown bread?	¿Te gusta el pan moreno?
[from the sun]	moreno(a)

brush n
hairbrush	un cepillo para el pelo
toothbrush	un cepillo de dientes
paintbrush	una brocha
artist's brush	un pincel

building n

a building	un edificio
[property]	un inmueble
[the process of building]	la construcción
building land	tierra [fem] para construcción
a building lot/plot/site	un solar
the building trade	la industria de la construcción

bulb n

[light bulb]	un foco [Mex]/una bombilla/una ampolleta [Chi]
[flower bulb]	un bulbo

bus n

a (city) bus	un autobús/un camión [Mex]/un colectivo [Arg]/un guagua [Cub]/un micro [Chi & Per]
a tour bus/coach	un autocar

business n

in general — el comercio/los negocios [Note: plural]

a business man/woman	un hombre/una mujer de negocios
a business meeting	una reunión/sesión de negocios
a business trip	un viaje de negocios
to be on business	estar de negocios
to go away on business	irse de negocios
to do business with sb	comerciar con alguien
Business is good.	Los negocios marchan bien.

affair, matter — el asunto/la cuestión

Mind your own business!	¡No es asunto tuyo!

a company — un comercio/una empresa/una casa

academic subject

business administration	la administración de empresas
business college/school	una escuela de comercio
business studies	estudios de la empresa/estudios empresariales

busy adj

general — ocupado(a)

Are you busy?	¿Estás ocupado(a)?
I'm busy tonight.	No estoy libre esta noche. Tengo mucho que hacer esta noche.
She was busy with her studies.	Estaba ocupada en sus estudios.
They were busy reading.	Estaban ocupados leyendo/en leer.

telephone

The line is busy.	La línea está ocupada. [LA]/Están comunicando. [Sp]

places — concurrido(a)

The street was very busy.	La calle estaba muy concurrida.

but conj

but	pero
[after a negative]	sino
He isn't in Colombia but in Ecuador.	No está en Colombia sino en Ecuador.

by *prep*

general, by means of

I paid by check.
Is this made by hand or by machine?
I know her by name/sight.
to do sth all by oneself

Pagué por cheque.
¿Está hecho a mano o a máquina?
La conozco de nombre/de vista.
hacer algo solo/hacer algo por sí

attributed to

He bought a painting by Goya.
Have you read any novels by
  Gabriel García Márquez?

de
Compró un cuadro de Goya.
¿Has leído unas novelas de Gabriel
  García Márquez?

manner

[means of transportation]
by bicycle/boat/bus/car/
  motorcycle/plane/train
[to send mail, goods]
We sent the goods by air/rail.

en
en bicicleta/barco/autobús/carro/
  moto(cicleta)/avión/tren
por
Enviamos los géneros por avión/
  ferrocarril.

measurement

The box measures two feet long
  by six inches wide.

por
La caja mide dos pies de largo por
  seis pulgadas de ancho.

place

[near to]
He lives by the beach.
[alongside]
by the sea/the lake/the river
to go/pass by
They went by the theater.
to come by *[to call, visit]*
Come by tonight.
Will you come by and pick me up?

cerca de
Vive cerca de la playa.
a orillas
a orillas del mar/del lago/del río
pasar por delante
Pasaron por delante del teatro.
pasar (por casa)
Pasa por casa esta noche.
¿Quieres pasar a recogerme?

rate

It is sold by the kilogram/
  liter/meter.
to pay by the hour/day/week

por
Se vende por kilo/litro/metro.

pagar por hora/día/semana

time

by day/by night
I like traveling by night.
You must finish it by this evening.
I must be in Madrid by the
  fifth of April.

de día/de noche
Me gusta viajar de noche.
Debes terminarlo para esta tarde.
Tengo que estar en Madrid antes del
  cinco de abril.

verb + by + gerund

He succeeded by working hard.

Tuvo éxito trabajando mucho.

**past participle + by + noun
descriptive state [with estar]**

to be covered by
to be surprised by
to be surrounded by
The house was surrounded by trees.

estar cubierto(a) de
estar sorprendido(a) de
estar rodeado(a) de
La casa estaba rodeada de árboles.

passive [with ser]

The house was surrounded by
  the police.
He was accompanied by his wife.

La casa fue rodeada por los
  policías.
Fue acompañado por su esposa.

C

cabin *n*

a (log) cabin   una cabaña (de madera)

Ø **la cabina** means "an aircraft cabin" or "cabin of a truck;" **una cabina telefónica/ de teléfono** is "a telephone booth."

call *v*

[to shout]	gritar
[to name]	llamar
[to telephone]	telefonear/llamar por teléfono
Who's calling? *[on telephone]*	¿De parte de quién?/¿Quién llama?

call *n*

telephone call   una llamada
long distance call   una llamada de larga distancia

camera *n*

a still camera   una máquina (fotográfica)
a movie/TV camera   una cámara

can *v*

[to be physically able to]   poder
He can't play tennis today. He   No puede jugar al tenis hoy. Se ha
   has broken his arm.   roto el brazo.
Can I *[may I]* help?   ¿Puedo ayudarte?
[to know how to]   saber
Can you swim?   ¿Sabes nadar?
I can't play chess.   No sé jugar al ajedrez.
[see also **could**]

can *n*

a can of tomatoes   un bote/una lata de jitomates
a can of beer   una lata de cerveza
a garbage can   un cubo para basuras/de la basura

cancel *v*

to cancel   cancelar/anular
to cancel a check   anular un cheque
I cancelled the meeting.   Anulé la reunión.

Ø **cancelar** is often used in Latin America to mean "to pay" (of bills, etc.).

car *n*

[an automobile]   un carro *[most of LA]*/un coche *[Sp,
     Arg & Uru]*/un automóvil

Ø **un autocar** is a "tour bus".

care *n & v*
to take care of, to look after
   [people]   cuidar de/atender
Their grandfather takes care   Su abuelo cuida de ellos(as).
   of them.

careful

Dr. Sosa is taking care of her.
Take care of yourself!
I can take care of myself.
[in store] Are you being taken
care of?

El doctor Sosa la atiende/asiste.
¡Cuídate bien!
Sé cuidar a mí mismo(a).
¿Le atienden a usted?

[things]

guardar/tener cuidado de/
encargarse de

You must take care of your
passport.
She takes good care of her clothes.
He'll take care of the arrangements.

Debes guardar tu pasaporte.
Tiene gran cuidado de su ropa.
Se encargará de los preparativos.

to be concerned about
He cares for her very much.
They really care about peace.
I don't care.
I couldn't care less.

querer/preocuparse de/tener interés en
La quiere mucho.
Se preocupan mucho de la paz.
Me es igual./No me importa.
Eso me trae sin cuidado./Me importa
un pepino./Me importa todo un rábano.

Who cares?

¿A quién le importa?/¿Qué más da?/
¿Quién se preocupa (por eso)?

to like, want something
Would you care for a drink?
Would you care to go to the movies?
She doesn't care for garlic.

querer/gustar
¿Te gustaría tomar algo?
¿Quieres ir al cine?
No le gusta el ajo.

to be careful
Take care!
Take care not to lose it!

tener cuidado
¡Atención!/¡Cuidado!/¡Ojo!
¡Ten cuidado, no lo pierdas!/
¡Guárdate de no perderlo!

Handle with care.
in care of (c/o) *[on letter]*
Mr. X care of Mrs. Y

Manéjese con cuidado.
en casa de
El Sr. X en casa de la Sra. Y

anxiety, worry
I haven't a care in the world.

un cuidado/una inquietud
No tengo ninguna preocupación en la
vida.

carefree
to be carefree

estar despreocupado(a)/libre de
preocupaciones

careful *adj*
cautious
a careful driver
Be careful what you say!

cuidadoso(a)/cauteloso(a)/prudente
un(a) conductor(a) prudente
¡Ten cuidado con lo que dices!

painstaking
a careful worker

cuidadoso(a)/esmerado(a)/competente
un obrero cuidadoso/esmerado

carpet *n*
a carpet

una alfombra

Ø **una carpeta** is "a file" *[in which letters, etc. are kept]*.

cartoon *n*
[animated film]
*[humorous drawing as in
newspaper]*
[comic strip]

los dibujos animados
un dibujo cómico/un chiste/una
caricatura
una tira humorística/cómica

34

[comic book/paper]	un libro de historietas [Mex & Par]/ una revista de historietas [Arg]/una comiquita [Ven]/un tebeo [Sp]
[art]	un cartón

case n

[container]	una caja
[suitcase]	una valija [LA]/un veliz [Mex]/ una maleta [Sp]
[instance]	un caso/un asunto
in this case	en este caso
This is a strange case.	Esto es un asunto raro.
[medical]	un caso
in case of	en caso de
in case they come	por si vienen/en caso de que vengan [Note: the subjunctive after en caso de que]
just in case	por si acaso
in any case	en todo caso/por todas formas

cash n

[money]	el dinero/la plata [LA]
[notes & coins]	el dinero contante/el efectivo
I don't have any cash on me.	No tengo dinero conmigo.
cash price	el precio al contado
to pay cash	pagar al contado/en efectivo
[see also money]	

cash v

to cash a check	cobrar un cheque
to cash a traveler's check	cambiar un cheque de viajero

casserole n

[the container]	la cacerola
[the food]	la cazuela

Ø **la cacerola** is also the general word for "saucepan."

casual adj/casually adv

[fortuitous]	fortuito(a)/casual/accidentado(a)
a casual meeting	un encuentro fortuito/casual
[clothing]	informal/de sport/corriente
to dress casually	vestirse de sport
casual clothes	la ropa de sport/el traje de calle
[off hand]	despreocupado(a)
[of work]	temporero(a)/eventual
a casual worker	un jornalero/un temporero
casual earnings	los ingresos ocasionales
[see also informal]	

catch v

[in general]	agarrar [In Spain only: coger]
to catch a ball	agarrar/parar/atrapar una pelota
[animals]	atrapar/entrampar un animal
I caught a salmon yesterday.	Capturé/tomé un salmón ayer.
[transportation]	tomar

I'll catch the train/bus.	Voy a tomar el tren/el autobús.
[a disease]	contagiarse de/contraer
She caught the flu.	Se contagió de/Contrajo la gripe.
I've caught a cold.	Me he resfriado/Me he acatarrado.
[to perceive]	comprender/oír
I didn't catch what he said.	No oí lo que dijo.

Ø The verb **coger**, which can cover almost all senses of "to catch," is in widespread use in Spain and in many Latin American countries, but should be avoided in Argentina, Paraguay, Uruguay, and parts of Mexico and Venezuela.

cave *n*
[natural]	la cueva
[man made]	la caverna

Ø **la cava** is the word used for Spanish sparkling wines made by the champagne method.

challenge *n*
a challenge	un reto/un desafío
[of job or opportunity]	un estímulo/un incentivo

chance *n*
fate, luck
by (sheer) chance	la casualidad/la suerte
	por (pura) casualidad

risk
to take a chance	un riesgo
	arriesgarse

possibility, probability
	la posibilidad/la probabilidad
The chances are that they will win the game.	Lo más probable es que ganen el partido. *[Note: subjunctive]*
I have a good chance of getting them.	Tengo buenas probabilidades de conseguirlos.
He hasn't got a chance.	No tiene posibilidad alguna.

opportunity
	la oportunidad/la ocasión
We have the chance of going to Peru.	Tenemos la ocasión de ir al Perú.
Give her a chance!	¡Dale la oportunidad!

Ø **chance** (m/f) may be encountered in Latin America meaning "chance/opportunity" *[an anglicism]* or "luck" *[a gallicism]*.

change *n*
[alteration/modification]	una modificación
[foreign exchange]	el cambio
[small change]	la moneda suelta/el suelto
[money returned]	el vuelto *[LA]*/la vuelta *[Sp]*
Keep the change!	¡Quédese con el vuelto/la vuelta!
	*[Note: **usted** form]*

change *v*
to change	cambiar
You haven't changed a bit!	¡No has cambiado en lo más mínimo!
[to exchange for]	cambiar por
You will have to change dollars for pesos.	Tendrás que cambiar dólares por pesos.
[clothes, mind, trains, etc.]	cambiarse de
to change one's clothes	cambiarse de ropa

I had to change my shoes.	Tuve que cambiarme de zapatos.
She's changed her mind.	Ha cambiado de opinión.
We change trains in Madrid.	Cambiamos de tren en Madrid.
[to change into]	transformarse en
It changed into a butterfly.	Se transformó en mariposa.

character *n*

[nature of sth/sb]	el carácter/el índole
[moral quality]	el carácter
a person of good character	una persona de buena reputación
He's a bad character.	Tiene mala fama/reputación.
[in film, story]	un personaje
[individual]	un tipo
He's an odd character.	Es un tipo raro.

charge *n*
responsibility

to be in charge of	estar encargado(a) de
the person in charge	el/la encargado(a)/la persona responsable
Who's in charge here?	¿Quién manda aquí?
to take charge of sth	encargarse de/hacerse cargo de

cost

admission charge	el precio de entrada
free of charge/no charge	gratis
There's no admission charge.	La entrada es gratis/gratuita.
an extra charge	un suplemento

charge *v*

How much do you charge?	¿Cuánto cobran ustedes?
The lawyer charged me $1000 for the advice.	El abogado me pidió/cobró mil dólares por el consejo.
You have charged me 1000 pesos too much.	Me has cobrado mil pesos de más.
to charge with a credit card	pagar con tarjeta de crédito
Charge it to my account.	Cárguemelo en mi cuenta.
Cash or charge?	¿Al contado o a crédito?

cheap *adj*

[inexpensive]	barato(a)
This tie was cheap.	Esta corbata fue barata.
[of travel tickets]	ecónomico(a)
He bought a cheap ticket to Mérida.	Sacó un boleto económico para Mérida.
cheaper *[less expensive]*	más barato(a)/menos caro(a)
It's just cheap junk.	No son más que baratijas.
a cheapskate	un(a) tacaño(a)

cheat *v*

to cheat at cards/in an exam	hacer trampas
to cheat sb	estafar/timar/defraudar a alguien
She cheated her brother out of the money.	Estafó el dinero a su hermano.
[be unfaithful]	engañar a/burlar de alguien
He cheated on his wife.	Engañó a su esposa.

check *n*

a bank check	un cheque

37

check

a traveler's check	un cheque de viajero
[in a restaurant]	una cuenta
[invoice]	una factura
Check! *[in chess]*	¡Jaque!
Check! *[OK!]*	¡Vale!

check v

to make sure

to make sure	chequear *[LA]*/comprobar/verificar
to check *[information]*	verificar
to check the date/the quality	verificar la fecha/la calidad
to check the accounts	chequear/verificar las cuentas
to check off *[list]*	marcar
to check a box *[on a form]*	marcar en un recuadro
[to count]	contar
to check on sb	investigar a alguien

traveling

to check passports/tickets	controlar los pasaportes/los boletos
[e.g., at an airport]	
to check in *[flights/hotel]*	registrarse
to check (in) *[luggage]*	facturar/chequear *[LA]* el equipaje
to check out	pagar la cuenta y marcharse
What time do you check out?	¿A qué hora te marchas?
to check one's coat	depositar/dejar el abrigo en el guardarropa

checker n

[in supermarket]	un(a) cajero(a)
[in cloakroom]	un(a) encargado(a) de guardarropa
checkers *[game]*	las damas

check-out n

| *[at supermarket]* | la caja |

checkup n

| *[medical]* | un reconocimiento general |
| I need a checkup. | Necesito un reconocimiento general. |

cigar/cigarette n

| cigar | un puro |
| cigarette | un cigarro/cigarrillo |

claim v

to claim	pretender
They claim to have done it.	Pretenden haberlo hecho.
She claims to be poor.	Pretende ser pobre.

Ø "to pretend" is translated by **fingir** or **imaginarse**.

class n

education

[a group of students]	una clase
the class of '85	la promoción de 1985
a classmate *[in school]*	un(a) compañero(a) de clase
to be classmates *[in university]*	estudiar juntos(as)
a former classmate	un(a) antiguo(a) compañero(a) de clase
a classroom	un aula *[fem]*/una clase/un salón de clases

38

[a course]	un curso
to take a class in Spanish	hacer un curso de lengua española
social class	la clase
the working/middle/upper class	la clase obrera/media/alta
class struggle/war	la lucha de clases

clerk *[see worker]*

climb *v*

to climb the stairs	subir (por) la escalera
I cannot climb those steps.	No puedo subir esos peldaños/esas gradas.
to climb a hill *[a slope]*	subir una cuesta/una colina
to climb a mountain	subir a/escalar una montaña
to climb a fence/tree/wall	trepar a una valla/un árbol/una tapia
to climb over a wall	franquear una tapia
to climb down	bajar por

close *adj*

[of relationships]	íntimo(a)
a close friend	un(a) amigo(a) íntimo(a)
a close family	una familia unida
The brothers are very close.	Los hermanos son muy unidos.
Juan and Pepe are very close (friends)	Juan y Pepe son muy amigos..
[of contests, etc.]	reñido(a)
a close election	una elección reñida

close *prep & adv*

He works close to the harbor.	Trabaja cerca del puerto.
The stadium is close by.	El estadio está muy cerca.
We're getting close to the airport.	Nos acercamos al aeropuerto.

closet *n*

[a cupboard]	un armario/un closet *[Mex]*
[for clothes]	un ropero

coat *n*

coat	un abrigo
coat of paint	una mano de pintura

coffee *n*

black coffee	un café negro *[LA]*/solo *[Sp]*
coffee with a little milk	un café cortado
coffee with milk	un café con leche
espresso coffee	un café exprés
coffee-colored	de color café
coffee pot	una cafetera

cold *adj*

It's (very) cold. *[weather]*	Hace (mucho) frío
I'm (very) cold.	Tengo (mucho) frío.
Your hands are cold.	Tienes las manos frías.
The water is (very) cold.	El agua está (muy) fría.

cold *n*

[temperature]	el frío
I can't stand the cold.	No puedo soportar el frío.

collect

[infection]	un resfriado/un constipado/un catarro
to have a cold	estar resfriado(a)/constipado(a)/ acatarrado(a)
to catch a cold	acatarrarse/resfriarse

collect *v*
[as a collector]	coleccionar
I used to collect stamps.	Coleccionaba estampillas.
[to pick up sth]	recoger
They collected firewood.	Recogieron leña.
[to pick up/fetch sth]	ir a buscar algo/ir por
He went to collect the mail.	Fue a buscar/Fue por el correo.
to call collect *[telephone]*	llamar a cobro revertido
a collect call	una llamada a cobro revertido

college *n*
a college	una universidad
to go to/be in college	ir a/estar en la universidad

Ø **un colegio** can be an elementary or high school.

color *n*
What color is it?	¿De qué color es?
It's a blue/red color.	Es de color azul/rojo.
color film/photography/TV	una película/una fotografía/un televisor en colores

come *v*
to come	venir
(I'm) coming!	¡Voy!
Come on!	¡Vamos!
[to happen]	pasar
Come what may.	Pase lo que pase.

come + adverb
to come back (home)	regresar a casa/volver a casa
to come by *[house]*	pasar por casa
to come by *[obtain]*	conseguir/adquirir
to come down/up	bajar/subir
to come in/out	entrar/salir
to come up *[to happen]*	ocurrir/pasar/suceder
I'm sorry I'm late. Something came up.	Siento llegar tarde. Algo sucedió.

comfortable *adj*
of furniture
	cómodo(a)
a comfortable bed	una cama cómoda
a comfortable armchair	un sillón cómodo

of people
to be/feel comfortable	encontrarse a su gusto
to make oneself comfortable	acomodarse a su gusto
Make yourself comfortable!	¡Acomódate a tu gusto!/¡Ponte cómodo(a)!

of income
	adecuado
to be comfortably off	tener unos ingresos adecuados/una renta adecuada

40

commencement n
[beginning, start]   el comienzo/el principio
[graduation ceremony]   la ceremonia de entrega de diplomas

commute n & v
to commute   viajar diariamente/a diario al trabajo
to commute from the suburbs to   viajar desde las afueras hasta el
  downtown.   centro.
the daily commute   el viaje diario
commute time   la duración del viaje diario
We have a half hour commute.   Tardamos media hora en hacer el
                                              viaje al trabajo.

Ø **conmutar** means "to commute a sentence" or "to commute a payment."

commuter n
commuter   un viajero(a) diario(a)/una persona
                                              que viaja diariamente al trabajo
There is no real equivalent in Spanish for "commuter."

company n
a business   un comercio/una empresa/una
                                              casa/una firma/una sociedad

people
[guests]   invitados
to have company   tener invitados/visita
I'm expecting company tonight.   Espero invitados/visita esta noche.
[military, theater]   una compañía
[ship's]   una tripulación
He's good company.   Es un compañero divertido.
to part company   separarse de

competition n
[contest]   un concurso
an international chess competition.   un concurso internacional de ajedrez
[in business]   la competencia
unfair competition   la competencia desleal

complain v
in general
to complain (about)   quejarse (de)
I can't complain!   ¡Yo no me quejo!
She's always complaining about   Siempre se queja de algo.
  something.

to make a formal complaint   formular/presentar una queja
                                            formular una reclamación
You should complain to the   Deberías presentar una reclamación
  police.   a la policía.
I complained to the manager   Presenté una queja del ruido al
  about the noise.   gerente.

of health   presentar síntomas de/sufrir de
He's complaining about his throat.   Sufre de la garganta.

concentrate v
to concentrate (on)   concentrarse en/concentrar la atención en

41

concern

You must concentrate on your work	Debes concentrarte en tu trabajo.
to concentrate on doing sth	concentrarse para hacer algo
She's concentrating on solving the problem.	Se concentra para resolver el problema.
I can't concentrate.	No sé concentrarme.
He has trouble concentrating.	Lo encuentra difícil concentrarse.

concern *v*

[to affect]	tener que ver con/interesar
That doesn't concern you.	Eso no tiene nada que ver contigo.
as far as I'm concerned	en cuanto a mí/por lo que a mí se refiere
[to be worried about]	inquietarse por/preocuparse de
We're concerned about him.	Nos trae preocupados(as).
to concern oneself with	interesarse por/ocuparse de

condominium *n*

a condominium	una copropiedad
a condominium apartment	un condominio *[LA]*/un apartamento en copropiedad

conductor *n*

orchestra conductor	un director de orquesta
a train conductor	un revisor
lightning conductor	un pararrayos

Ø **un conductor** means "a driver."

conference *n*

[assembly, meeting]	un congreso
a national conference	un congreso nacional
a conference center	un palacio de congresos

Ø **una conferencia** means "a lecture."

confidence *n*

[general]	la confianza
to have confidence in sb/sth	tener confianza en alguien/algo
I have every confidence in my colleagues.	Tengo entera confianza en mis colegas.

Ø **una confidencia** means "a personal secret/revelation."

confident *adj*

self-confident

	seguro(a) de sí mismo(a)/lleno de confianza
She was very confident.	Estaba muy segura de sí misma.
They look very confident.	Parecen llenos(as) de confianza.

certain

to be confident of sth	estar seguro(a) de algo
I am confident you will win.	Estoy seguro(a) de que ganarás.

Ø **un confidente** means "a confidant" or "an informer."

conflict *n*

[clash, dispute]	un conflicto
a conflict of evidence	una contradicción de testimonios
a conflict of interests	una incompatabilidad
conflicting engagement	un compromiso
I have a conflict.	Ya tengo compromiso.

confuse v
[to mix up] · confundir (con)
You are confusing Paraguay and Uruguay. · Confundes el Paraguay con el Uruguay.
to confuse the issue · complicar la cuestión

confused *adj*
to be confused *[situation]* · estar confuso(a)/desconcertante
to be confused *[person]* · estar perplejo(a)
He looks confused. · Parece perplejo.
to get confused · desorientarse
I'm confused *[don't understand]*. · No lo comprendo bien.

confusing *adj*
It's confusing. · Está confuso./No queda claro.
It's all very confusing. · Todo ello es muy difícil de comprender.

connect v
[on phone] · poner a alguien (en comunicación) con

connection *n*
geographical · la comunicación
The connections between the town and the coast are bad. · Las comunicaciones entre el pueblo y la costa son malas.

relation · la relación
There's no connection between his company and mine. · No hay ningunia relación entre su firma y la mía.
I used to have good business connections with Ecuador. · Tenía buenas relaciones de negocios con Ecuador.

transit · la correspondencia/el enlace
There is a connection in Lima for Cuzco. · Hay correspondencia en Lima para Cuzco.
[connecting line in the metro] · la correspondencia

Ø **una conexión** means "an electrical or mechanical connection."

conservative *adj*
conservative · conservador(a)
the conservative party · el partido conservador

Ø **conservativo** usually means "preservative."

considerate *adj*
considerate · considerado(a)/atento(a)
to be considerate towards sb · ser atento(a) con
They were very considerate towards me. · Fueron muy atentos conmigo.
That's very considerate of you. · Es muy amable de tu parte.

consist v
to consist of · consistir en/constar de
What does the collection consist of? · ¿En qué consiste la colección?
The meal consisted of five courses. · La comida constó de cinco platos.

contact v
to contact sb · ponerse en contacto con/comunicar con

I'll contact her tomorrow.   Me pondré en contacto con ella mañana.

contents *n*
the contents of the bag/bottle/safe   el contenido de la bolsa/de la botella/de la caja fuerte

[of book]   el índice de materias

controversial *adj*
controversial   controvertible/discutido(a)/discutible
a controversial speech   un discurso controvertible

convenient *adj*
practical   práctico(a)
This system is not very convenient.   Este sistema no es muy práctico.

suitable   conveniente/apropiado
It would be a convenient place for the factory.   Sería un sitio apropiado para la fábrica.
Friday is convenient for me.   El viernes me conviene.
When is it convenient for your clients?   ¿Cuándo les conviene a tus clientes?
It's not convenient for the manager.   No es conveniente al gerente.

convention *n*
[a meeting]   una asamblea/un congreso/una convención

a convention center   una sala/un palacio de congresos/un centro de convenciones

[social convention/custom]   una convención

Ø **una convención** can also mean "agreement."

cook *v*
[in general]   cocinar/guisar
[by boiling]   cocer
Cook the meat slowly.   Cocina la carne a fuego lento./Que se cocine la carne a fuego lento.

I do the cooking at home   Soy yo el/la que hace la cocina/que prepara las comidas en casa.

[with name of a meal]   preparar
to cook lunch/dinner   preparar la comida/la cena
What's cooking? *[slang]*   ¿Qué pasa?

copy *n*
[reproduction]   una copia
a photocopy   una copia/una fotocopia
[of a book]   un ejemplar
I've lost my copy of *Don Quixote*.   He perdido mi ejemplar de *Don Quijote*.
[of a journal]   un número
Is this the latest copy of "Time"?   ¿Éste es el número más reciente de "Time"?

corner *n*
[in a room]   un rincón
She was sitting in the corner.   Estaba sentada en el rincón.
[outside, e.g., on the street]   una esquina
I'll wait for you on the corner.   Te esperaré en la esquina.
Let's meet in the café on the corner.   Vamos a reunirnos en el café de la esquina.

[in soccer]	una esquina/un córner
to take a corner	sacar una esquina/un córner

correct adj
[in general]	correcto(a)
[exact, right]	exacto(a)/justo(a)
the correct change	la moneda exacta/el suelto exacto
the correct time	la hora exacta
Correct!	¡Exacto!/¡Justo!
to be correct	tener razón

could v
past tense
[was/was not able to]
I couldn't do it.	No podía hacerlo/No pude hacerlo.

[did/did not know how to]
I couldn't do it.	No sabía hacerlo.

conditional
[would/would not be able to]
I said I could do it tomorrow.	Dije que podría hacerlo mañana.

[would/would not know how to]
I told him you could do it.	Le dije que tu sabrías hacerlo.

conditional perfect
[would/would not have been able to]
I could have done it if I had tried.	Habría podido hacerlo si me hubiera esforzado.

imperfect subjunctive
[would/would be able to after **si** "if"]
I would do it if I could. *[was able to]*	Lo haría si pudiera.
I would do it if I could.	Lo haría si supiera.
[knew how to]	

*[see also **can**]*

country n
[nation]	la nación/el país
[motherland/fatherland]	la patria
[countryside]	el campo
[region]	la región/la tierra

couple n
a few
in a couple of minutos	unos pocos/unas pocas
just a couple of minutes	en unos pocos minutos
I'll be in Chile only a couple of weeks.	dos minutos nada más
	Estaré en Chile sólo un par de semanas.

a pair [of things]
I've got a couple of things to tell you.	un par (de)
	Tengo un par de cosas que decirte.

two people together
a married couple	una pareja
a young married couple	un matrimonio
	un matrimonio joven

course n
course of action	una línea de conducta/acción
course of events	la marcha de los acontecimientos

court

a class   un curso
to take a math course   hacer un curso de matemáticas

on a menu   un plato
the main course   el plato principal
the first course   el primer plato

sport
a golfcourse   una cancha de golf [LA]/un campo de golf
a racecourse [horse-racing]   un hipódromo

court n
[of law]   un tribunal
[in sport]   una cancha [LA]/una pista [Sp]
a tennis court   una cancha de tenis
[royal court]   una corte

cream n
[in general]   la crema
[on whipped cream]   la nata
strawberries and cream   fresas con nata
a cream cake   un pastel de nata
suntan cream   la crema de broncear/la bronceadora

credit n
to buy on credit   comprar a crédito/a plazos
a credit card   una tarjeta de crédito
to pay with a credit card   pagar con tarjeta de crédito
credits [cinema]   los títulos/rótulos de crédito

crowded adj
[in general]   concurrido(a)/lleno(a) de gente
The streets were crowded.   Las calles estaban concurridas.
The bus was crowded.   El camión iba muy lleno.
[room]   apretado(a)/atestado(a)
The lecture room was crowded.   El aula estaba apretada.

cry v
[to shout]   gritar
[to weep]   llorar

cup n
[drinking vessel]   una taza/un pocillo [Col]
[trophy]   una copa

Ø **una copa** also means "a wine glass."

curious adj
inquisitive   curioso(a)
odd   extraño(a)/raro(a)

cute adj
attractive   lindo(a)/mono(a)/chulo(a) [Mex]
She's really cute.   Es muy linda.

shrewd   astuto(a)/listo(a)
What a cute (clever) guy!   ¡Qué tío tan listo!

D

dance *n*

a dance *[social event]*	un baile
a formal dance/a ball	un baile de etiqueta
to go dancing	ir a bailar/ir al baile
ballet dancing	el baile clásico
folk dancing	el baile tradicional
[ritual or tribal]	una danza
a dance hall	un salón de baile

dark *n*

the dark	las tinieblas/la oscuridad
She's afraid of the dark.	Tiene miedo de las tinieblas.

dark *adj*

It's dark.	Anochece/Se hace de noche.
It'll be dark at eight.	Anochecerá a las ocho.
Their kitchen is very dark.	Su cocina es muy oscura.
[of a color]	oscuro
His suit is dark blue.	Su traje es azul oscuro.

date *n*

the date *[calendar]* — la fecha

What's the date today? — ¿A cuántos estamos hoy?/¿Cuál es la fecha de hoy?

a personal or business date — una cita

a date *[romantic]*	una cita amorosa
to have a date	tener una cita
to make a date with sb	citarse con/darse cita con

the person invited — *[Note: There is no real equivalent in Spanish for "a date" referring to a person although it can sometimes be translated by **el novio/la novia** meaning "fiancé(e)" or "boyfriend"/"girlfriend".]*

his/her date — la chica/el chico con quien sale

date *v*

We're dating.	Salimos juntos.
Who are you dating?	¿Con quién sales?
Have you started dating?	¿Has comenzado a salir con chicos(as)?
to date a document	poner la fecha
to be up to date (with work)	estar al día
to be up to date (with the news)	estar al corriente
to bring sb up to date	poner a alguien al corriente
to bring sth up to date	poner algo al día

to date *adv*

to date — hasta la fecha

Ø **una data** means "an item *[in commerce]*;" **un dato** is "a fact" or "piece of information;" **los datos** means "data."

dated [see old-fashioned]

day n

a day	el día [Note: masculine]
What day is it?	¿Qué día es?
the first day of the week	el primer día de la semana
I'll be back in three days.	Volveré dentro de tres días.
the day before	el día anterior
the day before yesterday	anteayer
the next day/the following day	el día siguiente/al día siguiente
the day after tomorrow	pasado mañana
all day	todo el día
every day	todos los días/cada día
by day	de día
a day off	un día libre/un día de descanso
this very day	hoy mismo
Mother's Day	el día de la madre
a work day	una jornada
They have a ten-hour work day.	Tienen una jornada de diez horas.
Have a good day!	¡Que le vaya bien!/¡Que tenga un buen día! [Note: **usted** forms]

*[See also **today**]*

deal n
a quantity

a good deal (of)	mucho(a)/muchísimo(a)
He has a good deal of money.	Tiene mucho dinero.
She sleeps a good deal.	Duerme mucho.
They have done a good deal of the work.	Han hecho gran parte del trabajo.

business

a business deal	un trato/un negocio/una transacción
It's a deal!	¡Trato hecho!

a bargain

Only 100 pesos! That's a really good deal.	¡Sólo cien pesos! Es una verdadera ganga.

an agreement

[political, diplomatic]	un convenio
[business]	un trato
to make a deal	hacer un trato
to close a deal	cerrar un trato

deal with v

[to see to arrangements, etc.]	ocuparse de
My wife dealt with the arrangements.	Mi esposa se ocupó de los preparativos.
[to behave towards sb]	portarse con/tratar
They dealt very fairly with you.	Se portaron muy bien contigo./Te trataron muy bien.
[to have business dealings with]	tratar con
He deals with big companies.	Trata con grandes empresas.
[to deal with sb]	encargarse de
I'll deal with him.	Me encargaré de él.
[to confront, to handle]	enfrentarse con

The policeman will deal with this situation.

El guardia se enfrentará con esta situación.

dear *adj & noun*

a dear friend (of mine)

un querido amigo mío/una querida amiga mía

She was very dear to us all.

Todos la queríamos mucho./Fue querida por todos nosotros.

my dear/my darling

querido mío/querida mía

in letters
Dear Sir/Dear Madam/Dear Sirs

Muy señor mío/Muy señora mía/Muy señores míos

[to a specific person not personally known to you]
Dear Mr. Mateos
Dear Mrs./Miss Ruiz
[to a colleague]
Dear Dr. Gómez
[to a friend]
Dear Peter

Distinguido(a) señor(a)

Estimado señor Mateos
Estimada señora/señorita Ruiz
Mi distinguido(a) colega
Estimado(a) Doctor(a) Gómez
Mi querido(a) amigo(a)
Mi querido Pedro/Querido amigo (Pedro)/Querido Pedro

Dear Mary

Mi querida María/Querida amiga (María)/Querida María

decision *n*

to make a decision

tomar una decisión *[Note: not **hacer**]*

definite *adj*
certain
Is it definite they're coming?

seguro(a)/cierto(a)
¿Es seguro que vienen?

exact, clear

claro(a)/concreto(a)/determinado(a)/ definitivo(a)

a definite date
a definite result

una fecha determinada
un resultado concreto/definitivo

grammar
the definite article

el artículo definido

definitely *adj*
[certainly]

desde luego/claro que sí

Ø **definitivamente** means "finally" or "once and for all."

degree *n*
university
to have/get a degree
to have a degree in arts/law
to get a degree in science
a bachelor's degree
a doctorate (degree)

un título
sacar un título
ser licenciado(a) en letras/derecho
licenciarse en ciencias
una licenciatura
un doctorado

[Note: The degree system in universities in Spanish-speaking countries differs from that in the USA. There is no equivalent term for "a master's degree."]

temperature
The boiling point of water is 212 degrees (Fahrenheit).

un grado
El punto de ebullición del agua es 100 grados (centígrados).

Normal body temperature is 98.6 degrees.
It was 86 degrees today.

La temperatura normal del cuerpo es 37 grados.
Registraba 30 grados hoy.

demand n
The president has many demands on his time.
I have many demands on my time.
by popular demand
on demand
demands for (health) insurance

Los asuntos le tienen muy ocupado al presidente.
Los asuntos me tienen muy ocupado(a).
a petición del público
a petición
la urgente necesidad de seguro

demand v
to call for
The union demanded an increase.

reclamar
El sindicato reclamó un aumento.

to insist on, to require
I demanded an explanation from the manager.
She demands that you leave at once.

exigir
Le exigí una explicación al gerente.
Exige que te marches al instante.
[Note: subjunctive]

Ø **demandar** means "to sue."

demonstration n
in general
She gave a demonstration of the new dishwasher.

una demostración
Hizo una demostración del lavaplatos nuevo.

a protest
to hold a demonstration
a violent demonstration

una manifestación
hacer una manifestación/manifestarse
un motín/un tumulto

den n
[animal's lair]
[study]

una guarida
un estudio

deny v
to deny
I don't deny it.

negar
No lo niego.

Ø **negarse** means "to refuse:" "He refused to pay." **Se negó a pagar**.

depart v
[people]
[trains, etc.]
We will depart at six.
The train departs at seven.

irse/marcharse/partir
salir
Nos iremos/marcharemos a las seis.
El tren sale a las siete.

department n
in a store
The household appliances department is in the basement.
a department store

el departamento
El departamento de electrodomésticos está en el sótano.
un gran almacén/grandes almacenes

in a business
the maintenance department
the accounting department

el departamento/el servicio
el servicio de conservación
el servicio de contabilidad

in a university
la sección
the Spanish department
la sección de español

in government
el ministerio
the State Department
el Departamento de Estado

deposit n
down payment
[on rent, hotel room]
una señal/un depósito
[on purchase]
un abono *[LA]*/un depósito/una señal
to pay/leave a deposit of $50
dejar una señal de 50 dólares
to put a deposit on an
dar una entrada para un apartamento
  apartment
to pay a deposit on sth
pagar el desembolso inicial

at a bank
to make a deposit
hacer un depósito/ingreso

depress v
to depress *[mentally]*
deprimir
to be depressed
estar deprimido(a)/desanimado(a)
to get depressed
deprimirse
I feel depressed.
Me siento deprimido(a).
This place depresses me.
Este lugar me deprime.
This is very depressing.
Esto es muy deprimente.

detour n
to make a detour
desviarse/hacer un rodeo
We made a detour via León.
Nos desviamos por León.
I made a detour because the
Hice un rodeo porque la carretera
  road was blocked.
  estaba cortada.
[rerouting of traffic]
una desviación

development n
event, happening
un acontecimiento/un hecho
a sad development
un acontecimiento triste

progress, expansion
el desarrollo
a development plan
un plan de desarrollo
a housing development
una urbanización
an industrial development
un complejo industrial
a high-rise development
una torre de apartamentos

discovery
un descubrimiento
the latest developments in physics.
los últimos descubrimientos de la física

diary n
[a journal of personal experiences]
un diario
[appointment book]
una agenda/una libreta

Ø **diario** is the usual word for "a daily newspaper;" the adjective **diario(a)** means "daily."

direction n
in the direction of
en (la) dirección a
in the opposite direction
en sentido contrario/opuesto
Is this the right direction
¿Es éste el camino al hospital?
  for the hospital?
You're going in the wrong direction.
Te has equivocado de camino.

51

director

She doesn't have much sense of direction.	Le falta sentido de orientación.
Could you give me directions to the university?	¿Cómo se va a la universidad, por favor?
directions for use	el modo de empleo/las instrucciones para el uso

Ø **dirección** also means "address," "management," and "steering" *[of a car]*.

director *n*
all senses	un director/una directora
the managing director	el director/la directora gerente
the board of directors	el consejo de administración/la junta directiva

disappoint *v*
to disappoint	decepcionar/desilusionar
The book disappointed me.	El libro me decepcionó.
The actors disappointed us.	Los actores nos decepcionaron.
You have really disappointed her.	La has decepcionado mucho.
It was a disappointing result.	Fue un resultado decepcionante.
I'm very disappointed to learn that you are leaving.	Siento mucho saber que te marchas.

disappointment *n*
What a disappointment!	¡Qué decepción!

Ø "deception" and "to deceive" are rendered in Spanish by **el engaño** and **engañar** respectively.

discuss *v*/discussion *n*
to discuss	discutir/hablar de/estudiar/tratar de
We must discuss it.	Debemos estudiarlo.
discussion	una discusión/una conversación

Ø **discutir** and **discusión** more often than not mean "to argue" and "argument."

dish *n*
a serving dish	una fuente
a bowl	un plato hondo
a course/dish on a menu	un plato
a set of dishes	la vajilla
to do/wash the dishes	lavar los platos/la vajilla
a dishwasher	un lavaplatos

dispute *[see argument]*

disturb *v*
to bother, interrupt sb	molestar a alguien
I'm sorry to disturb you.	Siento molestarte.
Please do not disturb.	Se ruega no molesten. *[Note: subjunctive]*
Do not disturb!	¡No se moleste!
Don't disturb yourself!	¡No te molestes!/¡No se moleste!

to upset sb	inquietar/perturbar a alguien
I am very disturbed by your comments.	Tus observaciones me inquietan mucho.

divorce n & v

to divorce/to get a divorce from sb	divorciarse de alguien
He/She is divorced.	Está divorciado(a)
They are divorced.	Están divorciados.
Both women are divorced.	Las dos mujeres están divorciadas.
I divorced my husband.	Divorcié a/Me divorcié de mi marido.
He got a divorce ten days ago.	Se divorció hace diez días.
We got divorced last year.	Nos divorciamos el año pasado.
You should ask for a divorce.	Deberías pedir el divorcio. *[Note: "the" divorce]*

do v

for emphasis
	*[Note: **hacer** is not used for this]*
I do want them to come.	Quiero mucho que vengan.
Will John come? I do hope so.	¿Vendrá Juan? Espero que sí.
If the team does win ...	Si en realidad/en efecto gana el equipo...

to have finished
	haber acabado/terminado
Are they done?	¿Han terminado/acabado?

in a question, a negative
	*[Note: **hacer** is not used]*
Do you want to go out?	¿Quieres salir?
Don't you know me?	¿No me conoces?
Did you visit the museum?	¿Visitaste el museo?

to do without
	pasarse sin/prescindir de
She can't do without the car.	No puede pasarse sin el coche.
They can't do without him.	No pueden prescindir de él.

to have to do with
	tener que ver con
I want to have nothing to do with you.	No quiero tener nada que ver contigo.
It's (got) nothing to do with it.	No tiene nada que ver con ello.

to fare
How is he doing?	¿Cómo le va?/¿Qué tal le va?

to be suitable
Will this shirt do?	¿Qué te parece esta camisa?
Yes, that one will do.	Sí, me quedo con ésa.

domestic adj

of the home
domestic work	las faenas domésticas/de casa
domestic life	la vida de familia

national
domestic affairs	los asuntos interiores
a domestic flight	un vuelo nacional/interior

dormitory n

a student dormitory	una residencia

Ø **un dormitorio** is a "bedroom."

double adj

a double bed	una cama de matrimonio
a double room	una habitación doble/para dos

down

down adv & prep

The theater is down the street.	El teatro está un poco más abajo de la calle.
Her office is down below.	Su oficina está abajo.
down the street	calle abajo

verb + down

to come/go down	bajar
She hasn't come down yet.	Todavía no ha bajado.
I went down the street.	Bajé la calle.
They ran down the street.	Bajaron la calle corriendo.
to get down from [to get off]	apearse de/bajar de
He got down from the train.	Se apeó del tren./Bajó del tren.
to take/bring sth down	bajar
Take the suitcases down, please	Haga el favor de bajar las maletas.
to fall down	caer/caerse al suelo
to lay/put sth down (on)	poner/deponer algo (en)
to lie down	acostarse/echarse

downstairs adv

to come/go downstairs	bajar la escalera ·
The dog sleeps downstairs.	El perro duerme abajo.

downtown n

downtown	el centro de la ciudad
to go downtown	ir al centro

dozen n

a dozen eggs	una docena de huevos

dress n

[in general]	el vestido
[clothes]	la ropa
casual dress	la ropa de sport
formal or evening dress	el traje formal [LA]/el traje de etiqueta [men]/el traje de noche [women]
They were all in evening dress.	Todos estaban/iban vestidos de etiqueta
street or business clothes	el traje de calle

dress v

to dress/get dressed	vestirse
to dress up [for an occasion]	vestirse de etiqueta
to dress well	vestirse con gusto
to dress up as	disfrazarse de
to be dressed in	estar/ir vestido(a) de

drink n

a drink	una bebida
a drink [alcoholic]	una copa
to have a drink	tomar una bebida
to have a drink [alcoholic]	tomar una copa/echar un trago
a before-dinner drink	un aperitivo/un cóctel
an after-dinner drink	un licor

drive *v*

to drive a car	manejar *[LA]*/conducir/guiar un coche
Can you drive?	¿Sabes manejar?
to drive to work	ir al trabajo en coche *[Note: When "to drive" just means "to go by car" use* **ir en coche**.*]*
Shall we drive or walk?	¿Vamos en coche o a pie?
to drive sb home	llevar a alguien a casa

drop *v*

to drop sth	dejar caer *[deliberately]*
	caerse *[accidentally]*
I dropped the glass.	Se me cayó el vaso.
to drop out of school	abandonar sus estudios

drugs *n*

prescription drugs	los medicamentos
[narcotics]	las drogas/los narcóticos
to take drugs	drogarse
drug addiction	la toxicomanía
a drug addict/user	un toxicómano/un drogadicto
drug traffic	el tráfico de narcóticos
a drug trafficker	un traficante en drogas

drugstore *n*

a drugstore	una farmacia

Ø **una droguería** is a store where cleaning products for the home are sold; you will not find medicine here.

due *adj*

time due

The invoice is due for payment right now.	La factura es pagadera ahora mismo.
When is the train due?	¿Cuándo debe llegar el tren?
He is due to be in New York tomorrow.	Tiene que estar en Nueva York mañana.

due to

due to *[because of]* the fog	debido a/por causa de la niebla
due to *[thanks to]* my sister	gracias a mi hermana

E

each *adj*

each man/each woman	cada hombre/cada mujer
each day/each night	cada día/cada noche
each time	cada vez

*[Note: **Cada** is invariable.]*
*[See also **every**.]*

each *pron*

each (one)	cada uno/cada una
Each of my sons will come.	Cada uno de mis hijos vendrá.
He gave us each 100 dollars.	Nos dio a cada uno cien dólares./
	Nos dio cien dólares por persona.
each (one) of us/them	cada uno(a) de nosotros(as)/ellos(as)
They're worth 500 pesos each.	Valen quinientos pesos cada uno(a).
To each his own.	A cada cual lo suyo.

each other/one another *pron*

each one/one another	nos/se *[Note: **el uno el otro/la una la otra/los unos los otros/las unas las otras** may be added for clarity.]*
We've never written each other.	No nos hemos escrito nunca.
They don't help each other.	No se ayudan (el uno al otro).
They should talk to one another.	Deberían hablarse (unos a otros).
We were sitting across from each other.	Estábamos sentados el uno enfrente del otro.

ear *n*

the ear *[external]*	la oreja
the ear *[internal/sense of hearing]*	el oído
She has an earache.	Tiene dolor de oídos./Le duele el oído.
I have a good ear for music.	Tengo buen oído para la música.
My daughter has no ear for languages.	Mi hija no tiene oído para los idiomas.
to play by ear *[music]*	tocar de oído
to play it by ear	improvisar sobre la marcha
ear of corn	una mazorca

early *adj & adv*

for a set time

	temprano/con tiempo/de anticipación
He always arrives early at the office.	Siempre llega temprano a la oficina.
The train left ten minutes early.	El tren salió con diez minutos de anticipación.
You must reserve your tickets early.	Debes reservar tus boletos con tiempo.

in a time period

I got up early.	Me levanté temprano.
as early as possible	lo más pronto posible/cuanto antes
the early morning	la madrugada
early in the morning	de madrugada/muy de mañana

56

at an early date *[letters]*	en fecha próxima
He/She's an early riser.	Es madrugador(a).
to take the early flight	tomar el primer vuelo del día
in the early eighties	al principio de los (años) ochenta
He's in his early thirties.	Tiene poco más de treinta años.

earth *n*

[planet]	la Tierra
[soil]	el suelo/la tierra

easy *adj*

easy	fácil/sencillo(a)
Take it easy!	¡Tranquilo!
an easy chair	un sillón

eat *v*

to eat out	comer fuera/en un restaurante
to eat up	comerse
to eat away *[metal]*	desgastar
to eat into *[fig]*	consumir
with name of a meal	*[Note: Do not use* **comer** *with the name of a meal.]*
to eat breakfast	desayunar/tomar el desayuno
to eat lunch	almorzar/tomar el almuerzo/tomar la comida
to eat dinner	cenar/tomar la cena

Ø **comida** can also be used to mean "dinner;" this usage can vary from country to country so it is best to follow the local practice.

edge *n*

[of a cliff]	el borde
[of the water]	la orilla
[of a cutting tool]	el filo/el corte
[of a page]	el margen
to have the edge on sb	llevar ventaja a alguien
My nerves are on edge.	Tengo los nervios de punta.
the edge of town	las afueras

editor *n*

newspaper editor	el editor/la editora *[LA]*
	el director/la directora *[Sp]*
text editor	el redactor/la redactora

Ø In Spain **editor** means "publisher."

educated *adj*

Where were you educated?	¿Dónde cursaste tus estudios?
I was educated at the University of Madrid.	Cursé mis estudios en la Universidad de Madrid.
a well-educated person	una persona culta
He's very well educated.	Es muy culto.

Ø **bien educado(a)** means "well-bred," "well-mannered;" **mal educado(a)** means "badly behaved," "rude."

education *n*

[in general]	la educación
[instruction in a school]	la enseñanza

educational

[vocational training]	la formación
primary/secondary education	la enseñanza primaria/secundaria
further education	la enseñanza superior/los estudios universitarios

educational adj

educational background	la formación
an educational film	una película instructiva
educational policy	la política educativa
educational television	la televisión educativa
educational texts [for schools]	los libros escolares

Ø **educacional** is an anglicism for "educational" which will sometimes be heard.

effective adj

come into operation

	en vigor
effective from 1 May	en vigor a partir del primero de mayo
The curfew became effective at eleven o'clock.	El toque de queda entró en vigor a las once.

efficient [of things]

	eficaz
Her medication is very effective	Su medicina es muy eficaz.

efficient [of people]

	capaz/eficiente/competente
She's a very effective worker.	Es una trabajadora muy capaz.

effort n

effort	un esfuerzo
[an attempt]	un intento

either (one) adj & pron

either (one)	cualquier... de los/las dos
	cualquiera de los/las dos
	uno u otro
Either one (will do).	Cualquiera de los dos me servirá./ Cualquiera de los dos valdría./No me importa cualquiera.
Either car will do.	Cualquier coche (de los dos) me servirá.
Which color do you prefer? – I'll take either.	¿Qué color prefieres? – Llevaré cualquiera/uno u otro.

in the negative

	no... ninguno/ni... ni
I don't want either of them.	No quiero ninguno de los dos.
She doesn't like either.	No le gusta ni el uno ni el otro.

either ... or conj

either ... or	o... o
I'll go either to Mexico or to Colombia.	Iré o a México o a Colombia.
You could either go to the game or watch it on TV.	Podrías o ir al partido o mirarlo en la televisión.

in the negative

She doesn't like wine or beer.	No le gusta ni el vino ni la cerveza.
They're not going either.	No van tampoco.

elective n

an elective course	un curso facultativo
an elective subject	una asignatura facultativa

elevator n
an elevator — un elevador *[LA]*/un ascensor *[Sp]*

else adv
something else — algo más/otra cosa
nothing else/not ... anything else — nada más *[+ no with verb]*
We don't need anything else. — No necesitamos nada más.
everything else — todo lo demás
somebody else — otro(a)/otra persona
nobody else/not ... anybody else. — nadie más
Nobody else can do it. — Nadie más (que tú/él, *etc.*) sabe hacerlo.
He didn't see anybody else. — No vio a nadie más.
everybody else — todos los demás/todos los otros
somewhere else *[with motion]* — a (cualquier) otro sitio/otra parte
somewhere else *[position]* — en (cualquier) otro sitio/otra parte
nowhere else *[with motion]* — a ningún otro sitio/a ninguna otra parte
nowhere else *[position]* — en ningún otro sitio/en ninguna otra parte
What else?/Anything else? *[in a store or café, etc.]* — ¿Algo más?
What else could I do? — ¿Qué más podría hacer?
Who else is coming? — ¿Quién más viene?
or else ... — si no...

embarrass v
to embarrass — apenar *[LA]*/avergonzar/desconcertar/turbar/azarar
to embarrass [deliberately] — poner en un aprieto
to be/feel embarrassed — apenarse *[LA]*/avergonzarse
sentirse confuso(a)/azarado(a)/avergonzado(a)/molesto(a)/violento(a)
She looked embarrassed. — Parecía confusa.
I'm really embarrassed about it. — Me siento algo avergonzado(a) por eso.
It was an embarrassing situation. — Fue una situación violenta.
We were embarrassed by his behavior. — Su comportamiento nos desconcertó.

Ø **embarazar** means "to hinder," "to obstruct," or "to make pregnant;" **embarazada** means "pregnant," not "embarrassed."

emotional adv
of a person
[warm-hearted] — emocional / sentimental
[taking things too hard] — demasiado sensible
[over-emotional] — exagerado(a)/exaltado(a)

relating to the emotions — emocional
an emotional experience/shock/state — una experiencia/una conmoción/un estado emocional

emphasis n/emphasize v
to accent — acentuar
In Spanish you put the accent on the next-to-the-last syllable. — En castellano se acentúa la penúltima sílaba.

to stress the importance — enfatizar
The guide emphasized the importance of not going into that area. — El guía enfatizó la importancia de no pasar por ese barrio.

He emphasized that we should arrive on time.

Enfatizó que deberíamos llegar a tiempo.

enclose v/enclosure n
to enclose something
enclosed
Please find enclosed ...
I enclose a check for 50 dollars.

adjuntar algo/remitir algo adjunto
adjunto(a)
Le mandamos adjunto(a)...
Remito un cheque de cincuenta dólares.

end n
opposite of beginning
the end of the century/the
  film/the paragraph/the week
at the end of the month

el fin
el fin del siglo/de la película/del
  párrafo/de la semana
a finales del mes

of a time or place
at the end of the corridor
at the other end of the street

el final
al final del pasillo
al otro extremo de la calle

other
from one end to another
a candle end
the end of a table
To what end?
to no end
You'll never hear the end of it.

de un extremo al otro
un cabo de vela
el extremo de una mesa
¿Con qué propósito?
en vano
No te dejarán olvidarlo nunca.

end v
to end [in general]
This word ends with a "t."
She ended by saying ...

terminar/acabar
Esta palabra termina en "t."
Terminó diciendo...

energetic adj
an energetic person

una persona enérgica

Ø **energético(a)** is an anglicism, often used in Latin America.

engaged adj/engagement n
to be engaged [to be married]
They got engaged yesterday.
She got engaged to a Peruvian.
to announce one's engagement

estar prometido(a)
Se prometieron ayer.
Se prometió con un peruano.
darse palabra de casamiento

business/social occasion
She has an engagement tonight.
You have an engagement at six.

Tiene un compromiso esta noche.
Tienes una cita a las seis.

engine n
[of a car]
[of a train]
a jet engine

el motor
la máquina/la locomotora
un motor de reacción

enjoy v
to possess
She enjoys good health.

disfrutar de/gozar de
Disfruta de buena salud.

to take pleasure in
I enjoyed the film.
Do you enjoy reading?

gustar/disfrutar con
Me gustó la película.
¿Te gusta leer?

He enjoys classical music.	Disfruta con la música clásica.
They enjoyed their vacation.	Se divirtieron en las vacaciones.

to enjoy oneself — divertirse/pasarlo bien
He enjoyed himself in the country. — Se divirtió en el campo.
I didn't enjoy myself in Chile. — No lo pasé bien en Chile.

enough *adj & adv*
You don't eat enough. — No comes bastante.
I don't have enough time. — No tengo suficiente tiempo.
He didn't have enough money. — No tenía suficiente dinero.
They are rich enough to pay for it. — Son bastante ricos para pagarlo.
It's good enough. — Está bien.
I've had enough. *[I'm fed up.]* — Estoy harto(a).
That's enough! — ¡Basta ya!
oddly enough — por extraño que parezca

enroll *v*
to enroll in a club — inscribirse en una sociedad
to enroll in a course — matricularse para un curso

entertain *v*
to hospitality, meals, etc. — agasajar/invitar
They entertained her at the Palace. — La agasajaron en el Palacio.

to amuse — divertir/entretener
He entertained the children. — Divirtió/Entretuvo a los niños.

entree *n*
the entree *[main course]* — el plato principal

errand *n*
an errand — un encargo/un recado/una diligencia *[Arg]*

escape *n*
[in general] — una fuga/una huída
[of gas] — un escape

escape *v*
[to make one's escape] — escaparse
He escaped from jail. — Se escapó de la cárcel.
[to avoid] — evitar/librarse de
to escape danger — librarse del peligro
They narrowly escaped death. — Por poco evitaron la muerte.

establish *v*
[proof] — demostrar
[facts] — constatar
[fame] — consolidar

estimate *n & v*
to assess — calcular
I estimate that it will cost too much. — Calculo que va a costar demasiado.

for work to be done — presupuestar/hacer un presupuesto
an estimate — un presupuesto

| He estimated for the building materials. | Hizo un presupuesto del material de construcción. |

Ø **estimar** means "to esteem," "to respect."

even *adj*
flat, level, smooth
| an even piece of land | llano(a)/liso(a) un terreno llano |
| an even surface | una superficie lisa |

uniform
| at an even pace | uniforme/regular a paso uniforme/regular |

equal
| The teams are even. | igual Los equipos son iguales. |

opposite of odd
| odd or even numbers | par números pares o impares |

even *adv*
even	aun/hasta/incluso
Even the President attended.	Hasta el Presidente asistió.
even at night	aun de noche
Everybody left, even the teachers.	Todos salieron, incluso los profesores.
even so	aun así
even on Saturdays	incluso los sábados

even if/even though
	aunque *[+ subjunctive]* si bien que *[+ indicative]*
I wouldn't help them even if I could.	No los ayudaría aunque pudiera.
Even though he bought a ticket he didn't go to the concert.	Si bien que sacó una entrada no asistió al concierto.
Even though it is easy he won't do it.	Aunque sea fácil no quiere hacerlo.

not even
| She didn't even read the instructions. | ni siquiera Ni siquiera leyó las instrucciones. |

evening *n*
the evening	la tarde
at seven o'clock in the evening	a las siete de la tarde
this evening/yesterday evening /tomorrow evening	esta tarde/ayer por la tarde/ mañana por la tarde
every evening	todas las tardes
all evening/the whole evening	toda la tarde
I always go out in the evening.	Siempre salgo por las tardes.
She's going out in the evening.	Sale por la tarde.
Good evening!	¡Buenas tardes!
during the evening	durante la tarde
a musical evening	una velada

Ø In the Spanish-speaking world the day is essentially divided into three: morning/before lunch **(la mañana)**, between lunch and darkness falling **(la tarde)** which corresponds to our afternoon and early evening, and night **(la noche)**.

event *n*
| an event/a happening | un suceso/un acontecimiento |

Ø **suceso** can also mean "accident" or "crime;" "success" is translated by **el éxito.**

eventful *adj*
eventful | memorable

eventually *adv*
[in time] | finalmente/al fin y al cabo/eventualmente [LA]
to do sth eventually | acabar por hacerlo
He'll do it eventually. | Lo hará con el tiempo/a la larga.

Ø **eventualmente** also means "by chance."

ever *adv*
Have you ever been to Peru? | ¿Has ido alguna vez al Perú?
forever | para siempre/por siempre

every *adj*
every | cada/todos los/todas las
every tourist | cada turista/todos los turistas
every Sunday | todos los domingos
every other day | cada dos días
every ten minutes | cada diez minutos
every half hour | cada media hora
every one | cada uno(a)
every one of them | todos ellos/todas ellas
every one of us | todos nosotros/todas nosotras

everybody/everyone *pron*
everybody | todo el mundo/todos
Everybody will be there. | Estará todo el mundo. [Note: singular verb]/Estarán todos.

everything *pron*
everything | todo
We sold everything. | Lo vendimos todo.
Everything's fine. | Todo va/está bien.
to do everything | hacer de todo
everything that | todo lo que
everything (that's) good | todo lo bueno
everything (that) you want | todo lo que quieras [Note: subjunctive]
I'll do everything I can. | Haré todo lo que pueda.

everywhere *adv*
everywhere in Mexico | en todas partes de México
There are tourists everywhere. | Hay turistas en todas partes.
We went everywhere in Spain. | Fuimos a todas partes de España.
She looked everywhere. | Buscó por todas partes.
everywhere they go | dondequiera que vayan

evidence *n*
[proof] | las pruebas
[signs] | los indicios
to give evidence | prestar declaración

evil *adj*
[of person] | malo(a)/malvado(a)
[of things] | malo(a)/pernicioso(a)

exam *n*
in school
	un examen
a final exam	un examen de fin de curso
an oral exam	un examen oral
to take an exam	hacer un examen/presentarse a un examen
to pass an exam	aprobar/ser aprobado(a) en un examen [Note: not **pasar**]
to fail an exam	suspender un examen [Note: not **faltar**]
You have failed.	Te han suspendido.

medical exam

un reconocimiento médico
He had a physical exam.   Le dieron un reconocimiento médico.

examine *v*
[in general]   examinar
[in jurisprudence]   interrogar

exchange *n & v*
I'd like to exchange this shirt for a larger size.   Quisiera cambiar esta camisa por una talla más grande.
The exchange rate of the dollar has gone up.   Ha subido el tipo de cambio del dólar.
foreign exchange   las divisas
Stock Exchange   la Bolsa
telephone exchange   la central telefónica
[of ideas]   un intercambio
in exchange for   a cambio de

excited *adj*
enthusiastic
to be excited   estar emocionado(a)
to be excited about   emocionarse por
     entusiasmarse con/por
I'm very excited about my new car.   Me entusiasmo con mi coche nuevo.
She was very excited about my news.   Se quedó muy entusiasmada por mis noticias./Mis noticias le hicieron mucha ilusión.

over-excited
The children were over-excited.   Los niños estaban nerviosas.
Don't get too excited!   ¡No te emociones tanto!/No te excites!

looking forward to
We're getting excited about our trip to Brazil.   Esperamos con ansia nuestro viaje al Brasil.
She was getting excited about the holidays.   Esperaba con mucha ilusión las vacaciones.

exciting *adj*
exciting   emocionante

excuse *v*
to interrupt
Excuse me. Could you please ...   Perdón, señor/señora/señorita. ¿Podría usted... ?
     Perdone usted, señor/señora/señorita. ¿Podría... ?

to apologize
Excuse me (for disturbing you)

Discúlpame por haberte molestado.
Discúlpeme por haberle molestado.
Me disculpo por molestarte/molestarle.
Te/le pido perdón por molestarte/
molestarle.

to seek permission
*[on leaving table, getting
off crowded bus/metro,
pushing through crowd, etc.]*

Con (su) permiso.

to justify
He cannot excuse his conduct.

justificar
No puede justificar su conducta.

to excuse sb from doing sth
I excused them from attending.

dispensar/eximir a alguien de hacer algo
Les dispensé de asisitir.

executive *n*
executive

un ejecutivo/una ejecutiva

exercise *n*
a written exercise
to do (physical) exercises

un ejercicio escrito
hacer ejercicios/hacer gimnasia/
practicar la gimnasia

exercise book

un cuaderno

exercise *v*
to exercise *[physically]*
to exercise the dog
to exercise rights/duties

hacer ejercicio físico/entrenarse
sacar el perro de paseo
ejercer derechos/obligaciones

exhaust *n*
an exhaust
exhaust fumes

un (tubo de) escape
los gases de combustible

exhaust *v*
to exhaust
The work exhausted me.

agotar
El trabajo me agotó.

exhibition *n*
[a show of art, etc.]
[an exhibition of sports]
to make an exhibition of oneself

una exposición
una exhibición
ponerse en ridículo

exit *n*
the exit

la salida

Ø **el éxito** means "success."

expect *v*
to await
I am expecting him shortly.
My wife is expecting a baby.

esperar
Lo espero dentro de poco.
Mi esposa espera un niño.

to anticipate sth
They didn't expect that.
We expect to see them soon.
He is expecting us to come.

esperar
No lo esperaban.
Esperamos verlos pronto.
Espera que vengamos. *[Note: subjunctive]*

expense

That is to be expected.	Es de esperar.
As was to be expected.	Como era de esperar./Como podía esperarse.

to plan to — contar con/tener la intención de
They expect to leave tomorrow.	Cuentan con salir mañana.
When do you expect to return?	¿Cuándo tienes la intención de volver?

to think likely
I expect so.	Supongo que sí.
I don't expect so.	Supongo que no.

expense n
expense	un gasto
at my expense	a costa mía/a mi costa
expense account	una cuenta de gastos de representación
to go to any expense	hacer todo lo posible
to meet expenses	hacer frente a los gastos

experience n
an experience	una experiencia
to learn by experience	aprender por la experiencia

experience v
to experience pleasure	experimentar placer
to experience pain/grief	sufrir dolor
to experience a loss	sufrir una pérdida
to experience difficulty	tener dificultad

experiment n
to do an experiment	hacer experimentos/pruebas
They do experiments on rabbits.	Hacen experimentos con conejos.

expire v
[to die]	morir/expirar
[contract]	vencer
[passport, driver's license]	caducar

express adj
special delivery — urgente
express mail	el correo urgente
an express package/letter	un paquete/una carta urgente

of transport
an express train	un rápido/un expreso

extend v
to extend [in general]	extender
[to enlarge]	ampliar
[to lengthen]	alargar
[to prolong]	alargar
to extend a visa	prorrogar una visa [LA]/un visado
to extend an invitation	invitar

extent n
extent	una extensión
[limit]	un límite

to a certain extent	hasta cierto punto
to a greater or lesser extent	en mayor o menor grado
to a large extent	en gran parte
to what extent?	¿hasta qué punto?

extra *adj*

[additional]	adicional
I need an extra blanket.	Necesito una cobija adicional.
[to spare]	de más/de sobra
some extra towels	unas toallas de sobra
two extra towels	dos toallas más
an extra charge	un recargo
[a supplement on a ticket]	un suplemento
an extra payment	un pago extraordinario

Ø **extra** can often mean "of superior quality."

extravagant *adj*

in spending
He's an extravagant person.

pródigo(a)/despilfarrador(a)
Es una persona pródiga.

exaggerated
She has extravagant ideas.
These prices are extravagent.

Tiene ideas extravagantes.
Estos precios son exorbitantes.

F

fabric *n*
[cloth]   el tejido/la tela

Ø **la fábrica** means "factory" and also "fabric" or "framework" [of a building].

fabricate *v*
[to make]   fabricar/labrar
to fabricate a story   forjar una historia
[documents, evidence, etc.]   falsificar

face *n*
[of a person]   la cara/el rostro
[countenance]   el semblante
[of a clock]   la esfera/el cuadrante
to make faces   hacer muecas/gestos
to wear a long face   poner mala cara
face value   el valor nominal
to keep a straight face   contener la risa
to tell sb to his/her face   decir a uno a rajatablas

face *v*
The library faces the river.   La biblioteca da al río.
My room faces south.   Mi cuarto da al sur.
They were (sitting) facing   Estaban (sentados) uno frente al
  each other.   otro./Estaban (sentadas) una
                                             frente a la otra.
to face (up) to a problem   afrontar/arrostrar/hacer frente a
                                             un problema
Let's face it.   Hay que reconocerlo.
She can't face it.   No tiene la resolución para afrontarlo.
to face the music   dar la cara/afrontar las consecuencias
[to put a new surface on]   revestir

facility *n*
a facility for music/math/   una facilidad para la música/las
  languages, etc.   matemáticas/los idiomas, etc.
a sports facility   unas instalaciones deportivas
transportation facilities   los medios de comunicación

fact *n*
in general   el hecho/la realidad
[data/information]   los datos
The fact of the matter is (that)   La verdad es (que)

in fact (emphasizing)   en efecto/efectivamente
I often go to see him; in   Voy a verlo frecuentemente; en
  fact, I went to see him   efecto fui a verlo hoy.
  today.

in fact (on the contrary)   en realidad/de hecho
They claim to be experts, but   Pretenden ser peritos, pero en
  in fact they know very little.   realidad/de hecho saben muy poco.

68

faculty n
[school or university staff]   el profesorado

Ø **la facultad** is a "school" or "college" in a Spanish-speaking university, e.g., **la facultad de derecho** "law school."

fade v
[color]   desteñirse/descolorarse
[flower]   marchitarse
[light]   apagarse
to fade away   desvanecerse
to fade in   aparecer progresivamente
to fade out   desaparecer progresivamente

fail v
to fail an exam   ser reprobado(a) [LA]/suspendido(a)
                                            en un examen [Note: not **faltar**]
[brakes, harvest, memory]   fallar
The brakes failed.   Fallaron los frenos.
to fail sb   fallar a alguien
not to fail to do sth   no dejar de hacer algo
I won't fail to tell him.   No dejaré de decírselo.
[of plans, events, etc.]   fracasar
The film/plan failed.   La película/El proyecto fracasó.

fair adj
[in appearance]   hermoso(a)
[of hair]   rubio(a)
[just]   justo(a)
[of weather]   bueno
The weather is fair.   Hace buen tiempo.
[of price]   razonable
fair play   el juego limpio

fall v
to fall   caer/caerse
[prices, temperature]   bajar
[date, night, silence]   caer
Night fell.   Cayó la noche/Anocheció/Se hizo de noche.
to fall down [person]   caerse
to fall down [building]   hundirse/derrumbarse/venirse abajo
to fall down the stairs   caer rodando por la escalera
to fall for sb   enamorarse de alguien
to fall through [plans, etc.]   fracasar

false adj
[mistaken, wrong]   falso(a)/erróneo(a)
[of teeth, hair, jewels]   postizo(a)
a false bottom   un doble fondo
a false ceiling   un cielo raso
false imprisonment   la detención ilegal
a false start   una salida nula
a false step   un paso en falso

familiar adj
well known   bien conocido/familiar
That's a familiar situation.   Es una situación bien conocida.

fan

They look familiar.	Me parece que los conozco.
His voice is familiar.	Me parece que conozco la voz.
a familiar story	un cuento de todos los días
That sounds familiar.	Eso me suena.
to be on familiar terms with sb	tener confianza con alguien

to be familiar with sth
[a place]	conocer
I'm not familiar with Puebla.	No conozco Puebla.
[facts/information]	estar enterado(a) de
She's not familiar with the facts.	No está enterada de los datos.

Ø **familiar** is also used as an adjective meaning "family,", e.g., **asuntos familiares** "family matters."

fan *n*
[a cooling device]	un abanico *[manual]*/un ventilador *[mechanical]*
[admirer of a star]	un(a) admirador(a)
[supporters of a team]	las hinchadas *[LA]*/los (las) hinchas/los (las) aficionados(as)
He's a supporter of Santa Fe.	Es hincha del Santa Fe.
[an enthusiast, a "buff"]	un(a) aficionado(a)/un(a) entusiasta
I'm a boxing/baseball fan.	Soy aficionado(a) del boxeo/béisbol.

far *adv*
far away/far	lejos
It's not far from the station.	No está lejos de la estación.
Is it far (from here)?	¿Está lejos?/¿Dista mucho (de aquí)?
It's too far to walk.	Está demasiado lejos para caminar/ir a pie.
Keep going as far as the park.	Sigue/Siga hasta el parque.
How far is it to San Juan?	¿Cuánto hay de aquí a San Juan?
We went as far as the bank.	Fuimos hasta el banco.
as far as I can tell	que yo sepa
She's by far the best.	Es con mucho la mejor.

farm *n*
a farm	una granja/una finca *[LA]*/una estancia *[LA]*/una hacienda/un cortijo/una quinta *[LA]*/un rancho *[Mex]*
cattle farm	una hacienda *[LA]*/un rancho *[LA]*/una estancia *[Arg]*
farmhouse	un cortijo/una alquería/una casa de labranza/una casa de hacienda *[LA]*

fast *adj*
[quick]	rápido(a)/ligero(a)
a fast train	un tren rápido
to be fast *[of a clock]*	adelantar
My watch is ten minutes fast.	Mi reloj adelanta diez minutos/está diez minutos adelantado.
fast colors	los colores sólidos

fast *adv*
[rapid]	de prisa/rápidamente
He speaks fast.	Habla de prisa.
She was going very fast.	Ella iba muy de prisa/con mucha velocidad.

Not so fast!   ¡Un momento!

fast *v*
to fast   ayunar

fat *adj*
of a person   gordo(a)/grueso(a)
to get/grow fat   engordar

of food   que tiene mucha grasa/grasiento(a)
It was too fat.   Tenía demasiada grasa.

fat *n*
for cooking
[lard]   la manteca de cerdo/el lardo
[suet]   el sebo

in meat   la grasa
There's a lot of fat in this   Hay mucha grasa en este cerdo./
  pork.   Este cerdo tiene mucha grasa.

faucet *n*
a faucet   un grifo/una llave/un caño [Per]

fault *n*
a weakness   un defecto
He has his faults.   Tiene sus defectos.

blame   la culpa
Whose fault is it?   ¿Quién tiene la culpa?
It's not my fault.   No es culpa mía.

geological
a fault   una falla

error
faults in spelling   errores de ortografía

Ø **falta** means "a fault" [in tennis], "a mistake," or "a lack."

fault *v*
to fault, find fault with   criticar
You cannot fault her taste.   No puedes criticar su gusto.

favorite *adj & n*
favorite   preferido(a)/favorito(a)
the favorite   el preferido/la preferida
This is my favorite opera.   Ésta es mi ópera preferida.
This song is my favorite.   Ésta es la canción que más me gusta.
She is her mother's favorite.   Es la hija predilecta de su madre.

fed up *adj*
to be fed up (with sth)   estar harto(a) (de algo)
We're fed up with traveling.   Estamos hartos(as) de viajar.

feel *v intrans*
health   sentirse
How do you feel?   ¿Cómo te sientes?
I don't feel very well.   No me siento muy bien.

71

feel

My wife feels sick.
[see also sick]

Mi esposa se siente enferma.

physical state
Do you feel hot/cold?
The children feel thirsty.

¿Tienes calor/frío?
Los niños tienen sed.

inclination
to feel like doing sth
Do you feel like going?

tener ganas de
¿Tienes ganas de ir?

emotional
I feel bad that ...

Siento que.../Me da lástima que.../
   Lamento que...

I feel bad that her father is ill.

Siento que su padre esté enfermo.
   [Note: subjunctive]

He feels bad that he upset you.
to feel good that ...

Le da lástima que te desconcertó.
estar contento(a)/satisfecho(a) *[+*
   subjunctive]

He feels good (that) you are
   better.
They feel good about the new
   house.

Está contento de que estés mejor.

Están satisfechos(as) de la casa
   nueva.

feel *v trans*
to touch
The doctor felt my ribs.
to feel sb's pulse

palpar
La médica me palpó las costillas.
tomar el pulso a alguien

to be aware of
I felt that somebody was in
   the room.

sentir
Sentí que alguien estaba en el
   cuarto.

to experience
They are feeling the effects
   of the earthquake.
to feel affection/pity for
to feel regret
I feel no interest in your
   affairs.

sentir/experimentar
Sienten los efectos/Se resienten de los
   efectos del terremoto.
sentir cariño/compasión por
sentirlo/sentir pesar
No me interesan tus asuntos.

to have the impression (that)
He feels they are talking about
   him.

tener la impresión (de) que
Tiene la impresión de que hablan de
   él.

to believe
She feels I am too old.
I feel you are lying.

creer/estar convencido(a)
Cree que soy demasiado viejo(a).
Estoy convencido(a) de que mientes.

fender *n*
[bumper]
[mudguard]

un parachoques
un guardabarros/un guardafango/una aleta

fertile *adj*
[soil]
[biologically]

fértil
fecundo(a)

few *adj*
in number
Few people came.

poco(a)/pocos(as)
Vino poca gente.

The town has few stores.　El pueblo tiene pocas tiendas.

some, several　unos(as)/algunos(as)/unos(as)
　　pocos(as)/unos(as) cuantas(as)

The town has a few bookstores.　El pueblo tiene unas cuantas librerías.

fewer adj
fewer ... (than)　menos... (que/de)
There are fewer tourists this　Hay menos turistas este año.
　year.
There are fewer tourists than　Hay menos turistas que el año
　last year.　　pasado.
I have fewer books than you.　Tengo menos libros que tú.
I have fewer books than you think.　Tengo menos libros de lo que piensas.
She has fewer than fifty.　Tiene menos de cincuenta.
the fewer the better　cuantos(as) menos mejor

fewest adj
the fewest　los(las) menos/el menor número de
This area has the fewest　Esta región tiene el menor número
　tourists.　　de turistas.

field n
[an open space]　un campo
[a soccer field]　una cancha[LA]/un campo de fútbol
a field of interest [a speciality]　un campo/un terreno de actividad
It's not my field.　No es mi terreno.
[magnetic, electric, accoustic]　un campo

fierce adj
[animal]　feroz/fiero(a)
[person]　cruel/violento(a)
[weather]　horroroso(a)

fight n & v
to fight physically　luchar/pelear/batirse con
to have a fight with sb　batirse con alguien
I had a fight with him.　Me batí con él./Peleé con él.
They were fighting in the street.　Peleaban/Se batían en la calle.

to quarrel　disputar/reñir
to have a fight with sb　reñir con alguien
We had a fight.　Reñimos.

to fight against　luchar contra
to fight against drugs　luchar contra las drogas
the fight against poverty　la lucha contra la pobreza

figure n
[a number]　un número/una cifra
to keep/lose one's figure　guardar/perder la línea
to have a good figure　tener buen tipo/tener un tipo
　　estupendo/tener buen físico [LA]

fill v
to fill a glass　llenar un vaso
to fill out a form　rellenar un formulario/completar un
　　formulario [Arg]

to fill up with gas	echar gasolina (al coche)
Fill her up!	¡Llénelo!
to fill a vacancy	cubrir un puesto
to fill a tooth	empastar una muela
to fill a crack	llenar una hendedura
to fill an order	despachar un pedido

film *n & v*

[cinema, photographic]	la película/el film/el filme
roll of film	un rollo/un carrete de fotografías
film star	un astro de cine *[man]*/una estrella de cine *[woman]*
film industry	la industria cinematográfica
silent film	una película muda
[thin layer]	una capa
[mist, smoke, etc.]	un velo
to film	filmar/rodar

final *adj & n*

[last]	último(a)/final
the final exam	el examen del fin de curso
the final *[in sports]*	la final
the final chapter	el último capítulo

finally *adv*

[at last]	al fin/por fin/finalmente
They have finally done it.	Por fin lo han hecho.

financial aid *n*

[in general]	la ayuda económica/financiera
[a grant]	una beca
[a loan in general]	un préstamo
[a commercial loan]	un empréstito

find *v*

to find *[general]*	encontrar
Have you found the keys?	¿Has encontrado las llaves?
No, I can't find them.	No, no las encuentro.
[to go and find]	ir a buscar
I'm going to find something to read.	Voy a buscar algo que leer.
[to surprise]	sorprender
I found him spying on us.	Lo sorprendí espiándonos.
[to establish]	comprobar
It has been found that ...	Se ha comprobado que...

fine *adj*

a fine meal	una comida excelente
a fine garden	un jardín hermoso
a fine dress	un vestido elegante
a fine afternoon *[occasion]*	una tarde agradable
a fine day *[weather]*	un buen día

finish *v*

to finish	acabar/terminar
She finished by bursting into tears.	Acabó por echarse a llorar.
I have finished writing.	He terminado de escribir.

fire *n*

a fire	un fuego/un incendio
to make/light a fire	encender un fuego
to be sitting by the fire	estar sentado(a) al lado de la chimenea
to be on fire	estar ardiendo/en llamas
to catch fire	encenderse
to set fire to	pegar fuego a/incendiar
to put out a fire	apagar un fuego
the fire department	los bomberos/el cuerpo de bomberos
fireworks	los fuegos artificiales

fire *v*

to fire at *[with a gun]*	tirar a/hacer fuego a
to open fire	abrir fuego
Fire!	¡Fuego!
[to dismiss sb]	despedir a/echar a alguien

first *adj*

first	primero(a)
the first time	la primera vez
the first row	la primera fila
the first chapter	el primer capítulo *[Note: **primero** shortens to **primer** before a noun]*
the first six months	los seis primeros meses *[Note word order]*
the first of March	el primero de marzo
Charles I (the first)	Carlos I° (primero) *[Note: no article]*

first *adv*

(at) first/first of all	en primer lugar/ante todo/primero
first and foremost	antes que nada/ante todo
head first	de cabeza
ladies first	las señoras primero
My family comes first.	Mi familia es lo primero.
We first went there last month.	Fuimos allí por primera vez el mes pasado.
[before]	antes/primero
You must see me first.	Tienen que verme primero.

first *pron*

the first	el primero/la primera
They were the first to arrive.	Llegaron primeros.

fish *n & v*

a fish *[alive in the water]*	un pez
a fish *[food]*	un pescado
to fish	pescar
to go fishing	ir a pescar/ir de pesca
fishing	la pesca

fix *v*

[to repair sth]	reparar algo
to fix a meal	preparar una comida
to fix *[arrangements, etc.]*	arreglar

Ø **fijar** has numerous meanings, e.g., "to fix," "to secure," "to stick down," "to focus," etc.

flat *n*
a flat *[tire]*

una ponchadura *[LA]*/un pinchazo *[Sp]*/una llanta baja

flavor *n*
taste
This coffee has a bitter flavor.

el gusto/el sabor
Este café tiene un sabor amargo.

flavoring
I want an ice-cream with a chocolate flavor.
This cake has an orange flavor.

Quiero un helado con sabor a chocolate.
Este pastel tiene sabor a naranja.

flight attendant
flight attendant/stewardess

la aeromoza *[LA]*/la azafata *[Sp]*

floor *n*
the floor *[beneath one's feet]*
on the floor
dance floor
floor show

el piso *[LA]*/el suelo *[Sp]*
en el suelo
una pista (de baile)
atracciones (en la pista de baile)/un espectáculo de caberet

[of ocean]

el fondo

floor level *[storey]*

el piso/la planta *[Note: Numbering in Spanish-speaking countries is different from U.S.]*

the first floor
the second floor
the top floor
His office is on the 50th floor.

la planta baja
la planta primera/el primer piso
el piso alto
Su oficina está en el piso cincuenta.

flu *n*
flu

la gripe/el trancazo *[Sp]*

fly *v*
of planes, birds
The plane was flying from Los Angeles to Caracas.

volar
El avión volaba desde Los Angeles hasta Caracas.

passengers
She flew to New York yesterday.
I prefer flying to driving.

ir en avión
Fue en avión a Nueva York ayer.
Prefiero ir en avión que en coche.

food *n*
general
They lacked healthy food.
[for animals]
food poisoning

el alimento/la comida
Les faltaba el alimento sano.
el pasto
la intoxicación alimenticia

to eat
I want some food.
I enjoy my food.
to give food to sb
She has to give the workers their food.
It is forbidden to give food to the animals.

Quiero algo que comer.
Me gusta comer.
dar de comer a alguien
Tiene que dar de comer a los obreros.
Se prohíbe dar de comer a los animales.

edibles
los comestibles
I keep the food in the food cupboard.
Guardo los comestibles en la despensa.
You must keep the frozen food in the freezer.
Debes guardar los comestibles congelados en el congelador.
Do they sell food?
¿Venden comestibles?
What do you think of the price of food?
¿Qué piensas del precio de los comestibles?

cuisine
la cocina
I love Mexican food.
Me gusta mucho la cocina mexicana.
The food's good in this restaurant.
Se come bien en este restaurante./ La cocina es muy buena en este restaurante.

foot *n*
[human]
el pie
[animal, furniture]
la pata
foot of the page
la parte inferior/el pie de la página

for *prep*
destined for
He has just left for Spain.
Acaba de salir para España.
This bus is for Toluca.
Éste es el autobús para/de Toluca.
Is this book for me?
¿Este libro es para mí?
The train for Barcelona has gone.
El tren con destino Barcelona ya ha salido.

purpose
What is that machine for?
¿Para que sirve esa máquina?
It's for washing the clothes.
Sirve para lavar la ropa.
a cure for AIDS
una cura contra el SIDA
What will you have for dessert?
¿Qué vas a tomar de postre?
for sale
se vende
for rent
se renta/se alquila
for example
por ejemplo
to go for a walk
darse un paseo

motive
for this reason
por esta razón
the reason for her arrival
el motivo de su llegada
He shouted for joy.
Gritó de alegría.
for fear of
por miedo de *[+ infinitive]*
for fear that
por miedo de que *[+ subjunctive]*
famous for
célebre/famoso(a) por
She went to the market for fruit.
Fue al mercado por fruta.

in exchange for
in exchange for sth
a cambio de algo
I want to exchange this one for that one.
Quiero cambiar éste por aquél.
I'll give you 100 dollars for the picture.
Le daré cien dólares por el cuadro.
What is the Spanish for "salt"?
¿Cómo se dice "salt" en castellano?
to thank for
dar las gracias por
We thanked him for his help.
Les dimos las gracias por su ayuda.

on behalf of
He did it for you.
Lo hizo por ti.

For God and country	Por Dios y la Patria

for distance covered

He walked for miles and miles *[E]*.	Caminó/Anduvo kilómetros y kilómetros *[Sp]*.

considering

She is very tall for her age.	Es muy alta para su edad.

respect for

They have no respect for their teachers.	No tienen ningún respeto para con sus profesores.

time

It's time for dinner.	Es la hora de cenar
I have no time to go to the movies.	No tengo tiempo para ir al cine.
forever	para siempre/por siempre
forever and ever	para siempre jamás
I've been living here for six months *[and still am]*.	Hace seis meses que vivo aquí./ Vivo aquí desde hace seis meses.
I lived in Madrid for a year *[but no longer do]*.	Viví en Madrid durante un año.
He had been living there for six months when he became ill.	Vivía allí desde hacía seis meses cuando se enfermó.
I am going to Puerto Rico for a month.	Voy a Puerto Rico para un mes.
She has reserved a room for two weeks.	Ha reservado una habitación para quince días.
They will be in Peru for most of the summer.	Estarán en el Perú durante gran parte del verano.
I waited for hours.	Esperé horas y horas.

verb + for

	[Note: "for" is often not translated]
to ask for	pedir
to hope for	esperar
to look for	buscar
to pay for	pagar
to pray for	rogar/orar por
to send for	enviar a buscar/mandar a buscar
to send for a doctor	llamar a un médico
to thank for	agradecer
to wait for	esperar

foreign *adj*

foreign	extranjero(a)
foreign trade	el comercio exterior
foreign affairs	los asuntos exteriores
foreign currency	las divisas

forget *v*

to forget	olvidar/olvidarse de
He forgot to buy the paper.	Se olvidó de comprar el diario.
I've forgotten the color.	He olvidado el color.
[to leave behind]	dejar
I forgot my umbrella in the café.	Dejé (olvidado) mi paraguas en el café.
And don't you forget it!	¡Que no se te olvide!

form *n & v*

form *[shape, style, method]*	la forma
[vague outline]	una figura

[document]	un formulario/una hoja
to fill out a form	llenar una hoja
[manner]	la manera
in this form	de esta manera
to form	formar

formal adj
formal dress	el traje formal [LA]
	el traje de etiqueta [men]
	el traje de noche [women]
They were all in formal [evening] dress.	Todos estaban/iban vestidos de etiqueta.
to dress formally	vestirse de etiqueta
[person's manner]	ceremonioso(a)/estirado(a)/formalista
Don't be so formal!	¡No te andes con tantos cumplidos!/
	¡No seas tan formalista!
She spoke to me in a formal manner.	Me habló de una manera ceremoniosa.
a formal visit	una visita oficial/de cumplido
a formal invitation	una invitación formal

Ø **formal** has a number of meanings including "reliable," e.g., **Es un hombre muy formal**. "He's a very reliable man."

former adj
[past, previous]	ex-/antiguo(a) [Note: precedes noun]
the former president	el ex-presidente/el antiguo presidente
the former capital of Spain	la antigua capital de España

former pron
[opposite of "the latter"]	aquél/aquélla
	el primero/la primera
Of the two hotels I prefer the former.	De los dos hoteles prefiero aquél.

fortune n
[fate, luck]	la fortuna/la suerte
[wealth]	una fortuna/un caudal
to cost a fortune	costar un dineral

frame n & v
[framework]	una estructura/un esqueleto
[of eyeglasses]	la montura/la armadura
[of door, window, picture]	el marco
to frame a picture	poner un marco a/enmarcar un cuadro
to frame sb	incriminar a alguien dolosamente

free adj
free of charge
free of charge	gratis/gratuito(a)/sin gastos
a free ticket	una entrada gratis
a free copy [of book]	un ejemplar gratuito
I got in free.	Entré sin pagar.
duty free	exento/libre de derechos de aduana
post free	franco de porte
tax free	exento/libre de impuestos

released, loose
released, loose	suelto(a)
The terrorists are free.	Los terroristas están sueltos.

One of the lions is free.	Uno de los leones está suelto.

commerce
a free port
free trade
a free gift

libre/franco(a)
un puerto franco
el libre cambio
una prima

available
Are you free tonight?
Is this table free?

libre
¿Estás libre esta noche?
¿Está libre esta mesa?

independent
the free press
free speech
free expression
the free world
free and easy

libre
la prensa libre
la libertad de palabra
la libertad de expresión
el mundo libre
despreocupado(a)

-free preceded by noun
fat-free foods
lead-free gasoline

sin + noun
alimentos sin grasa
la gasolina sin plomo

other
a free translation
to have a free hand/rein

una traducción libre
tener campo libre/carta blanca

freeze/frozen v
It's freezing.
I was frozen to the bone.
frozen foods

Hiela./Hay helada.
Estaba helado(a) hasta los huesos.
los alimentos/comestibles congelados

freezer n
a freezer
[for ice-cream making]

un fríser [LA]/un congelador
una heladera

friend n
a friend

un amigo/una amiga/un(a) camarada/
un compañero/una compañera/un(a)
compinche [fam]

a close friend
a friend of mine
He's no friend of mine.
my boyfriend
my girlfriend

un amigo íntimo/una amiga íntima
un amigo mío/una amiga mía
No es de mis amigos.
mi novio
mi novia

from prep
a place
from the city
from the school
from the stores
from the provinces
Where are you from? [place of
origin/birth, etc.]
Where have you come from?
[i.e., arrived from]

de la ciudad
del colegio
de los almacenes
de las provincias
¿De dónde eres?

¿De dónde vienes?

with geographic names
from Buenos Aires
from Colombia

de Buenos Aires
de Colombia

from Peru   del Perú
from Mexico City   de la Ciudad de México/de México Distrito Federal

with transport
The train from Santiago has just arrived.   El tren procedente de Santiago acaba de llegar.

to take sth from somewhere
to take sth from the drawer   sacar algo del cajón
Go and get water from the well.   Ve a buscar agua al pozo.

time
from three o'clock to six   De las tres a las seis/desde las tres hasta las seis

from nine o'clock on   a partir de las nueve
from Monday/starting Monday   a partir del lunes
five years from now   dentro de cinco años
from start to finish   desde el principio hasta el final
from then on   desde entonces
from now on   desde ahora en adelante

position
from above   desde arriba/encima
from afar   desde lejos
from below   desde abajo

on behalf of   de parte de
Say hello to your father from me.   Salúdale a tu papá de mi parte.
He spoke to them on my behalf.   Les habló de parte mía.

other expressions
from bad to worse   de mal en peor
to know good from bad   saber distinguir entre el bien y el mal/saber el bien del mal/saber lo bueno de lo malo

from my point of view   desde mi punto de vista

verb + from
They took my father's watch.   Le quitaron el reloj a mi padre.
I'm going to borrow a ladder from my cousin.   Voy a pedir prestado una escalera a mi primo.
He bought the camera from his neighbor.   Compró la máquina a su vecino.
She stole it from me.   Me lo robó.

front *prep, adv, adj & n*
preposition
in front of   delante (de)
It was in front of us.   Estaba delante de nosotros.

adverb
in front   (por) delante
The mayor was walking in front.   El alcalde iba por delante.
in front *[in a vehicle]*   delante/en la parte delantera

adjective
    delantero(a)/de delante
the car in front   el coche de delante
[forward part]   delantero(a)
the front seat   el asiento delantero

[first] — primero(a)
I want to sit in the front row. — Quiero sentarme en (la) primera fila.
The photo was on the front page of the paper. — La foto estaba en (la) primera plana del diario.

noun
[of vehicle] — la parte delantera
[of shirt, dress, etc.] — la pechera
[business, organization] — una tapadera
His company is just a front. — Su empresa no es más que una tapadera.
the front *[military]* — el frente
the popular front *[political]* — el frente popular

Ø **la frente** means "forehead".

fruit *n & adj*
[botanical] — el fruto
[for eating] — la fruta
I like fruit. — Me gusta la fruta.
I'll have fruit for dessert. — Voy a tomar fruta de postre.
a piece of fruit — alguna fruta/una porción de fruta
a fruit tree — un árbol frutal
fruit salad — una macedonia de fruta
a fruit dish — un frutero

full *adj*
filled — lleno(a)
The glasses were full. — Los vasos estaban llenos.

no more room
[in bus, theater, restaurant] — completo(a)/lleno(a)
We are full. — Completo./Estamos completos./No caben más.

full to overflowing — lleno(a) hasta el tope
full house *[theater]* — el lleno
"House full" — "No hay localidades"

from eating
I'm full. — No puedo más.

other expressions
full speed — a toda velocidad
full employment — el pleno empleo
in full color — a todo color
full moon — la luna llena
full board — la pensión completa
full-length — de cuerpo entero
full-length *[of film]* — de largo metraje
full-scale — de tamaño natural

fun *n*/funny *adj*
[strange, odd] — curioso(a)/raro(a)
[amusing] — cómico(a)/divertido(a)/gracioso(a)
The play was very funny. — La comedia fue muy cómica.
to have fun — divertirse/pasarlo bien
They had a lot of fun. — Se divirtieron./Lo pasaron bien.
to make fun of sb — burlarse de alguien

fur n
fur
[of dead animal]
a fur coat

el pelo/el pelaje
la piel
un abrigo de pieles

furniture n
[in general]
He sells furniture.
a piece of furniture

los muebles/el mobiliario
Vende muebles.
un mueble

future adj
[next]
the future champion
the future tense

futuro(a)/venidero(a)
el futuro campeón
el (tiempo) futuro

future n
the future
He has a promising future in
  the company.
in the future
in the near future

el porvenir/el futuro
Tiene un porvenir prometedor en la
  compañía.
en el futuro/en lo futuro/en lo sucesivo
en un futuro próximo/en fecha próxima

fuzzy adj
[of hair]
[blurry]

rizado/crespo
borroso

G

gain *n*
[profit, earning]   un logro/una ganancia/un beneficio
[increase]   un aumento

gain *v*
[to earn, win]   ganar
to gain an objective   lograr/conseguir un objetivo

game *n*
in general   el juego
the Olympic Games   los Juegos Olímpicos (los JJ.OO.)

board & card games   una partida
a game of cards   una partida de cartas/naipes
a game of chess   una partida de ajedrez

ball games   un partido
a game of soccer/tennis/ice   un partido de fútbol/tenis/hockey
  hockey   sobre hielo
game, set and match   juego, set y partido

garage *n*
a garage   un garaje/un garage [spelling often
                    found in Latin America]

garbage *n*
household garbage   la(s) basura(s)/los desperdicios
[industrial waste]   los residuos/los vertidos
[litter, trash]   la basura
Don't litter!   ¡No tiren/dejen papeles!
a garbage can   un cubo de (la) basura
They collect the garbage on Recogen la basura los viernes.
  Thursdays.

gas *n*
a vapor   el gas
a gas stove   la cocina de gas

gasoline   la gasolina/la bencina
                  [Chi]/la nafta [Arg & Uru]
to fill up with gas   echar gasolina (al coche)
regular/super/unleaded gas la gasolina normal/súper/sin plomo
                  [Note: In Venezuela **la nafta** means
                  "super."]

gentle *adj*
[of character]   amable/benévolo(a)/bondadoso(a)
[mild]   suave
a gentle wind   un viento suave
a gentle slope   una cuesta suave
[soft, sweet]   dulce
a gentle voice   una voz dulce

Ø **gentil** has a number of meanings including "pleasant," "charming," "graceful," and "gentile."

gentleman   n

This gentleman is leaving now.	Este señor se marcha ahora.
Ladies and gentlemen!	¡Señoras y señores!
He's a real gentleman.	Es un cumplido caballero.

Ø **gentilhombre** means "a gentleman at court."

get   v

	[Note: Reflexive verbs often express the idea of "get."]
to get drunk	emborracharse
to get organized	organizarse
to get undressed	desnudarse
to become	[See under **become** for use of **llegar a ser, hacerse, ponerse,** and **volverse.** Alternative forms are often used for "get" in the sense of "become."]
to get excited	emocionarse
to get damaged	dañarse
to get sad	entristecerse
to get wet	mojarse

[See also **angry, big, bored, fat, hungry, interested, old, sick, sleepy, thin, thirsty, tired, used to.**]

to obtain	obtener/conseguir/lograr/procurar/comprar/sacar
She got her boss's permission.	Obtuvo el permiso de su jefe.
Where did you get your degree?	¿Dónde sacaste el título?
I'll try to get tickets.	Trataré de conseguir localidades.
I got her the raise.	Le procuré el aumento.
We got the books downtown.	Compramos los libros en el centro.
I got a television for my birthday.	Me regalaron un televisor para mi cumpleaños.
to receive	recibir
She gets lots of mail.	Recibe muchas cartas.
You always get good grades.	Siempre sacas buenas notas.
to go, to arrive	
How do I get to the town hall?	¿Cómo puedo llegar al ayuntamiento?
How do you get to San Juan from here?	¿Cómo se llega/se va a San Juan desde aquí?
We can get there by bus.	Podemos ir en autocar.
When will you get here?	¿Cuándo llegarás?
to get sb to come	ir a buscar a/hacer venir a/llamar a
I need to get the doctor.	Hace falta llamar al médico.
Go and get a policeman.	Ve a buscar a un guardia./Haz venir a un guardia./Llama a un guardia.
to go and get sth	ir a buscar
I'll go and get something to drink from the kitchen.	Iré a buscar algo que beber en la cocina.
to grasp (mentally)	comprender/entender
I don't get the joke.	No comprendo/entiendo el chiste.

85

I've got it!	¡Ya lo comprendo!/¡Ya lo entiendo!
I didn't get her name.	No oí/no llegué a oír su nombre.

to get the chance

She gets to drive the car.	La permiten manejar el coche.
When he's older he'll get to go to the university.	Cuando sea mayor, podrá ir a la universidad.
I got to see the film.	Fui a ver la película./Conseguí ver la película.

to have tener

Have you got the money?	¿Tienes el dinero?
No, I haven't got it with me.	No, no lo traigo/llevo.

impersonal expressions

It's getting hot/cold.	Empieza a hacer calor/frío.
It's getting dark.	Empieza a hacerse de noche./Se va anocheciendo.
It's getting light.	Empieza a hacerse de día.

to get + adverb

to get about/around	viajar mucho
to get ahead	adelantar
to get along/by	arreglárselas
to get along with sb	llevarse bien con alguien
to get down *[lift down]*	bajar
to get out *[of a place]*	salir (de)/bajar (de)/escaparse (de)
to get out *[news]*	hacerse público
[See also away, back, in, off, on, up]	

to get + past participle ser + past participle

to get arrested/paid/robbed	ser detenido(a)/pagado(a)/robado(a)
She got fired by the manager.	Fue despedida por el gerente.

gift *n*

[a present]	un regalo/un obsequio
[a talent]	un don/un talento/dotes *[fem pl]*
I have a gift for languages.	Tengo un don de lenguas.
He has a gift for management.	Tiene talento para la administración.
She has artistic gifts.	Tiene dotes artísticas.

girlfriend *n*

his girlfriend	su novia
[a woman friend]	una amiga

give *v*

to give	dar
[as a present]	regalar
[to donate]	donar
[to pay for]	pagar
to give up *[hand over]*	ceder
to give up *[to stop]*	dejar de
to give up smoking	dejar de fumar
to give up *[surrender]*	rendirse/entregarse
to give up for dead	dar por muerto

glass *n*

[material]	el vidrio/el cristal
It's made of glass.	Es de vidrio/cristal.

glass [window] pane	una luna
glass case	una vitrina
[glassware]	la cristalería/los artículos de vidrio
looking glass [mirror]	un espejo
drinking glass [water, etc.]	un vaso
wine glass	una copa
sherry glass	una copita
beer glass	una caña
eyeglasses	las gafas/los lentes
dark glasses	las gafas negras
sunglasses	las gafas de sol
[binoculars]	los gemelos/los prismáticos

go v

to go (someplace)	ir (a cualquier parte)
Let's go to the beach.	Vamos a la playa.
Let's go!	¡Vámonos!
Go ahead/Go on.	Adelante./Sigue.
It's time to go.	Es la hora de salir.
Things are going well.	Todo marcha bien.
to go abroad	ir al extranjero
to go near to	acercarse a
to go through	pasar por
to go through [endure]	sufrir/experimentar
to go to one's head	subirle a la cabeza
The victory went to his head.	La victoria le subió a la cabeza.
to go under	pasar por debajo de algo
to go under [sink]	hundirse [ship]/ desaparecer por debajo del agua [person]
to go wrong	andar fallando

[see also **away, down, in, out, up**]

to go + infinitive

They're not going to sell the house.	No van a vender la casa.
I wasn't going to see her.	No iba a visitarla.
Go and see who it is.	Ve/Vaya a ver quién es.
I went out to talk with them.	Salí a hablar con ellos.

goal n

[an aim]	un fin/un objeto/una meta
[ambition]	una ambición
[in sports]	un gol/un tanto
to score a goal	marcar un tanto

good adj

[in general]	bueno(a)
[healthy, wholesome]	sano(a)
Have a good day!	¡Que te vaya bien!
Be good! [well-behaved]	¡Pórtate bien!
a good man/fellow/guy	un buen chico/un buen tío/un buen tipo
a good woman	una buena chica/mujer/persona
to be good at chemistry	ser fuerte en la química
She's good with animals.	Entiende de animales.
He's a good teacher.	Es un buen profesor
She's a good teacher.	Es una buena profesora.
Good Friday	Viernes Santo

good

It's good to be here.	Es agradable estar aquí.
It's good to see you.	Me alegro de verte.
to be good [kind] to sb	ser amable con
It's very good [nice] of you to ...	Eres muy amable de...
to have a good time	divertirse/pasarlo(la) bien
Have a good time!	¡Que lo pases bien!/¡Que te diviertas!
They had a good time.	Lo pasaron bien./Se divirtieron.
good for nothing	inútil
a good deal of	bastante
as good as done	prácticamente terminado

verb + good

to look good [health]	parecer bien
She looks good today. [well-dressed]	Está muy elegante hoy.
to be good-looking	ser guapo(a)/ser de buen parecer
to feel good [health]	sentirse bien
to feel good [emotion]	estar contento(a)/satisfecho(a)
I feel good about my work.	Estoy satisfecho de mi trabajo.
to smell good	oler bien
The meat smells good.	La carne huele bien.
to taste good	ser sabroso(a)

good *n*

good and evil	el bien y el mal
to do good	hacer bien
It's for your own good.	Es por su propio bien.
It'll do you good.	Te sentará bien.
It's no good complaining.	De nada sirve quejarse./No sirve para nada quejarse.
What's the good of it?	¿Para qué sirve?
It's no good worrying about it.	No vale la pena inquietarse por ello.
for good [for ever]	para siempre
goods	los bienes
goods [commerce]	los géneros/los artículos

grade *n*

[in school]	el curso/la clase
to be in sixth grade	estar en el sexto curso
[a score]	una nota
to get bad grades	sacar malas notas
to make the grade	tener éxito/llegar al nivel necesario

Ø **grada** means "step," "stair;" **grado** means "degree" (temperature).

graduate *n & adj*

| to be a graduate of the University of Santiago | ser licenciado de la universidad de Santiago |
| to do graduate studies | hacer estudios graduados |

grand *adj*
great, large

| | grande |
| the grand hall | la gran sala |

magnificent

	magnífico(a)/espléndido(a)/grandioso(a)
a grand occasion	una función magnífica
a grand piano	un piano de cola

88

grant *n & v*
[scholarship]   una beca
[subsidy]   una subvención
[to concede]   conceder
[to admit]   reconocer
to take sth for granted   dar algo por sentado

gray *adj*
gray   gris
[hair]   cano/canoso
[gloomy]   triste

great *adj*
in general   grande
a great man   un gran hombre
a great novel   una gran novela
                             *[Note: **Grande** shortens to **gran** before a noun.]*

They are great paintings.   Son grandes/magníficos cuadros.
to be great friends   ser muy amigos
with great care   con mucho cuidado
with great pleasure   con mucho gusto

excellent   estupendo(a)/maravilloso(a)
a great match   un partido estupendo
a great song   una canción maravillosa
That's great!   ¡Magnífico!/¡Estupendo!/¡Macanudo! *[Arg]*

gross *adj*
[large, fat]   grueso(a)
[coarse, vulgar]   grosero(a)/ordinario(a)/brusco(a)
                             [Ven]/guarango(a) *[Arg, Chi & Uru]*/
                             basto(a) *[Sp]*
[of error]   craso(a)
[injustice]   flagrante
[commerce]   bruto(a)
gross pay   el salario bruto

ground *n*
[earth, soil]   la tierra/el suelo
[terrain]   el terreno
football ground   un campo de fútbol
on the ground   en/sobre el suelo
the ground floor   la planta baja
[see also *floor*]
[reason]   la causa/el motivo/la razón
grounds [gardens]   los jardines

grow *v intrans*
to grow [people and things] crecer
My son has grown a lot.   Mi hijo ha crecido mucho.
She's letting her hair grow. Deja crecerse el pelo.
to grow up   hacerse mayor/hombre/mujer
When they grow up ...   Cuando se hagan mayores...
to grow old   envejecer(se)

of plants   cultivarse

89

Roses grow well in my garden.	Las rosas se cultivan bien en mi jardín.

to increase
The population has grown by ten per cent.	aumentar
	La población ha aumentado el 10 por ciento.

to grow + adjective: *[see get]*

grow   *v trans*
to grow plants	cultivar
We grow strawberries and raspberries.	Cultivamos fresas y frambuesas.

guard   *n & v*
[sentry]	un centinela
[escort]	una escolta
[soldier]	un guardia
the guard *[squad]*	el guardia
to be on guard	estar de guardia
a guard dog	un perro guardián
to be on one's guard	estar en guardia/alerta
off one's guard	desprevenido(a)
to guard *[place]*	guardar/proteger
to guard *[person]*	vigilar

guess   *v*
to believe, suppose
	creer/imaginar/suponer
I guess it's all right.	Creo que está bien./Estará bien, supongo.
Has he arrived? – I guess so.	¿Ha llegado? – Creo que sí.
I guess not.	Creo que no.

to make a guess
	adivinar
Guess where she's calling from!	¡A ver si adivinas de dónde llama!
to guess right	acertar
You've guessed right.	Has acertado.

guest   *n*
the person invited	el convidado/la convidada
	el invitado/la invitada
We have guests on Saturday.	Tenemos invitados el sábado.
Be my guest.	Invito yo.
[at a hotel]	el huésped/la huéspeda

guilty   *adj*
[guilty of a wrongdoing]	culpable
to have a guilty conscience	estar lleno de remordimiento
to feel guilty	sentir remordimiento

guy   *n*
[colloquial for a boy or man]	un tío/un tipo
a nice guy	un buen chico/un buen tío/un buen tipo

90

H

habit *n*

a habit	una costumbre/un hábito
What are his habits?	¿Cuáles son sus costumbres?
to be in the habit of doing sth	acostumbrar/soler hacer algo
I usually go to bed late.	Acostumbro/Suelo acostarme tarde.
to get into the habit	acostumbrarse a
from/out of habit	por costumbre

Ø **el hábito** usually means "habit" in the sense of clothing, e.g., "a nun's habit."

hair *n*

hair *[of the head]*	el pelo/los cabellos
a single hair	un pelo
to have brown/blond(e) hair	tener el pelo castaño/rubio
to have red hair	ser pelirrojo(a)
grey/white hair	las canas
My hair was all wet.	Tenía el pelo todo mojado.
He cut his hair.	Se cortó el pelo.
He had his hair cut.	Se cortó el pelo./Se hizo cortar el pelo.
a haircut	un corte de pelo
to comb one's hair	peinarse
to do one's hair	arreglarse el pelo
to have one's hair done	hacerse arreglar el pelo
a hairstyle	un peinado
a hairdresser	un peluquero/una peluquera
a hairdresser's	una peluquería
hair *[on chest, arms, etc.]*	el vello

half *adj*

half-	medio(a)
a half-brother/sister	un medio hermano/una media hermana
a half-liter of olive oil	medio litro de aceite de oliva
a half dozen	media docena
a half owner	un propietario a medias
half ... half ...	mitad... mitad...
half man half beast	mitad hombre, mitad animal
half alive	medio muerto(a)
half past two	las dos y media
halfway	a medio camino
halfway measures	medidas parciales

half *n*

a half	la mitad
I ate half the orange.	Comí la mitad de la naranja.
I will pay half (of) the cost.	Pagaré la mitad del coste.
the first half *[in sport]*	el primer tiempo

hall *n*

[a passage, a corridor]	un corredor *[LA]*/un pasillo
[entrance in house]	un hall*[LA]*/un vestíbulo
[a hotel or theater lobby]	el hall/el vestíbulo

91

[an exhibition or concert hall]	una sala de exposiciones/conciertos

Halt! ¡Alto!

hand *n*

a hand	la mano *[Note: feminine]*
the right hand/the left hand	la mano derecha/izquierda
[on a ship]	un tripulante
[worker]	un(a) trabajador(a)/operario(a)
[of clock or watch]	una manecilla
[of writing]	la escritura
to give sb a big hand	darle a alguien una gran ovación/un gran aplauso
on the other hand	por otro lado/por otra parte
She is weak in math; on the other hand she is strong in history.	Es floja en (las) matemáticas; por otro lado es fuerte en (la) historia.
on one hand ... on the other hand	por una parte... por otra parte/por un lado... por otro lado
to be on hand	estar a la mano
one last hand! *[cards]*	¡la última mano!
not to lift a hand	no mover un dedo
on hands and knees	a gatas/a cuatro patas

Ø **una mano** is used in many Latin American countries to mean "one-way" with regard to traffic.

handle *n*

[of bag, basket, cup]	un asa *[fem]*
[of bicycle]	un puño
[doorknob]	un pomo
[of drawer]	un tirador
to fly off the handle	salirse de sus casillas

handle *v*

to touch tocar
Please do not handle the goods. Por favor no toque/manosee la mercancía.
"Handle with care." "Manéjese con cuidado."
to handle a boat dirigir un barco

to take care of, to deal with encargarse de/tratar
We'll handle everything. Nos encargaremos de todo.
I don't know how to handle this problem. No sé cómo tratar este problema.

to control controlar/saber dominar
He cannot handle the students. No puede con los estudiantes.

to handle oneself comportarse
She handled herself well in that situation. Se comportó bien en esa situación.

handlebar *n*
[of bicycle] un manillar

handsome *adj*
[of appearance] guapo(a)/hermoso(a)/apuesto(a)/elegante
[considerable] considerable/bueno(a)
a handsome amount una cantidad considerable
a handsome salary un sueldo muy bueno

handwriting   n
[one's own]   la letra
[writing done by hand]   la escritura
handwritten   escrito(a) a mano

hang   v
[to kill by hanging from the neck]   ahorcar
to hang wallpaper   pegar/poner papel pintado
[to decorate, to hang pictures]   adornar con cuadros
to hang one's head   bajar la cabeza
to be hanging [pending]   estar pendiente
to leave a question hanging   dejar pendiente una cuestión
to hang around   vagar
to hang on   mantenerse firme/resistir/
                                                   aguantar

hangover   n
a hangover   un(a) crudo(a) [Mex]/una jaqueca
                                                   [Arg & Uru]/un guayabo [Col &
                                                   Ecu]/un chucháqui [Col & Ecu]/
                                                   un ratón [Ven]/una resaca [Sp]

hang-up   n/**hang up**   v
to have a hang-up   tener un complejo/una obsesión
to hang up [the phone]   colgar

happen   v
to happen, occur   acontecer/ocurrir/pasar/suceder
What happened?   ¿Qué pasó/sucedió?
That always happens.   Eso siempre ocurre/sucede.
These things happen.   Son cosas que pasan.

to a person
What happened to you?   ¿Qué te pasó?
What happened to [became of]   ¿Que habrá sido de ella?
  her?

by chance   por casualidad
                                                 si acaso [+ subjunctive]
If you happen to see her ...   Si la ves por casualidad...
                                                 Si acaso la veas...

Ø **suceder** only means "to succeed" in the sense of "to succeed to a title."

happy   adj
[fortunate]   (ser) feliz/dichoso(a)/afortunado(a)
[contented]   (estar) contento(a)/satisfecho(a)
[cheerful]   (estar) alegre
[appropriate]   (ser) feliz/oportuno(a)

hard   adj
[of a substance]   duro(a)
[of a person]   severo(a)/inflexible
[of a situation]   difícil
to have a hard time doing sth   costarle a uno hacer algo/encontrar
                                                   difícil hacer algo
He gave us a hard time.   Nos hizo todo muy difícil.

93

hard *adv*
to work hard
to study hard
to try hard to do sth
to try one's hardest to do sth

trabajar mucho
estudiar mucho/empollar *[fam]*
intentar hacer algo
esforzarse para/por/en hacer algo
hacer todo lo posible para hacer algo

hardly *adv*
[barely]
I hardly heard him.
hardly anyone
hardly anything
hardly ever

apenas
Apenas lo oí.
casi nadie
casi nada
casi nunca

hardness *n*
[difficulty]
[of winter]
[of heart]

la dificultad
el rigor
la insensibilidad

have *v*
to possess
I have three children.
Have you got any money?

He's got a house by the beach.

tener
Tengo tres hijos.
¿Tienes dinero? *[Note: There is no equivalent in Spanish of "got".]*
Tiene una casa cerca de la playa.

auxiliary verb
I have seen your brother.
Have you been to Mexico?

haber
He visto a tu hermano.
¿Has estado en México?

to have sth done
I have had a tooth out.
He should have his watch repaired.
We'll have it done tomorrow.
He had us read it.

hacer hacer algo/mandar hacer algo
Me han sacado una muela.
Debería mandar reparar su reloj.
Mandaremos hacerlo mañana.
Nos hizo leerlo.

have to *v*
to have to (do sth)

tener que/deber/hay que/hace falta

in the present
I have to leave immediately.

Tengo que/Debo/marcharme al instante/en seguida.

in the past (habitually)
When we lived in Lima I had to work on Sundays.
She had to visit her aunt every day.

Cuando vivíamos en Lima tenía que trabajar los domingos.
Debía visitar a su tía cada día.

in the past (a specific occasion)
I had to tell you the truth.
They had to pay the fine.

Tuve que decirte la verdad.
Debieron pagar la multa.

in the future
You will have to sell the car.
I will have to help them.

Tendrás que vender el coche.
Deberé ayudarlos.

with a negative
You don't have to come with us.

No es necesario acompañarnos./No tienes que acompañarnos. *[Note: **No debes acompañarnos** would mean "You must not come with us."]*

to have to do with	tener que ver con

hazard n
[danger] · el peligro
[risk] · el riesgo
a health hazard · un peligro/un riesgo para la salud
It's hazardous for your health. · Es peligroso para la salud.

he pron
he · él
He's on vacation at present. · Actualmente está de vacaciones.
He and his wife have gone to Brazil. · Él y su esposa han ido al Brasil.
[Note: **Él**, like all the other subject pronouns, is usually omitted; it is used for emphasis and clarification.]

Ø **él** meaning "he" has an accent to distinguish it from **el** meaning "the;" it can also mean "him" following a preposition, e.g., "It's for him" is translated by **Es para él.**

healthy adj
[of a person] · sano(a)/en buena salud
They are healthy. · Gozan de buena salud.
[of things] · sano(a)
healthy food · el alimento sano

Ø "sane" is translated by **cuerdo(a)**.

hear v
to hear · oír
to hear from sb · tener noticias de/recibir cartas de alguien
I haven't heard from her. · No he tenido sus noticias.
to hear of sb/sth · oír hablar de alguien/algo
I've never heard of her. · Nunca he oído hablar de ella.
to hear that · oír decir que
We heard you had gone away. · Oímos decir que te habías marchado.
I heard he was sick. · Supe/Me enteré que estaba enfermo.
I heard you coming in. · Te oí entrar.
I can hear them. · Los oigo.

heat n & v
heat · el calor
I don't like the heat. · No me gusta el calor.

heating · la calefacción
to turn the (central) heating on/off. · encender/apagar la calefacción central

in cooking
on low heat · a fuego lento
to heat (up) the soup · calentar la sopa

heavy adj
weight · pesado(a)
This case is heavy. · Esta maleta está pesada.
How heavy is he? · ¿Cuánto pesa?

other
The traffic was very heavy. · Había mucho tráfico./El tráfico estaba muy denso.

a heavy schedule · un programa cargado

heel

He's a heavy drinker.	Bebe mucho.
It's a heavy rain.	Está lloviendo fuerte.

heel n
[of foot]	un talón
[of shoe]	un tacón
[a person – slang]	un canalla/un sinvergüenza

hello excl
[in greeting]	¡Hola!/¡Hola, buenos días!
[on the telephone]	¡Bueno! [Mex]/¡Haló! [Ven, Per, Ecu, Bol]/ ¡Holá! [Arg & Uru]¡Diga!/¡Dígame! [Sp]

help v
to help/assist	ayudar
Can I help you? [in shop]	¿En que puedo servirle?

Ø **asistir** means "to attend," "to be present at."

help n
I am grateful for your help.	Te agradezco tu ayuda.
Help!	¡Socorro!

helpful adj
[of a person]	atento(a)/servicial/amable
He's a very helpful waiter.	Es un camarero muy atento.
The doctors were very helpful.	Los médicos eran muy amables.
[of a thing]	útil/provechoso(a)
This book will be most helpful.	Este libro será muy útil.
It would be very helpful to us if you could do it.	Nos serviría mucho si pudieras hacerlo.

her adj
[singular: masc & fem]	su
[plural: masc & fem]	sus
her husband and son [Note: adjective repeated.]	su esposo y su hijo [Note: adjective repeated.]
She lost her books and jewelry.	Perdió su ropa y sus joyas.

Ø As **su** can also mean "his," "its," "your," and "their," you can add **de ella** after the noun if the meaning is not entirely clear, e.g., **su casa de ella** "her house."

her pron
[direct object]	la
[indirect object] to her	le
[disjunctive]	ella/sí
Can you see her?	¿La ves?
Did you give her the money?	¿Le diste el dinero?
Yes, I gave it to her.	Sí, se lo di. [Note: When **le** is followed by **lo, la, los,** or **las** it changes to **se.**]
I lent it to her.	Sí, se lo presté a ella. [Note: As **se** has so many possible meanings you can add **a ella** after the verb to stress that here it means "to her."]
He sat behind her.	Estaba sentado detrás de ella.
She looked around her.	Miró alrededor de sí. [Note: **Sí** is used instead of **ella** as it refers to the same person as the subject of the verb.]

She took the money with her.

Llevó el dinero consigo. *[Note the special form of **sí** used after **con**.]*

here *adv*
here
Come here!
Here is/are ...

aquí/acá
¡Ven aquí!
Aquí está/están...
He aquí...

Here are your documents.
Where's the money? – Here it is.
Is the boss here today? – No,
  he isn't here.

He aquí tus papeles.
¿Dónde está el dinero? – Aquí lo tienes.
¿Está el jefe hoy? – No, no está.
  [Note: no Spanish equivalent of "here" used in this sense.]

around here
in here
near here
right here

por aquí
aquí dentro
aquí cerca
aquí mismo

hers *pron*
[singular]
[plural]
We all had our passports but
  Carmen had lost hers.
Is this ring yours? – No, it's hers.

el suyo/la suya
los suyos/las suyas
Todos teníamos nuestros pasaportes
  pero Carmen había perdido el suyo.
¿Es tuya esta sortija? – No, es suya.
  *[Note: definite article omitted after the verb **ser**]*

Ø As **suyo/a/os/as** could also mean "his," "yours," or "theirs," you can replace them with **de ella** if there is any chance of confusion, e.g., "It's hers". **Es de ella.**

herself *[see self]*

high *adj*
[general]
The tower is very high.
How high is this building?

alto(a)
La torre es muy alta.
¿Qué altura tiene este edificio?/
¿Cuánto mide este edificio de alto?

It's 10 meters high.
a high price
He has a high fever.
a high-rise *[building]*
high and dry
high and low
high and mighty
higher education

Tiene diez metros de alto/altura.
un precio elevado
Tiene una fiebre fuerte.
un rascacielos
sin recursos
de arriba abajo/por todas partes
arrogante
los estudios universitarios/la enseñanza
  superior

hill *n*
a hill
You can see the top of the
  hill from my room.

un cerro *[LA]*/una colina *[Sp]*
Se puede ver la cumbre/la cima del
  cerro desde mi cuarto.

a hillside, a slope
There are olive trees on the hills.
He went up the hill in search
  of the children.
downhill/uphill

una cuesta
Hay olivos en las cuestas.
Subió la cuesta en busca de los
  niños.
cuesta abajo/cuesta arriba

They ran downhill to see me.	Corrieron cuesta abajo a verme.

him *pron*
[direct object]

lo/le [Note: **Lo** is far more common than **le** in Latin America; **le** is frequently used in Spain.]

[indirect object] to him	le
[disjunctive]	él/sí
Do you know him?	¿Lo/le conoces?
Did you lend him the car?	¿Le prestaste el coche?
I read it to him.	Se lo leí. [Note: When **le** is followed by **lo**, **la**, **los**, or **las** it changes to **se**.]
	Se lo leí a él. [Note: As **se** has so many possible meanings you can add **a él** after the verb to stress that here it means "to him."]
Do you remember him?	¿Te acuerdas de él?
He looked around him.	Miró alrededor de sí. [Note: **Sí** is used instead of **él** as it refers to the same person as the subject of the verb.]
He took the money with him.	Llevó el dinero consigo. [Note the special form of **sí** used after **con**.]

himself [see **self**]

his *adj*

[singular: masc & fem]	su
[plural: masc & fem]	sus
his wife and daughter	su esposa y su hija [Note: adjective repeated.]
He sold his house and car.	Vendió su casa y su coche.

Ø As **su** can also mean "her," "its," "your," and "their," you can add **de él** after the noun if the meaning is not entirely clear, e.g., **su casa de él** "his house."

his *pron*

[singular]	el suyo/la suya
[plural]	los suyos/las suyas
I've got my keys but my husband has lost his.	Tengo mis llaves pero mi esposo ha perdido las suyas.
Is this newspaper yours? – No, it's his.	¿Es tuyo este diario? – No, es suyo. [Note: definite article omitted after the verb **ser**]

Ø As **suyo/a/os/as** could also mean "hers," "yours," or "theirs," you can replace them with **de él** if there is any chance of confusion, e.g., "It's his." **Es de él.**

hit *v*

[strike]	golpear/pegar
to hit [targets]	alcanzar/acertar/hacer blanco en/dar en
to hit it off with sb	congeniar con/hacer buenas migas con alguien
to hit the ceiling	enojarse/perder los estribos
to hit the hay	irse a la cama
to hit the jackpot	sacar el premio gordo
to hit the nail on the head	acertar
to hit the road	ponerse en camino/largarse

holiday n

a day's holiday	un día libre/un día de descanso
a public holiday	un día feriado [LA]/un día de fiesta/un día festivo
a religious holiday	una fiesta
the Christmas holidays	las Navidades/las Pascuas
the Easter holidays	la Pascua/las Pascuas

home adv

at home	en casa
I was at home last night.	Estaba en casa anoche.
Is your brother at home?	¿Está tu hermano?
Yes, he is.	Sí, está. [Note: The verb **estar** alone is sufficient in such situations.]
home [involving movement]	a casa
Go home at once!	¡Vete a casa en seguida!
I go home at seven o'clock.	Voy/Vuelvo a casa a las siete.
He got home at midnight.	Llegó a casa a medianoche.
She left home in May.	Salió de casa en mayo.

home n

[the building]	la casa
She has a home in Acapulco.	Tiene una casa en Acapulco.
Make yourself at home.	Estás en tu casa.
[the sentiment, the concept]	el hogar
home, sweet home	hogar, dulce hogar
[place of residence]	el domicilio
His home is in Buenos Aires.	Vive en/Es de Buenos Aires.
my home town	mi ciudad natal
the homeland	la patria
a homemaker	un ama de casa [Note: **Un** is used although the noun is feminine, because it begins with a stressed **a**.]
to be homeless	estar sin casa ni hogar
homework	los deberes

hope v

to hope	esperar
I hope to come tomorrow.	Espero venir mañana.
I hope you can come.	Espero que puedas venir. [Note: use of subjunctive.]

Ø **esperar** can also mean "to wait for" or "to expect."

hot adj

[weather, body heat]	el calor [noun]
It was very hot.	Hacía mucho calor.
I'm hot.	Tengo calor.
[things]	caliente
The soup is too hot.	La sopa está demasiado caliente.
There is no hot water.	No hay agua caliente.
a hot day	un día caluroso/de calor
Your head is hot.	Tienes la cabeza caliente.
[of spicy food]	picante
The sauce is very hot.	La salsa es muy picante.
hot line	una línea directa

house *n*

a house	una casa
[commercial]	una casa/una firma
a detached house	una casa independiente/un chalet
housewares	los artículos de uso doméstico/los utensilios domésticos
housework	los quehaceres domésticos
full house [theater]	el lleno
"house full"	"no hay localidades"

house *v*

to house [a person]	alojar/hospedar
to house [public]	proveer viviendas para

housing *n*

[act]	el alojamiento/la provisión de viviendas
[houses, apartments]	las casas/las viviendas
the housing shortage	la crisis de la vivienda
They need housing.	Necesitan alojamiento.
student housing	una residencia estudiantil
low-income housing	viviendas a un precio bajo

how *adv*

How are you?	¿Cómo estás?/¿Cómo está usted?/ ¿Cómo están ustedes?
How's it going?	¿Qué tal?/¿Cómo te va?/¿Cómo le va? /¿Cómo te anda?/¿Cómo le anda?
How do you say "help" in Spanish?	¿Cómo se dice "help" en castellano?
How do you spell it?	¿Cómo se lo escribe?

an exclamation

How beautiful they are!	¡Qué hermosos(as) son!
How terrific!	¡Qué estupendo!

a question: how + adjective

How big is the house?	¿Cómo es de grande la casa?
How big is it?	¿De qué tamaño es?
How far is it to Cancún?	¿Cuánto hay de aquí a Cancún?
How fast was the car going?	¿A qué velocidad iba el coche?
How heavy is the crate?	¿Cuánto pesa el cajón?
How high is the church?	¿Cuánto mide de alto la iglesia?
How long is the corridor?	¿Cómo es de largo el pasillo?
How long is the movie?	¿Cuánto dura la película?
How long is it since you were in Chile?	¿Cuánto tiempo hace desde que estabas en Chile?
How long did they live in Mexico City?	¿Cuánto tiempo vivieron en la Ciudad de México?
How long have you lived here?	¿Desde cuándo vives aquí?/¿Cuánto tiempo hace que vives aquí?
How long did he take to do it?	¿Cuánto tiempo tardó en hacerlo?
How much is it?	¿Cuánto es?/¿Cuánto cuesta?
How much is it worth?	¿Cuánto vale?
How much are the tickets?	¿Cuánto son/cuestan/valen las localidades?
How much does the baby weigh?	¿Cuánto pesa el niño?
How much sugar did you buy?	¿Cuánto azúcar compraste?
How much flour did you buy?	¿Cuánta harina compraste?
How many bulls do they have?	¿Cuántos toros tienen?

How many cows do they have?   ¿Cuántas vacas tienen?
How often did you visit her?   ¿Cuántas veces la visitaste?
How often do the buses leave   ¿Con qué frecuencia salen los
  for León?   autobuses para León?
How old are you?   ¿Cuántos años tienes/tiene usted?
How tall is she?   ¿Cuánto mide?
How well do you know him?   ¿Lo conoces bien?
How wide is the river?   ¿Cuánto tiene de ancho el río?

however   adv

However you do it, it's all   De cualquier modo/manera que lo
  the same to me.   hagas, me es igual.
However intelligent you are,   Por inteligente que seas, lo
  you will find it difficult.   encontrarás difícil.
However much he tries, he   Por mucho que se esfuerce, nunca
  never succeeds.   tiene éxito.

however   conj

[nevertheless]   no obstante/sin embargo
I can't come today; however I   No puedo venir hoy; sin embargo te
  will see you on Friday.   veré el viernes.

hug   n & v

to hug sb/to give sb a hug   abrazar a/dar un abrazo a alguien
I gave her a big hug.   Le di un fuerte abrazo.
We hugged each other.   Nos abrazamos.

Ø **abrazo** is often used to sign off personal, informal letters, e.g., **un abrazo cordial de...** and at the end of a phone conversation.

humor   n/humorous   adj

humor   el humor
to have a sense of humor   tener un sentido del humor
She has no sense of humor.   No tiene sentido del humor.
humorous [amusing of person,   divertido(a)/gracioso(a)/
  book, remark, etc.]   chistoso(a)
He's a very humorous person.   Es una persona muy divertida.
a humorous poet   un poeta cómico

Ø **humor** also means "mood" or "temperament," e.g., **de buen/mal humor** meaning "in a good/bad mood."

hundred   n & adj

a hundred   ciento
a hundred dollars   cien dólares [Note: **Ciento** shortensto **cien**
   before a noun.]

I have two hundred dollars and   Tengo doscientos dólares y trescientas
  three hundred pesetas.   pesetas. [Note: The hundreds agree
   with the noun they modify.]

hundreds of people   centenares de personas

hunger   n/hungry   adj

hunger   el hambre [fem]
to be very hungry   tener mucha hambre
to get hungry   empezar a tener hambre

hurry *v*

to hurry — apurarse *[LA]*/darse prisa *[Sp]*/ apresurarse

Hurry up! — ¡Apúrate!/¡Date prisa!
to be in a hurry — tener prisa/estar de prisa

hurt *v*
[to cause bodily injury] — hacer daño a/hacer mal a/lastimar
to hurt oneself/to get hurt — hacerse daño/lastimarse
I hurt my leg. — Me lastimé la pierna./Me hice daño a la pierna.

My shoes hurt. — Mis zapatos me hacen daño.
[to cause physical pain] — doler
My head hurts. — Me duele la cabeza.
Does it hurt? — ¿Te duele?
My feet hurt. — Me duelen los pies.
Where does it hurt (you)? — ¿Dónde te duele?
[to wound] — herir
[to hurt sb's feelings] — ofenderle a alguien
[to hurt sb mentally] — doler/herir
— causar pena a alguien

Your news hurt her deeply. — Tus noticias le causaron mucha pena.

husband *n* — el esposo/el marido
[Note: *Marido* is more common in Spain than in Latin America.]

I

I *pron*

I don't want to go to the
theater; my brother does.
Who is it? – It's me/It is I.
My husband smokes. I don't.

yo *[Note: Like all the subject pronouns*
yo *is normally only used with a verb for*
emphasis or in case of confusion.]
Yo no quiero ir al teatro; mi
hermano sí que quiere ir.
¿Quién es? – Soy yo.
Mi esposo fuma. Yo no.

ice *n & v*

ice	el hielo
ice cream	un helado
ice-cream parlor	una heladería
ice cube	un cubito de hielo
iced *[of cake]*	escarchado(a)
[of drink]	con hielo/enfriado(a)
ice hockey	el hockey sobre hielo
ice skating	el patinaje sobre hielo
icing *[on cake]*	la alcorza/la escarcha/la garapiña
icing sugar	el azúcar de alcorza
to ice	helar
to ice up	helarse
to ice *[drinks]*	enfriar/echar cubitos de hielo a
to break the ice	romper el hielo
to tread on thin ice	pisar un terreno peligroso

ID *n*

identification card

un documento/una tarjeta de identidad/una
cédula *[Col, Ven & Arg]*/una cartilla *[Mex]*/
un carnet de identidad *[Sp]*

Your ID, please.
*[see also **identity**]*

Sus papeles/documentos, por favor.

idea *n*

[belief]
[plan]
That's the idea!
not to have the foggiest/slightest
idea
What's the big idea?

la idea
un plan/un proyecto
¡Eso es!/¡Exacto!
no tener la menor idea

¿A qué viene eso?

identity *n*

identity
mistaken identity
*[see also **ID**]*

la identidad
la identificación errónea

if *conj*

If he comes, I will tell him.
I will do it if I can.
He only drinks water if he's thirsty.
If she has done it, she will tell us.

si
Si viene, se lo diré.
Lo haré si puedo.
Sólo bebe agua si tiene sed.
Si lo ha hecho, nos lo dirá.

If I arrived early, I would [i.e., used to] see him.	Si llegaba temprano, lo veía.

[The above are all examples of open conditions, where the action may or may not take place.]

If he came, I would tell him.	Si viniera, se lo diría.
I would do it if I could.	Lo haría si pudiera.
He would only drink water if he were thirsty.	Sólo bebería agua si tuviera sed.
If she had done it, she would tell us.	Si lo hubiera hecho, nos lo diría.
If she had done it, she would have told us.	Si lo hubiera hecho, nos lo habría dicho.
If I arrived early, I would see him.	Si llegara temprano, lo vería.
If only Marta were here.	Ojalá estuviera Marta.

[The above are examples of unfulfilled conditions where the action is unlikely or even impossible. In all these cases si is followed by the imperfect subjunctive.]

ignore *v*

to ignore	no hacer caso de/hacer caso omiso de/desconocer
She ignored my advice.	No hizo caso de mi consejo.
Your brother ignored me.	Tu hermano hizo caso omiso de mí./ Tu hermano me desconoció.
Ignore him!	¡No le hagas caso!

to fail to take into account

They ignored the fact that we had changed our plans.	No tuvieron en cuenta que habíamos cambiado de proyecto.

to omit, to leave out

He ignored the details.	Pasó por alto los detalles.

Ø **ignorar** normally means "not to know" or "to be ignorant of," although it will be heard in Latin America meaning "to ignore."

ill *[see sick]*

ill at ease *adj*

ill at ease	molesto(a)/intranquilo(a)
She felt ill at ease in the woods.	Se sintió intranquila en el bosque.

impress *v*

to impress	imprimir
to impress [on sb's mind]	grabar/convencer de
I tried to impress on her the importance of coming on time.	Traté de convencerle de la importancia de llegar a la hora.
I'm not easily impressed.	No me dejo impresionar fácilmente.
He impressed us favorably.	Nos hizo una buena impresión.
How did the product impress you?	¿Qué impresión te produjo el producto?

improve *v*

to improve sth

They want to improve their working conditions.	Quieren mejorar sus condiciones de trabajo.
She needs to improve her Spanish.	Necesita perfeccionar sus conocimientos del castellano.

to undergo improvement

The economy has improved.	La economía se ha mejorado.

My health is improving.   Mi salud se mejora.
Your Spanish has improved.   Has hecho progresos en el castellano.

in   *prep*
in most senses   en
in Mexico/in New York/in May   en México/en Nueva York/en mayo

time within   dentro de
I'll do it in two hours.   Lo haré dentro de dos horas.
Come back in 20 minutes.   Vuelve dentro de veinte minutos.

in time
in time   a tiempo

time of day
in the morning/in the afternoon   por la mañana/por la tarde
in the evening/in the night   por la tarde/por la noche
eight o'clock in the morning   las ocho de la mañana
five o'clock in the afternoon   las cinco de la tarde
seven o'clock in the evening   las siete de la tarde
in the daytime   de día/durante el día

weather
in the rain   bajo la lluvia
in the sun   bajo el sol
30 degrees in the shade   treinta grados a la sombra
in this weather   con el tiempo que hace
in this heat   con este calor

after a superlative
the biggest country in the world.   el país más grande del mundo
the best team in the league   el mejor equipo de la liga

manner
in this way   de esta manera/de este modo
in writing   por escrito
in ink/in pencil   escrito con tinta/lápiz
painted in white   pintado(a) de blanco
to be in mourning   estar de luto
in alphabetical order   por orden alfabético
covered in   cubierto de
in fashion   de moda
in uniform   de uniforme
dressed in   vestido de

place
in the distance   a lo lejos
in prison   en la cárcel
in bed   en la cama
to arrive in   llegar a
to come/get/go in   entrar en

ratio
one in ten   uno sobre diez

inclined   *adj*
to be inclined to [tendency]   inclinarse/tener tendencia a
She's inclined to lie.   Tiene tendencia a mentir.
to be inclined to [choice]   estar dispuesto(a) de
I'm inclined to believe you.   Estoy dispuesto(a) de creerte.

include v
to include	incluir
The price includes tax.	El precio incluye impuestos.
The bill includes service.	La cuenta incluye el servicio.
[with a letter]	adjuntar/enviar adjunto

included
[with a letter]	adjunto
service included	servicio incluido/comprendido

including
	incluso/inclusive/con inclusión de
Including this one I have six.	Con la inclusión de éste tengo seis.
We're all going, including my grandfather.	Vamos todos, incluso mi abuelo.
	[Note: **Incluso** can often be translated by "even."]

income n
annual income	los ingresos anuales
gross income	la renta bruta
net income	la renta neta
national income	la renta nacional
income tax	el impuesto sobre la renta
He can't live on his income.	No puede vivir con lo que gana.
to live beyond one's income	gastar más de lo que se gana

inconvenient adj
[not convenient]	incómodo(a)/poco práctico(a)
It will be a very inconvenient journey for my boss.	Será un viaje muy incómodo para mi jefe.
[time]	malo(a)/inoportuno(a)
It was an inconvenient time for the meeting.	Fue una hora inoportuna para la reunión.
If it's not inconvenient for you ...	Si no te molesta...

infant n
[a baby]	una criatura [Note: used for male or female]
[a small child]	un niño/una niña
[a new-born]	un recién nacido/una recién nacida
infant mortality rate	la mortalidad infantil

Ø **infante** and **infanta** are respectively "prince" (son of a king) and "princess" (daughter of a king or wife of an infante).

informal adj
informal dress	el traje de calle
[person's manner]	sencillo(a)/desenvuelto(a)/afable/ poco ceremonioso(a)
an informal meeting	una reunión no oficial
She spoke to me informally.	Me habló en tono de confianza.
an informal visit	una visita de confianza
an informal dinner/party	una cena/reunión entre amigos

Ø **informal** usually means "unreliable," "untrustworthy," "bad mannered." It is rarely used of things.

information n
information	la información/los informes/los datos
a piece of information	una información/un dato/una noticia

[news]	las noticias
classified information	la información secreta
to ask for information	pedir informes
information office	el centro de informaciones
information desk	las informaciones
information technology	la informática

injure v

to injure oneself	hacerse daño/lastimarse
I injured my arm.	Me lastimé el brazo./Me hice daño al brazo.
to be injured	estar lesionado
Ten people were injured when the bomb went off.	Diez personas quedaron lesionadas cuando estalló la bomba.
They took the injured to hospital.	Llevaron a los heridos al hospital.

[see also **hurt**]

injury n

an injury	una herida/una lesión
the injured party	la persona ofendida/perjudicada

Ø **una injuria** means "an insult," "an offence;" **injuriar** means "to insult."

in-laws [see law]

inside adv

to wait inside	esperar dentro
Shall we go inside?	¿Vamos adentro?/¿Entramos?
Come inside.	Pasa, por favor.
Look inside.	Mira hacia dentro.
It's very warm inside.	Hace mucho calor por dentro.

inside prep

inside	en/dentro de
They're inside the house.	Están dentro de la casa.
Put it inside the box.	Ponlo en la caja.

insist v

to insist on sth	insistir en algo
to insist on doing sth	insistir en hacer algo
to insist that	insistir en que [+ subjunctive]
I insist that you pay me now.	Insisto en que me pagues ahora.

instead adv

I bought a car instead.	En cambio/En lugar de eso compré un coche.
Her brother went instead.	Su hermano fue en su lugar.

instead of prep

instead of	en lugar de/en vez de
I ordered fish instead of meat.	Pedí pescado en lugar de carne.
They went to Peru instead of Mexico.	Fueron al Perú en vez de México.

insurance n

fire insurance	el seguro contra/de incendios
fully comprehensive insurance	el seguro a/contra todo riesgo
life insurance	el seguro de vida/sobre la vida

third party insurance	el seguro contra terceros/contra tercera persona
insurance agent	un agente de seguros
insurance company	una compañía de seguros
insurance coverage	los riesgos cubiertos
insurance policy	una póliza de seguros
insurance premium	una prima de seguros

insure v
to insure sth against	asegurar algo contra

intend v
to intend to	tener la intención de/pensar
I intend to do it tomorrow.	Pienso hacerlo mañana.
She intends to go alone.	Tiene la intención de ir sola.

Ø **intentar** means "to try," e.g., **Intentó hacerlo.** "He tried to do it."

interest v
to interest	interesar
to be/get interested in	interesarse en/por
He's not interested in baseball.	No le interesa el béisbol./No se interesa en el béisbol.
to be interested in [financially]	estar interesado(a) en

intermission n
[interruption]	una intermisión/una interrupción
[in movies]	el descanso
[in theater]	el descanso/el entreacto

intoxicated adj
[drunk]	borracho(a)/ebrio(a) [more formal, legal term]

Ø **intoxicado(a)** usually has the sense of "poisoned."

introduce v
to introduce sb to sb	presentar alguien a alguien
May I introduce my wife?	Permíteme presentarte a mi esposa./ Te presento a mi esposa.
He introduced me to his sister.	Me presentó a su hermana.
Let me introduce myself.	Me presento.
I'd like to introduce Alfonso.	Quisiera presentarte a Alfonso./Te presento a Alfonso.
to introduce a new fashion/ product	introducir una moda nueva/un producto nuevo
[to insert]	introducir
She introduced the key into the lock.	Introdujo la llave en la cerradura.

involve v
to concern	concernir/atañer
This problem involves you too.	Este problema te atañe a ti también.
those involved	los interesados

to imply	suponer
This job involves living abroad.	Este trabajo supone que tengo que vivir al extranjero.

to require
Your plan will involve a lot
of money.

requerir/exigir
Tu proyecto requerirá mucho dinero.

to implicate
He was involved in the murder.

implicar/meter/involucrar
Estaba implicado/metido/involucrado
en el homicidio.

to get involved in
They got involved in the
argument.
Don't get involved in that!
[to have an affair with sb]
He got involved with an actress.

meterse en/enredarse en/embrollarse en
Se metieron en la disputa.

¡No te metas en eso!
tener un lío con alguien
Tuvo un lío con una actriz.

involved *adj*
[complex]
This is very involved.

complicado(a)
Esto es muy complicado.

issue *n*
a question, a topic
It's a political issue.

una cuestión/un asunto/un problema
Es una cuestión política.

a copy of a publication
in this issue of the magazine

un número
en este número de la revista

shares, stamps, notes
an issue of shares

una emisión
una emisión de acciones

it *pron*
[subject]

él *[masculine]*
ella *[feminine]*
ello *[neuter]*
*[Note: Even more than the other subject
pronouns, **él, ella,** and **ello** meaning "it"
are usually omitted.]*

Where's the money? – It's on
the table.
Have you seen my scarf? – Yes,
it's in the car.
I didn't like it. *[the whole
business]*
It was all over and done with.

¿Dónde está el dinero? – Está en la
mesa.
¿Has visto mi bufanda? – Sí, está
en el coche.
Ello no me gustó.

Ello se acabó. *[Note: **Ello** does not
refer to a specific object but to an idea,
concept, the whole business, etc.]*

[direct object]

lo *[masculine & neuter]*
la *[feminine]*

My passport? I've lost it.
Your jacket? I haven't seen it.

¿Mi pasaporte? Lo he perdido.
¿Tu chaqueta? No la he visto.

[indirect object]
Give it a kick!

le
¡Dale una patada!

[disjunctive]

él/sí *[masculine]*
ella/sí *[feminine]*
ello/sí *[neuter]*

He'll see to it.

Se ocupará de ello.

its *adj*

[singular: masc & fem]	su
[plural: masc & fem]	sus
its main street	su calle mayor
its rivers and mountains	sus ríos y sus montañas *[Note: adjective repeated]*

it's (it is) *[see it]*

itself *pron*

	él mismo/ella misma/ello mismo
	sí/sí mismo(a)
in itself/per se	de por sí/en sí

J

jacket n
a jacket   un saco *[LA]*/una chaqueta/una americana
[a sport coat]   una americana de sport
[of woman's suit]   una chaqueta
[of pajamas]   una chaqueta
a sheepskin jacket   una chamarra

jam n
[food]   la mermelada
a traffic jam   un embotellamiento
[a blockage]   un atasco
[fig.]   un apuro/un lío
to be in a jam   estar en un apuro
to get into/out of a jam   meterse en/salir de un apuro

jam v
to jam sth into   meter algo a la fuerza en

jeans n
jeans   el bluyín *[LA]*/los tejanos/
                                         los pantalones vaqueros *[Sp]*

jerk n
[sudden movement]   una sacudida
[sudden pull]   un tirón
[a shove]   un empujón
[a fool]   un idiota

job n
a job   un trabajo/un empleo/un puesto
to look for a job   buscar trabajo/un empleo
to lose one's job   perder su trabajo
to be laid off *[from a job]*   ser despedido(a)
to do a good job   hacer un buen trabajo/hacer algo bien
to be out of a job   estar sin trabajo/estar desocupado(a)
a full-time job   un trabajo de jornada completa/de
                                         plena dedicación

a part-time job   un trabajo a media jornada/de
                                         dedicación parcial

join v
[two things together]   unir/juntar/poner juntos
[a club or society]   ingresar en/hacerse socio de
[a political party]   afiliarse a/hacerse miembro de
[the armed forces]   alistarse en
[to meet someone]   reunirse con/unirse a/juntarse con
I'll join you at six.   Me reuniré contigo a las seis.
They joined him at the café. Se reunieron con él en el café.
Would you like to join us?   ¿Te gustaría acompañarnos?
May I join you?   ¿Se permite?
Join the club!   ¡No faltaba más!

journey   n
a journey   un viaje
Ø **una jornada** means "a working day."

juice   n
[in general]   el jugo
[fruit juice]   el jugo *[LA]*/el zumo *[Sp]*
[gas]   la gasolina
[electricity]   la corriente

junior   adj & n
[in age]   menor/más joven
[in terms of service on staff]   más nuevo(a)
[of a championship]   juvenil
the junior soccer championship   el campeonato juvenil de fútbol
a junior   un(a) menor/un(a) joven

at the university
the junior year   el tercer año
a junior   un/una estudiante de tercer año
He's a junior.   Es estudiante del tercer año.
Ø Spanish has no real equivalent for a "junior" at high school.

junk   n
[cheap goods]   las baratijas
That car is junk.   Ese coche es una porquería.
The film was a load of junk.   La película era una porquería.
You're talking a lot of junk.   No dices más que tonterías.
a junk market   un rastro
a junkshop   un baratillo

just   adv
It's just what I wanted.   Es exactamente lo que quería.
It's just the same.   Es exactamente igual.
She's just leaving.   Sale ahora mismo.
I was just leaving.   Estaba a punto de salir.
It's just here.   Está aquí mismo.
The library is just past the   La biblioteca está un poco más allá
  museum.   del museo.
just a little (bit)   un poquito
just a few   unos pocos/unas pocas
I'm just as capable as you.   Soy tan capaz como tú.
He plays the piano just as   Toca el piano tan bien como su
  well as his brother.   hermano.
She just missed the train.   Acaba de perder el tren.
They arrived just in time.   Llegaron justamente con tiempo.
Just a moment!   ¡Un momentito!
They were here just now.   Estaban aquí hace un momento.
just around the corner   a la vuelta de la esquina
just because   porque sí
Why don't you do it? – Just because.   ¿Por qué no lo haces? – Porque no.

to have just   acabar de *[+ infinitive]*
I have just seen her.   Acabo de verla.
He had just left the office   Acababa de salir de la oficina
  when I telephoned.   cuando telefoneé.*[Note: **acabar de** is only used in two tenses, the present and the imperfect, and translates "have just" and "had just" respectively.]*

K

keep *v intrans*

to keep quiet	callarse
Keep quiet!	¡Cállate!
Keep straight ahead for the hotel.	Sigue todo derecho para el hotel.
Keep to the left/right.	Sigue por la izquierda/derecha.
Keep out!	¡Prohibida la entrada!
Keep off the grass!	¡No pisar la hierba! *[Note: Public signs often use the infinitive form instead of the imperative.]*

to keep at it	perseverar
to keep fit	mantenerse en forma
to keep in mind	tener en cuenta/tener presente

to keep (on) doing sth

She kept on talking.	Siguió hablando.
Keep on looking for it!	¡Sigue buscándolo!

to last — conservarse/durar

These apples won't keep.	Estas manzanas no se conservarán frescas.
Buy some fruit that will keep.	Compra fruta que durará.

keep *v trans*

to keep a promise/one's word	cumplir una promesa/lo prometido
to keep an appointment	acudir a una cita
to keep company with	tener relaciones con
to keep house	llevar la casa
to keep one's chin up	no desanimarse
to keep order	mantener/imponer orden
to keep the ball rolling	mantener el interés/animar la conversación
to keep sb waiting	hacer esperar a alguien/hacer que alguien espere *[Note: use of subjunctive]*
She kept me waiting an hour.	Me hizo esperar una hora./Hizo que esperara yo una hora.
to keep sb informed/posted about sth	tener a alguien al corriente de algo
Keep me informed!	¡Tenme/Téngame al corriente!
I don't know where she keeps her jewels.	No sé dónde guarda sus joyas.
[to keep domestic animals]	tener
They keep a dog and two cats.	Tienen un perro y dos gatos.
[to rear animals]	criar
He keeps sheep and cows.	Cría ovejas y vacas.

to save — tener guardado(a)/reservar

He was keeping the book for me.	Tenía guardado el libro para mí.
Keep me a seat!	¡Resérvame un asiento!

to retain

Keep the change!	¡Quédese con la vuelta!

to keep sth hot/cold — tener algo caliente/frío

I've kept the soup hot.	He tenido caliente la sopa.
You must keep this juice cold.	Debes tener frío este jugo.

113

to keep (sb) warm
You must keep (yourself) warm.

abrigar(se)/mantener(se) el calor
Debes mantener el calor del cuerpo.
/Debes abrigarte.

This blanket will keep you warm.

Esta cobija te mantendrá el calor.
/te abrigará.

kid *n*
a kid *[child]*

un(a) chaval(a) *[LA & Sp]*/un(a)
chamaco(a) *[Mex]*/un(a) pibe *[Arg & Uru]*/
un(a) patojo(a) *[Gua]*/un(a) guambito(a)
[Col]/un(a) nene(a) *[Arg, Uru, Sp]*

kill *v*
to kill
He killed his wife.
He killed himself.
The President has been killed.

matar
Mató a su esposa.
Se mató.
Le han matado al Presidente./Se
mató al Presidente.

to kill time

pasar el rato

kind *adj*
to be kind
You're very kind./That's very
kind of you.
to be kind to
He's very kind to me.
to be kind to animals
Please be so kind as to ...
Would you be so kind as to ...?

ser amable/bondadoso(a)
Eres/Es usted muy amable.

ser amable con
Es muy amable conmigo.
tratar bien a los animales
Ten/Tenga la bondad de...
¿Me haces/hace el favor de... ?

kind *n*
a kind
What kind of car do you have?
He's interested in animals of
that kind.
I'm not that kind of person.
He's the sort of person who
would not do that.
I like films of all kinds.

una clase/una especie/un género/un tipo
¿Qué clase/tipo de coche tienes?
Le interesan los animales de esa
especie/ese género.
No soy de esa clase de personas.
Es de los que no podrían hacer eso.

Me gustan películas de toda clase./
Me gusta toda clase de películas.

all kinds of people
She's a kind of detective.
It's kind of awkward.

toda clase de gente
Es algo así como una detective.
Es algo difícil.

kiss *n & v*
a kiss
to kiss sb/give sb a kiss
to kiss sb goodbye
They kissed.

un beso
besar/dar un beso a alguien
dar un beso de despedida a alguien
Se besaron./Se dieron un beso.

knock *n & v*
to knock
to knock at the door
There's a knock at the door.
Did you hear a knock?

golpear
llamar a la puerta
Llaman/Se llama a la puerta.
¿Oíste una llamada (a la puerta)?

114

know *v*

to be acquainted with
Do you know my boss?
I know him by name/sight.
I've known your parents for
  twenty years.

She knows Spain very well.
I don't know Gabriel García
  Márquez's novels.

to get to know (people/places)
We got to know them last
  summer.

to recognize
I knew them at once.

to know facts
Do you know how much it costs?
He doesn't know the price.
Do they know German?
Who knows?
How should I know?
to know sth by heart
If only I had known ...!

to let know
I'll let you know.
Why didn't you let me know?

to get to know sth
How did you get to know that?

to know how to
Does he know how to swim?
She doesn't know how to play
  the piano.
I don't know how to repair it.

to know about/to understand
He knows all about cars.

to know one's business/job

not to know/be unaware of
I didn't know about their
  problems.

conocer
¿Conoces a mi jefe?
Lo conozco de nombre/vista.
Conzco a tus padres desde hace
  veinte años./Hace veinte años que
  conozco a tus padres.
Conoce bien España.
No conozco las novelas de Gabriel
  García Márquez.

(llegar) a conocer
Los conocimos/Llegamos a conocerlos
  el verano pasado.

reconocer
Los reconocí en seguida.

saber
¿Sabes cuánto cuesta?
No sabe el precio.
¿Saben alemán?
¿Quién sabe?
¿Qué sé yo?
saber algo de memoria
¡De haberlo sabido antes...!

avisar
Te avisaré.
¿Por qué no me avisaste?

enterarse de algo
¿Cómo te enteraste de eso?

saber
¿Sabe nadar?
No sabe tocar el piano.

No sé cómo repararlo.

entender de
Entiende mucho de coches.

conocer/saber su oficio

ignorar/no saber
Ignoraba sus problemas.

L

label *n*
[on goods, clothes, bottles]   una etiqueta/un rótulo

Ø **etiqueta** also means "etiquette," "formality."

lady *n*
a lady	una señora
a lady [distinguished, old]	una dama
the ladies' restroom	las señoras
Ladies and gentlemen!	¡Señoras y señores!
The First Lady	La primera dama
Our Lady	Nuestra Señora

land *n*
[in general]	la tierra
[nation]	un país
[region]	una región/una tierra
[soil]	la tierra/el suelo
[property]	tierras/una estancia [LA]/una hacienda [LA]/una finca
[countryside, agricultural]	el campo
[piece/tract of land]	un terreno
native land	la patria

land *v*
[of aircraft]	aterrizar
to land a job	conseguir un trabajo

lane *n*
[in the country]	un camino/una vereda
[in town]	un callejón/una callejuela
[traffic]	un carril/una vía/una banda/una senda
the left-hand lane	el carril de la izquierda
[in track and field, swimming]	una calle/una banda
[in bowling]	una pista

language *n*
[of country or region]	la lengua/el idioma
the Spanish language	la lengua castellana/el idioma castellano/el español
modern languages	las lenguas modernas/los idiomas modernos
to be good at languages	ser fuerte en los idiomas
[faculty of speech]	el lenguaje
bad language	el lenguaje indecente/las palabrotas
scientific/technical language	el lenguaje científico/técnico

large *adj*
large	grande
a large house	una casa grande
a large family	una familia grande/numerosa

a large quantity
a large sum of money
*[see also **big**]*

una gran cantidad
una gran cantidad de dinero

Ø **largo** means "long."

last *adj*
final
in the last days of the war
It was Galdós' last novel.
It will take place on the last
  Sunday of the month.
the last three numbers
the last straw

último(a) *[Note: precedes the noun]*
en los últimos días de la guerra
Fue la última novela de Galdós.
Tendrá lugar el último domingo del
  mes.
las tres últimas cifras *[Note the word order.]*
la última gota/el final/el colmo *[Sp]*

most recent
last Saturday
last month
last year
last week
last night
the night before last
Did you like her last film?

pasado(a)
el sábado pasado
el mes pasado
el año pasado
la semana pasada
anoche/ayer en la noche
anteanoche
¿Te gustó su película más reciente?

late *adj & adv*
to arrive/be late
[person]
She is always late.
I'm sorry I'm late.
[of transportation]
The train arrived ten minutes
  late.
His plane will be half an hour
  late.

llegar tarde
Siempre llega tarde.
Siento llegar tarde.
llegar con retraso
El tren llegó con diez minutos de
  retraso.
Su avión llegará con media hora de
  retraso.

It's late.
It was getting late.
to work late at the office

late at night/in the night
late into the night
late in the afternoon
in the late eighties

Es tarde.
Se estaba haciendo tarde.
trabajar en la oficina después de la
  hora acostumbrada/hasta una
  hora tardía
ya muy entrada la noche
hasta muy entrada la noche
a última hora de la tarde
en los últimos años ochenta

to be late (in) doing something
I was late (in) getting up.

tardar en hacer algo
Tardé en levantarme.

miscellaneous
to be in one's late thirties
See you later!
at the latest
the latest fashion
my late husband/wife

acercarse a los cuarenta
¡Hasta pronto!/¡Hasta más tarde!
a lo más tarde/a más tardar
la última moda/la moda más reciente
mi esposo difunto/mi esposa difunta

latter *pron*
[as opposed to former]
Of the two dishes, I prefer
  the latter.

éste/ésta/éstos/éstas
De los dos platos, prefiero éste.

law n

the law(s) *[of a country]*	la ley/las leyes
[subject for study, body of law]	el derecho/la jurisprudencia
civil/commercial/constitutional/ criminal/international law	el derecho/civil/mercantil/político penal/internacional
martial law	la ley marcial/el gobierno militar
by law	según la ley
court of law	un tribunal (de justicia)
to study law	estudiar derecho
law school	una escuela/facultad de derecho
to practice law	ejercer de abogado
the law of gravity	la ley de la gravedad
in-law	político(a)
brother-in-law	el cuñado/el hermano político
sister-in-law	la cuñada/la hermana política
father-in-law	el suegro/el padre político
mother-in-law	la suegra/la madre política

lawyer n

[an attorney]	un(a) abogado(a)
[out-of-court legal adviser]	un(a) licenciado(a) *[Mex]*
[notary]	un(a) notario(a)

lazy adj

lazy	flojo(a) *[LA]*/perezoso(a)

least adj, adv & n

adverb — menos

the least important matter	el asunto menos importante
the least expensive shirts in the store	las camisas menos costosas de la tienda *[Note: **de** after a superlative]*
These are the least expensive.	Éstos/Éstas son los/las menos costosos(as).
This is the least interesting.	Éste/Ésta es el/la menos interesante.
He's the one who works least.	Es él que trabaja menos.
She did it least efficiently.	Fue ella quien lo hizo menos eficientemente.

adjective — menos/menor/(más) mínimo(a)

He has the least money.	Es el que tiene menos dinero.
I have the least chance of going to Colombia.	Tengo la menor oportunidad de ir a Colombia.

noun — lo menos

The least you can do is ...	Lo menos que puedes hacer es...
to say the least	para no decir más
not in the least!	¡en absoluto!/¡de ninguna manera!

least (at) adv

at least	a lo menos/al menos/por lo menos
He's at least fifty.	Tiene por lo menos cincuenta años.
At least it's not raining.	Por lo menos no llueve.
At least, that's what I think.	De todos modos, eso es lo que pienso yo.

leave v

to go away — irse/marcharse

They left yesterday.	Se fueron/marcharon ayer.

to leave a place
We left Madrid this morning.

salir de
Salimos de Madrid esta mañana.

to take one's leave
I must leave you now.

despedirse de
Tengo que despedirme de ustedes ahora.

to leave sb or sth somewhere
They left me at the airport.
I left your money on the table.

dejar
Me dejaron en el aeropuerto.
Dejé su dinero en la mesa.

to leave for good
My friend has left his wife.

abandonar
Mi amigo ha abandonado a su esposa.

to leave unintentionally
I left my umbrella in the
 train.
I've left my books behind.
They left their friends behind.

dejar (olvidado)/olvidar/dejar atrás
Dejé (olvidado) mi paraguas en el
 tren.
He olvidado mis libros.
Dejaron atrás a sus compañeros.

to leave + adjective
She left the door open.
Leave me alone!

dejar
Dejó abierta la puerta.
¡Déjame en paz!

to bequeath
His father left him 50,000
 dollars.

dejar/legar
Su padre le legó cincuenta mil
 dólares.

lecture n
[in general]
[university lecture]
to go to a lecture
to go to lectures on ...
a lecture hall

una conferencia
una clase
asistir a una conferencia
seguir un curso sobre/de...
una sala de conferencias/un aula *[fem]*

Ø **lectura** means "reading."

left adj, adv & n
opposite of right
your left arm
the left(-hand) drawer
on the left
to the left
to keep to the left
the left-hand side
left turn
left-handed
to be on the left *[politics]*
left-winger

izquierdo(a)
tu brazo izquierdo
el cajón de la izquierda
a la izquierda
a la izquierda
circular por la izquierda
la izquierda
una vuelta a la izquierda
zurdo(a)
ser de izquierdas
un(a) izquierdista

remaining
to be left
Is there any money left?
We have enough money left.
I'm sorry, there's no rice
 left.
to be left over *[to spare]*
Is there any fruit left over?
There was a lot of food left.
I have no time left.
leftovers

quedar
¿Queda dinero?
Nos queda bastante dinero.
Lo siento, no queda arroz.

sobrar
¿Sobra fruta?
Sobraba mucha comida.
No me sobra tiempo.
las sobras/los restos

lend *v*
to lend sth to sb
Will you lend me the car?
to lend a hand

prestar algo a alguien
¿Quieres prestarme el coche?
echar una mano

less *adj, adv & n*
in comparisons
I have less money than you.
He is less intelligent than
  his sister.
It cost less than 10 dollars.

menos... que
Tengo menos dinero que tú.
Es menos inteligente que su
  hermana.
Costó menos de diez dólares. *[Note:
  use of **de** when a number follows.]*

the less ... the less
The less you work, the less
  you earn.

mientras/cuanto menos... menos
Mientras menos trabajas, menos
  ganas.

less and less
I am less and less interested
  in business.

cada vez menos
Me interesan cada vez menos los
  negocios.

let *v*
to allow
Let me help you!
He didn't let me go to the game.
Let us in!
Let them come in!

dejar/permitir
¡Déjame ayudarte!/¡Permíteme ayudarte!
No me permitió ir al partido.
¡Déjanos pasar!
¡Déjalos pasar!/¡Que pasen!

in suggestions
Let's go!
Let's go to the beach!
Let's see!
Let's play tennis!

¡Vamos!
¡Vamos!/¡Vámonos!
¡Vamos a la playa!
¡Vamos a ver!/¡A ver!
¡Vamos a jugar al tenis!

to let go [set free]
They are letting the prisoners go.

soltar
Sueltan a los prisioneros.

to let go of
He let go of the rope.

soltar
Soltó la cuerda.

to let sb down
The train let me down.
Her brother let us down.

fallar/desilusionar/defraudar a alguien
El tren me falló/defraudó.
Su hermano nos falló/defraudó.

other
Let's face it!

¡Seamos realistas!

let alone *adv*
let alone
He can't go for a week, let
  alone a month.

mucho menos
No puede ir por una semana, y mucho
  menos un mes.

letter *n*
[correspondence]
[of alphabet]

la carta
la letra

library *n*
a library

una biblioteca

Ø **una librería** means "bookstore."

120

license   n

[general]	una licencia/un permiso/una autorización
driver's license	un brevete *[Per]*/un carnet *[Chi & Sp]*/una libreta *[Arg & Uru]*/una licencia *[Mex]*/un carnet de conducir *[Sp]*/un título *[Ven]*
license plate *[of car]*	una placa (de matrícula)
license number	la matrícula/el número de matrícula

light   adj & adv

not heavy
	liviano(a) *[LA]*/ligero(a)
lightweight clothes	ropa liviana/ligera
a light wind	un viento suave
to be a light sleeper	tener un sueño ligero
to travel light	viajar con poco equipaje

not dark
	claro(a)
a light room	una habitación clara
light blue	azul claro/azul celeste
a light complexion	una tez blanca
to grow light	amanecer/hacerse de día
[illuminated/well lit]	bañado(a) de luz/con mucha luz

light   n

in general
	la luz
daylight	la luz del día
sunlight	la luz del sol

lighting
	la iluminación
[lamp]	una luz/una lámpara
to turn on the light	encender la luz
to turn off the light	apagar la luz
floodlight	un foco
street light	un farol
traffic lights	los semáforos
the red/green light	la luz roja/verde
headlight *[car]*	un faro/una linterna *[Col]*
rear light *[car]*	un piloto/una calavera *[Mex]*/un cocuyo *[Ven]*
lighthouse	un faro

flame
	el fuego/la lumbre
Do you have a light? *[for a cigarette, etc.]*	¿Tienes fuego?
pilot light *[in an oven]*	un mechero/un encendedor

light   v

to set light to	pegar fuego a/encender
to light a fire/the gas/a match	encender un fuego/el gas/una cerilla
to light a room	iluminar una habitación

like   v

to find pleasurable
	gustar(le) a uno/agradar(le) a uno *[Mex]*
I like fruit.	Me gusta la fruta.
He likes potato chips.	Le gustan las papas fritas.

We like swimming.	Nos gusta nadar.
Do you like it/them?	¿Te gusta?/¿Te gustan?

acquaintances
Do you like Mr. Ramírez?

gustar(le) a uno
¿Te gusta el señor Ramírez?/¿Le tienes simpatía al señor Ramírez?/¿Te es simpático el señor Ramírez?

close friends, relations
Do you like your cousins?
She likes my brother.

querer/gustar(le) a uno
¿Quieres a tus primos?
Le gusta mi hermano.

to want
Would you like an ice-cream?
I'd like some strawberries.
They would like to stay.

querer/gustar(le) a uno
¿Quieres un helado?/¿Te gustaría un helado?
Quisiera unas fresas.
Les gustaría quedarse.

likely *adj*
likely
It's quite likely.

probable
Es muy probable.

likewise *adv*
likewise

igualmente

line *n*
[in general]
a dotted line
a straight line
to draw a line
a line of poetry
lines *[of a play]*
a line of traffic
to stand/wait in line
to line up

una línea
una línea de puntos
una línea recta
dibujar/trazar una línea
un verso
el papel
una cola de coches
hacer cola
alinearse/ponerse en fila

liquor *n*
[alcoholic]
hard liquor

el licor/las bebidas alcohólicas
el licor espiritoso

Ø **licor** is also used to mean "a cordial."

listen *v*
to listen to

escuchar a *[people]*
escuchar *[Note: no preposition when used with objects]*

He never listens to his boss.
I want to listen to the music.

Nunca escucha a su jefe.
Quiero escuchar la música.

litter *[see garbage]*

little *adj, adv & n*
small
It's a small house.

chico(a) *[LA]*/pequeño(a)
Es una casa chica.

not much
He eats very little.
She has little patience.

poco
Come muy poco.
Tiene poca paciencia.

a small amount/quantity

un poco (de)

I have a little bread.	Tengo un poco de pan.
Would you like a little wine?	¿Te gustaría un poco de vino?
– Yes, just a little.	– Sí, sólo un poco/un poquito.
a little bit (of)	un poquito (de)
little by little	poco a poco

live *v*

to live	vivir
They live in this appartment.	Viven en este apartamento.
to live a happy life	llevar/tener una vida feliz
to live well	darse buena vida/vivir en el lujo
as long as I live	mientras viva
Long live the president!	¡Viva el presidente!

living *n*

to make a living	ganarse la vida
to work for a living	ganarse la vida trabajando
What do you do for a living?	¿Cómo te ganas la vida?/A qué te dedicas?
the cost of living	el coste de vida

loan *n*

a loan *[between people]*	un préstamo
a loan *[commercial]*	un empréstito
on loan	prestado(a)
[see also **borrow** *and* **lend**]	

lobby *n [see* **hall**]

locate *v*

to locate	encontrar
to locate a place on the map	encontrar un sitio en el mapa
Where is it located?	¿Dónde se encuentra?/¿Dónde está?

location *n*

[a site]	una localización/un solar
a location for the factory	un solar para la fábrica
It's in a good location.	Está bien situado(a).
to be on location *[filming]*	estar rodando

lock *n & v*

to lock	cerrar con llave
The doors are locked.	Las puertas están cerradas con llave.
to lock sb or sth in	encerrar a alguien/encerrar algo
I'll lock my money in the drawer.	Voy a encerrar mi dinero en el cajón.
to lock up *[in prison]*	encarcelar
a lock	una chapa *[LA]*/una cerradura

lonely *adj*

[general]	solitario(a)/solo(a)
to feel lonely	sentirse solo(a)
It's a lonely life.	Es una vida solitaria.
[place]	aislado(a)/remoto(a)
We live in a lonely place.	Vivimos en un sitio aislado.

long *adj*

long	largo(a)

long

a long journey	un viaje largo
a long story	una historia larga
She has long hair.	Tiene el pelo largo.

long *adv*

[for a long time]	mucho tiempo
I've been waiting a long time.	Hace mucho tiempo que estoy esperando.
I won't be long. *[returning]*	Vuelvo pronto.
I won't be long. *[finishing]*	Termino pronto.
a long time ago	hace mucho tiempo
He cannot wait any longer.	No puede esperar más (tiempo).
I'll wait a little longer.	Esperaré un poco más (tiempo).
How much longer must I wait?	¿Hasta cuándo tengo que esperar?

how long ... ?

	¿desde hace cuánto tiempo... ?/¿cuánto tiempo hace que... ?
How long has he lived in San Juan?	¿Desde hace cuánto tiempo vive en San Juan?/¿Cuánto tiempo hace que vive en San Juan?
How long did he live in San Juan?	¿Durante cuánto tiempo vivió en San Juan?

as long as

As long as you work here, you will do what the boss says.	Mientras trabajes aquí harás lo que diga el jefe.
Stay as long as you like.	Quédate hasta cuando quieras.
[provided that]	con tal que *[+ subjunctive]*
You can go to the dance as long as you are back by midnight.	Puedes ir al baile con tal que vuelvas antes de medianoche.

long *v*

to long for sth	anhelar algo
I'm longing for her return.	Anhelo su regreso.
to long to do sth	anhelar hacer algo
She's longing to see you again.	Anhela verte otra vez.

look *v*

to seem

	parecer
That book looks interesting.	Ese libro parece interesante.
You look ill.	Pareces enfermo(a).

to look like

	parecerse a
She looks like her aunt.	Se parece a su tía.

to look at

	mirar a *[people]*
	mirar *[Note: no preposition when used with objects]*
Look at Maria!	¡Mira a María!
I was looking at the photos.	Miraba las fotos.
He was looking out of the window.	Miraba por la ventana.

to look after sb

	cuidar de alguien
He looks after his parents.	Cuida de sus padres.

to look up

	consultar/buscar
I looked up that word in the dictionary.	Busqué esa palabra en el diccionario.

to look up to

	respetar/admirar
They look up to their teacher.	Respetan a su profesor(a).

to look forward to *[see forward]*

lost adj
to get lost — perderse/extraviarse
They got lost in the woods. — Se perdieron en el bosque.
I think they're lost. — Creo que se han perdido.
the lost and found department — la oficina de objetos perdidos

lot adv
[a great deal] — mucho
She smokes a lot. — Ella fuma mucho.
I liked the hotel a lot. — Me gustó/agradó mucho el hotel.

lot(s) n
[much; many] — mucho/mucha/muchos/muchas
They have a lot/lots of money. — Tienen mucho dinero.
I have a lot/lots of relations — Tengo muchos parientes en Cuba.
  in Cuba.

loud adj
loud — alto(a)/fuerte/ruidoso(a)
a loud voice — una voz fuerte
a loud noise — un ruido fuerte
He spoke in a loud voice. — Habló en voz alta.
The music is very loud. — La música está muy alta.
[noisy] — ruidoso(a)
a loud district — un barrio ruidoso
loudspeaker — un altoparlante/un altavoz/una magnavoz

love v & n
to love sb — querer a alguien
He loves his children. — Quiere a sus niños.
to fall in love with sb — enamorarse de alguien
She fell in love with him. — Se enamoró de él.
to be in love in with sb — estar enamorado(a) de alguien
I'm not in love with her. — No estoy enamorado de ella.
to make love (to sb) — hacer el amor (a alguien)
to love sth — adorar algo/encantarle a uno algo
I love Mexican food. — Adoro la comida mexicana.
I love Chinese food. — Me encanta la comida china.

lovely adj
of appearance — lindo(a) [LA]/bonito(a)/hermoso(a)/
  precioso(a)

How lovely she is! — ¡Qué linda es!
It's a lovely beach. — Es una linda playa.

of personal qualities — encantador(a)
His father is a lovely person. — Su padre es una persona encantadora.

pleasant — agradable
It was a lovely trip. — Fue un viaje agradable.
to have a lovely time — pasarlo muy bien/divertirse
We had a lovely time in Spain. — Lo pasamos muy bien en España.

lover n
a lover — un/una amante
to be lovers — ser amantes
[an enthusiast] — un(a) aficionado(a)

lucky

a lover of soccer

She's a music lover.
She's a great lover of the guitar.

un(a) aficionado(a) al fútbol/un(a)
  hincha del fútbol
Es aficionada a la música.
Tiene mucha afición a la guitarra.

lucky adj
lucky
He's a very lucky person.
to be lucky
You were very lucky.
She was lucky enough to get
  tickets.
How lucky!
a lucky charm
It's not my lucky day.

afortunado(a)
Es una persona afortunada.
tener suerte
Tuviste mucha suerte.
Tuvo la suerte de conseguir
  entradas.
¡Qué suerte!
un amuleto que trae suerte
Hoy no traigo buena estrella.

luggage n
luggage
hand luggage
excess luggage
a piece of luggage
luggage check-in
luggage locker

el equipaje/las maletas
los bultos de mano/el equipaje de mano
el exceso de equipaje
una maleta
la consigna
la consigna automática

luxury adj & n
luxury
a luxury apartment/hotel
to live in luxury
I can't afford luxuries.

el lujo
un apartamento/hotel de lujo
vivir en (el) lujo
No tengo con que comprar artículos
  de lujo.

Ø **la lujuria** means "lust."

M

mad adj
angry
She'll be mad if you arrive late.
to be mad at sb
to get mad at sb

furioso(a)
Estará furiosa si llegas tarde.
estar furioso(a) con alguien
enojarse/enfadarse/ponerse enojado(a)/
    ponerse enfadado(a) con alguien

crazy
His father is mad.

Are you mad?

[idea, plan]
[hurriedly]
to go mad
a mad dog

loco(a)
Su padre es loco. *[Note: Ser is used to
    refer to a permanent state of insanity.]*
¿Estás loco(a)? *[Note: Estar is used where
    permanent insanity is not referred to.]*
insensato(a)
precipitadamente
volverse loco(a)
un perro rabioso

enthusiastic
to be mad about
I'm mad about her.
He's mad about music.

andar/estar loco(a) por
Ando loco por ella.
Está loco por la música.

mail n
[in general]
[letters]
airmail
by airmail

el correo/la correspondencia *[Arg]*
las cartas/la correspondencia
el correo aéreo
por avión/por correo aéreo

mail v
[to send through the mail]
[to put in mail box]

echar/mandar por correo
echar/depositar al buzón

main adj
main course
main office
main street

el plato principal
la oficina central
la calle mayor

major n
academic studies
What is your major?
to change one's major

la especialidad
¿Cuál es tu especialidad?
cambiarse de especialidad

person studying
He is a chemistry major.

Se especializa en la química.

military rank
a major

un comandante

major v
to major in *[a subject at a
    university]*
She majored in Spanish.

especializarse en

Se especializó en español.

make *n*
a make *[brand]*   una marca

make *v*
[general]   hacer
to make a journey/a noise   hacer un viaje/un ruido
[manufacture]   fabricar
They make cars here.   Fabrican coches aquí.
"Made in Venezuela"   "Fabricado en Venezuela"
to make a mistake   equivocarse/cometer una falta
to make money   ganar dinero
to make an appointment with   citarse con/darse una cita con
to make friends with   trabar amistad con/hacerse amigo de
to make up one's mind   decidirse
to make a meal   preparar una comida
to make fun of sb   burlarse de alguien
to make good grades   sacar buenas notas
to make a living   ganarse la vida

to make sb do sth   hacer/obligar a alguien
to make sb leave   obligar a alguien a salir
She made him cry.   Le hizo llorar.
I made him apologize to the   Le hice disculparse con el cliente.
  customer.

to cause/provoke   causar
to make trouble   causar problemas

to cause to be
to make sb ill/sad   poner a alguien enfermo(a)/triste
Don't make me laugh!   ¡No me hagas reír!
to make sb hungry/thirsty   darle hambre/sed a alguien

to make out
I can't make that out.   No lo entiendo./No me lo explico.
Can you make out his writing?   ¿Puedes descifrar su letra?

to make up
[with cosmetics]   maquillarse/pintarse
[after a quarrel]   hacer las paces
to make up for lost time   recuperar el tiempo perdido
to make up a story   inventar un cuento
You're making it up!   ¡Puro cuento!

to make up for   compensar

make-believe *n*
make-believe   la fantasía/la invención

male *n*
[animal, plant]   un macho
[person]   un varón
[adj: male sex]   masculino

manage *v*
to run *[a business]*   administrar/dirigir/llevar
He manages three businesses.   Dirige tres empresas.
My daughter manages a hotel in   Mi hija lleva un hotel en Cancún.
  Cancún.

to manage one's own affairs	llevar sus negocios
to succeed (in getting)	conseguir
He managed to get a good job.	Consiguió un buen trabajo.
to succeed in doing sth	conseguir/lograr hacer algo
They managed to find the museum.	Consiguieron/lograron encontrar el museo.
Did you manage to see the doctor?	¿Conseguiste ver al médico?
to handle a tricky situation	arreglarse
How did you manage at the meeting?	¿Cómo te arreglaste en la reunión?
I managed very well.	Me arreglé muy bien.
to manage people	manejar/manejarse con
She manages her employees very well.	Maneja muy bien a sus empleados./Se maneja muy bien con sus empleados.
They can't manage the children.	No pueden con los niños.

manager n

[of a company]	el director/la directora
	el/la gerente
	el encargado/la encargada
[owner, boss of small business]	el dueño/la dueña
[of estate]	el administrador/la administradora
sales manager	el gerente de ventas
[of sports team]	el/la entrenador(a)

Ø **el mánager** is also used to refer to a "manager" in the sport and entertainment fields.

mane n

[of a horse]	una crin
[of a lion]	una melena

man-made adj

[lake]	artificial
[fabric, etc.]	sintético(a)

manners n

bad manners	la mala educación
good manners	la educación
He has good manners.	Tiene educación.
You have no manners.	No tienes educación.
It's bad manners to interrupt.	Es de mala educación interrumpir.

manufacture v

[in general]	fabricar
[for clothes]	confeccionar
[for food]	elaborar

many adj & pron

There are many people in the square.	Hay mucha gente en la plaza.
I have many friends in Spain.	Tengo muchos amigos en España.
Many houses have air conditioning.	Muchas casas tienen aire acondicionado.
Many of them/us/you	Muchos de ellos/nosotros/ustedes
	Muchas de ellas/nosotras/ustedes

many times	muchas veces

as many as
She has as many friends as you.
I have as many as you.

tantos(as) como
Tiene tantos amigos como tú.
Tengo tantos como tú.

map   n
[general]
a map of the world
[of town/streets/transport system]
a map of the subway

un mapa [Note: masculine]
un mapamundi
un plano
un plano del Metro

march   n
[military]
[walk]
[demonstration]
[of time]

una marcha
una caminata
una manifestación
una marcha/un paso

march   v
to march in and out
to march past

entrar y salir enojado
desfilar

mark   n
[stain]
[imprint]
[from a blow]
[education]
On your marks!
to make one's mark

una mancha
una huella
una señal
una nota/una calificación
¡Preparados!
distinguirse

market   n
[general]
an open-air market
[stock market]
a supermarket
a hypermarket
[small grocery store]
the corner market
to be on the market

el mercado
un mercado al aire libre
la bolsa
un supermercado
un hipermercado
una tienda de ultramarinos
la tienda de la esquina
estar a la venta

marry   v
to marry/get married
Peter is marrying Teresa today.
We are getting married on Saturday.
They got married in Las Vegas.

casarse con
Pedro se casa con Teresa hoy.
Nos casamos el sábado.
Se casaron en Las Vegas.

**to conduct the marriage
  ceremony**
The priest married them.
The bishop will marry my sister.

casar a

El cura los casó.
El obispo casará a mi hermana.

to be married
I am not married.
They've been married for fifty years.

estar casado(a)(os)(as)
No estoy casado(a).
Hace cincuenta años que están
  casados.

master's   [see degree]

match n

[game]	un partido/un encuentro
[for striking]	un fósforo/un cerillo [Mex]/una cerilla [Sp]
a box of matches	una caja de fósforos
[marriage]	un partido
to be a good match	ser un buen partido

match v

to equal igualar/corresponder a
Her words don't match her Sus palabras no corresponden a sus
    actions.   acciones.

of clothes/colors hacer juego con/ser a tono
His tie matches his shirt. Su corbata hace juego con su camisa.
These colors do not match. Estos colores no son a tono/no hacen juego.

material n & adj

[information, ideas]	el material
[cloth]	el tejido/la tela
[substance]	la materia
raw materials	las materias primas
writing materials	los efectos de escritorio
[important]	material

matter n & v

[substance]	la materia
[subject, affair]	el asunto/la cuestión
as a matter of fact ...	en realidad.../el caso es que...
What's the matter?	¿Qué hay?/¿Qué pasa?
What's the matter with you?	¿Qué te pasa?/¿Qué tienes?/¿Te pasa algo?
Nothing's the matter.	No pasa nada.
It doesn't matter.	No importa./Da igual.
It's a matter of opinion.	Es cuestión de opinión.
It's a matter of time.	Es cuestión/cosa de tiempo.
It's a serious matter.	Es cosa seria.
no matter how	como sea
No matter where I go ...	Dondequiera que vaya...

matter-of-fact adj

matter-of-fact práctico(a)/realista

mature adj

[person, fruit]	maduro(a)
a mature person	una persona madura/de edad madura
[commerce, finance]	vencido(a)

may v

permission poder/permitir a alguien
May I ... ? ¿Me permite(s)... ?
You may go in now. Puedes entrar/pasar ahora.
May I come in? ¿Me permite(s) pasar?/¿Se puede pasar?

possibility es posible que/puede ser que
I may be able to help you. Es posible que pueda ayudarte.
    [Note: subjunctive]
She may have said so. Es posible que lo haya dicho.
    [Note: subjunctive]/Puede haberlo dicho.

131

me *pron*

[direct object]	me
[indirect object] to me	me
[disjunctive, object of preposition]	mí
He saw me in the street.	Me vio en la calle.
She gave the money to me.	Me dio el dinero.
Give it to me!	¡Dámelo!
Don't give them to me!	¡No me los des!
These are for me.	Éstos son para mí.
He came with me.	Vino conmigo.

mean *adj*

petty
mezquino(a)
It's very mean of you.
Es muy mezquino de tu parte.

bad/unkind
malo(a)/antipático(a)
a mean trick
una mala jugada
Her boss was a very mean guy.
Su jefe era un tío muy malo.

with temperature
medio(a)
the mean temperature
la temperatura media

mean *v*

to signify
querer decir/significar
What does this mean in English?
¿Qué quiere decir esto en inglés?
These instructions don't mean anything.
Estas instrucciones no significan nada.

to intend
They mean well.
Tienen buenas intenciones.
Do you mean it?
¿Lo dices en serio?
I didn't mean to do it.
Lo hice sin querer.
Does she mean to be difficult?
¿Quiere ser difícil?

means *n*

[manner]
el medio/la manera
[resources]
los medios
economic means
los recursos económicos
a person of means
una persona acaudalada
By all means!
¡Naturalmente!

medicine *n*

field of study
la medicina

medication
el medicamento/la medicina
You must take this medicine twice a day.
Debes tomarte esta medicina dos veces al día.

meet *v*

to get to know
conocer
I met them in Acapulco.
Los conocí en Acapulco.
We met at the university.
Nos conocimos en la universidad.
I'm very pleased to meet you.
Tengo mucho gusto en conocerte/lo/la.
Juan, meet Lola.
Juan, quiero presentarte a Lola.
Pleased to meet you!
¡Mucho gusto!/Encantado(a)/ Encantado(a) de conocerte/lo/la.

by arrangement
reunirse (con)/ir a recibir/esperar/venir a buscar/entrevistarse con

Let's meet later.	Vamos a reunirnos más tarde.
We can meet them at the café.	Podemos reunirnos con ellos en el café.
I'm meeting my wife at the airport.	Voy a recibir a mi esposa en el aeropuerto.
They're meeting me at the museum.	Vienen a buscarme en el museo.
I'll meet you at the theater.	Te espero en el teatro.
The President is meeting them at four o'clock.	El Presidente se entrevista con ellos a las cuatro.

accidentally encontrar/encontrarse con

I met my cousin in the street. Encontré a mi primo en la calle./Me encontré con mi primo en la calle.

We met in the market. Nos encontramos en el mercado.

meeting *n*
a group of people	una reunión/una sesión
a mass meeting	una reunión/un mitin popular
to hold a meeting	celebrar una reunión/sesión

individuals
[accidental]	un encuentro
[arranged]	una cita

mellow *adj*
[voice]	suave
[person]	sereno(a)

memorize *v*

to memorize aprender de memoria

memory *n*
the mental faculty
I have a good memory.	la memoria
	Tengo buena memoria.
He has a bad memory for names.	No recuerda bien los nombres.

something remembered
We have happy memories of Mexico. Tenemos felices recuerdos de México.

menu *n*
the menu	la lista de platos/la carta
[fixed price]	el menú/el cubierto [Mex]
today's menu	el menú del día
tourist menu	el menú turístico
What's on the menu?	¿Qué hay de comer?

middle *n*
in the middle of en medio de
in the middle of the field	en medio del campo
in the middle of the night	en medio de la noche
in the middle of summer	en pleno verano
in the middle of June	a mediados de junio
in the middle of Bogotá	en el centro de Bogotá
the middle class	la clase media
the Middle Ages	la Edad Media

to be busy doing sth estar + gerund

They were in the middle of
lunch when I arrived.

Estaban comiendo cuando llegué.

might *v*
It might be true.
It might be that he'll come
  tomorrow.
She said she might be able to
  help you.
She might have said so.

Podría ser verdad.
Podría ser que viniera mañana.
  [Note: subjunctive]
Dijo que pudiera ayudarte. *[Note:
  subjunctive]*
Podría haberlo dicho.

mind *n*
mind
What's on your mind?
to be out of one's mind
to change one's mind
It crossed my mind that ...
to go out of one's mind
to make up one's mind to
Have you made up your mind?

la mente
¿Qué es lo que te preocupa?
estar fuera de juicio
cambiar de opinión
Se me ocurrió...que
volverse loco
decidirse a
¿Te has decidido?

mind *v*
Do you mind if I open the window?
Where do you want to go? – I
  don't mind.
I don't mind waiting.
Would you mind ... ?

¿Te molesta si abro la ventana?
¿Adónde quieres ir? – Me es igual./
  No me importa.
No tengo inconveniente en esperar.
¿Serías tan amable de... ?

mine *pron*
[possessive]

His house is bigger than mine.
These books are mine.

Is this your glass? – No, mine
  is in the kitchen.
a friend of mine

el mío/los míos
la mía/las mías
Su casa es más grande que la mía.
Estos libros son míos.
*[Note: The definite article is omitted
  after the verb **ser**.]*
¿Es tuyo este vaso? – No, el mío
  está en la cocina.
un amigo mío/una amiga mía

minister *n*
[religious title]
[political]

el pastor
el ministro

miserable *adj*
[sad]
[unfortunate]
[wretched]
a miserable room

triste
desdichado(a)/desgraciado(a)
miserable
una habitación miserable

miss *v*
to fail to catch
They missed the bus.

perder
Perdieron el autobús.

to be absent
They missed the meeting.

faltar a
Faltaron a la reunión./No asistieron a
  la reunión.

She missed her appointment.	Faltó a su cita./No asistió a su cita.
to miss the boat	perder el tren
to be missing	faltar
Two people are missing.	Faltan dos personas.
[absent]	ausente
There are three students missing.	Tres estudiantes están ausentes.
[lost]	perdido(a)
Four tourists are missing in the desert.	Cuatro turistas están perdidos en el desierto.
to feel the absence of	echar de menos
We miss her.	La echamos de menos.
I missed you this morning.	Noté tu ausencia esta mañana.

mistake n

a mistake	una equivocación/un error/una falta
a spelling mistake	una falta de ortografía
There must be some mistake.	Ha de haber algún error.
to make a mistake	equivocarse/cometer un error/pelarse *[Ven]*

mistake v

to mistake sb for sb else	tomar a alguien por/confundir a alguien con/equivocar a alguien con
I mistook her for her sister.	La tomé por su hermana.

mix v

to mix a drink	preparar una bebida
a mixed salad	una ensalada mixta
to mix *[socially]*	llevarse bien con la gente
He doesn't mix well.	No se lleva bien con la gente.
to mix up	mezclar/confundir
He gets the two brothers mixed up.	Confunde a los dos hermanos.
I mix up *ser* and *estar*.	Confundo ser con estar.
to be mixed up	estar totalmente confuso(a)
to be mixed up in sth	estar metido en algo
to get mixed up in sth	meterse en algo

mixed adj

mixed	variado(a)
[with feelings]	contradictorio(a)

model n

a model	un modelo
[of plane, ship, etc.]	en miniatura
[exemplary]	un ejemplar
a model home	una casa piloto

money n

[in general]	el dinero/la plata *[in many parts of LA]*
paper money	el papel moneda
ready money	el dinero contante
money payment	un pago en metálico
to make money	ganar dinero

Ø **la moneda** means "currency," "coinage", and "coin:" note **la moneda suelta** meaning "small change."

monitor

monitor *n & v*

a monitor [TV, computer]	un monitor
[student]	un estudiante responsable
[to listen to]	escuchar
[to follow]	seguir de cerca

mood *n*

to be in a good/bad mood	estar de buen/mal humor
to be in the mood to do sth	tener ganas de hacer algo
I'm not in the mood to do it.	No tengo ganas de hacerlo.

more *adj, adv & pron*

in comparisons

	más... que
	más... del que/de la que/de los que /de las que/de lo que
He has more money than you.	Tiene más dinero que tú.
They drink more wine than beer.	Beben más vino que cerveza.
She is more intelligent than her brother.	Es más inteligente que su hermano.
I have more money than she thinks.	Tengo más dinero del que piensa.
They visited more factories than they expected.	Visitaron más fábricas de las que esperaban.
He is more intelligent than you think.	Es más inteligente de lo que piensas.

*[Note how the forms **del que/de la que/de los que/de las que** are used when the comparison is made between a noun and a following clause; **de lo que** is used when the comparison is between two clauses.]*

before a number

I have more than 50 dollars.	Tengo más de cincuenta dólares.
More than 100,000 people went to the game.	Más de cien mil personas asistieron al partido.
more than half	más de la mitad

additional

four more	cuatro más
Would you like some more wine?	¿Quieres más vino?
a few more days	algunos días más
I have one more thing to do.	Tengo una cosa más que hacer.
once more	una vez más

remaining

Is there any more coffee?	¿Queda café?
There are more potatoes left.	Quedan papas.

in negative sentences

I have no more money.	No tengo más dinero.
She doesn't go to the beach any more.	Ya no va a la playa.
There are no more than five left.	No quedan más de cinco.

more and more

	cada vez más
He became more and more excited.	Se puso cada vez más emocionado.

the more ... the more ...

	cuanto más... (tanto) más
The more you study the more you learn.	Cuanto más estudias (tanto) más aprendes.
the more the merrier	cuantos más mejor

136

morning   n

the morning	la mañana
[before dawn]	la madrugada
in the morning	por la mañana
in the morning [with time by the clock]	de la mañana
at eight o'clock in the morning	a las ocho de la mañana
early in the morning	muy de mañana
very early in the morning	muy de madrugada
this morning	esta mañana
tomorrow morning	mañana por la mañana
yesterday morning	ayer por la mañana
I spent every morning in the library.	Pasaba todas las mañanas en la biblioteca.
I spent the whole morning at the office.	Pasé toda la mañana en la oficina.
Good morning!	¡Buenos días! [Note: plural]

Ø **mañana** also means "tomorrow."

most   adj, adv & n
with a noun

[with a singular noun]	**más**
My brother has the most money.	Mi hermano tiene más dinero.
[with a plural noun]	los más/las más/la mayor parte de/ la mayoría de
Most students will be there.	La mayoría de los estudiantes estarán allí.

with an adjective

	más
It's the most enjoyable film I have seen.	Es la película más divertida que he visto.
It's the tallest building in the world.	Es el edificio más alto del mundo. [Note: **de** is used to mean "in" after a superlative.]
[meaning "very"]	muy
The film was most enjoyable.	La película fue muy divertida.

with a verb or adverb

His sister spent the most.	Es su hermana que ha gastado más.

most (of)   n

[with a singular noun]	la mayor parte (de)
most of the time	la mayor parte del tiempo
He paid for most of the wine.	Pagó la mayor parte del vino.
at the very most	como máximo
[with a plural noun]	la mayoría de
Most of these teachers are from Mexico.	La mayoría de estos profesores son de México.

mostly   adv
for the most part

They are mostly Peruvians.	en su mayor parte/en su mayoría En su mayoría son peruanos.

mainly

	casi siempre/la mayoría de las veces generalmente/en general/por lo general
We mostly go to the movies.	Generalmente vamos al cine.
He mostly drinks coffee.	Casi siempre bebe café.

mother   n & v

a mother

una madre/una mamá [Note: In Mexico the word **madre** is very often used in an insulting fashion; it is therefore better to use **mamá** to refer to one's mother.]

mother country
la madre patria

to mother
mimar

mother tongue
la lengua materna

mountain   n

a mountain
una montaña/un monte

The Appalachians
Los Montes Apalaches

a chain/range of mountains
una sierra/una cordillera

Let's go to the mountains.
Vamos a la sierra.

I spent my vacation in the mountains.
Pasé las vacaciones en la sierra.

mouth   n

a mouth
una boca

[of a river]
una desembocadura

by word of mouth
de palabra

to keep one's mouth shut
no decir esta boca es mía/tener la boca cerrada

to mouth [to articulate]
articular

move   v trans

physical
mover

I couldn't move the piano.
No pude mover el piano.

emotional

to move to tears
hacer llorar a alguien

The music moved me to tears.
La música me hizo llorar.

move   v intrans

to move
moverse

Don't move!
¡No te muevas!/¡No se mueva!/¡No se muevan!

to move house
mudarse de casa

They moved last week.
Se mudaron de casa la semana pasada.

She's moved to San Diego.
Se ha trasladado a San Diego.

to move in
instalarse en una casa

When did you move in?
¿Cuándo se instalaron ustedes?

movie   n

a movie
una película

a movie theater
un cine

to go to the movies
ir al cine

a movie star
un astro de cine [man]/una estrella de cine [woman]

much   adj, adv & pron

He doesn't sleep much.
No duerme mucho.

I don't drink much coffee.
No tomo mucho café.

There isn't much to do here.
Aquí no hay mucho que hacer.

How much do you need?
¿Cuánto necesitas?

in comparisons
as much as
I didn't eat as much as you.
as much ... as
They don't buy as much fruit
  as they used to.

tanto como
No comí tanto como tú.
tanto(a)... como
No compran tanta fruta como antes.

so much
He drank so much coffee that
  he couldn't sleep.
There is so much to do.

tanto(a)
Bebió tanto café que no pudo
  dormir.
Hay tanto que hacer.

too much
[adj]
They eat too much rice.
[adv & pro]
You smoke too much!
She has too much to do.

demasiado(a)
Comen demasiado arroz.
demasiado
¡Fumas demasiado!
Tiene demasiado que hacer.

musical adj
a musical instrument
She is very musical.
I come from a musical family.
a musical [show]

un instrumento músico
Tiene mucho talento para la música.
Soy de familia de músicos.
una comedia musical

must v
obligation
I must speak to him at once.
You must not go alone.

deber/tener que
Debo/Tengo que hablarle en seguida.
No debes ir solo(a).

probability
They must be very rich.
You must have been mistaken.

deber de
Deben de ser muy ricos.
Debías de haberte equivocado.

my adj
[masc & fem]
my son/family
my parents/sisters

mi/mis
mi hijo/familia
mis padres/hermanas

myself [see self]

139

N

nail   *n & v*

[finger, toe]	una uña
[animal's claw]	una garra
[metal]	un clavo
to be as hard as nails	ser muy resistente/tener el corazón de piedra
to bite one's nails	comerse las uñas
to hit the nail on the head	dar en el clavo/acertar
to nail	clavar
to nail together	fijar con clavos

name   *n*

[general]	el nombre
first name	el nombre de pila
family name/surname	el apellido
maiden name	el apellido de soltera
married name	el apellido de casada
nickname	el apodo
pet name	el nombre cariñoso
by name	de nombre
I know her by name.	La conozco de nombre.
a man named Morales	un hombre de nombre/llamado Morales
What's your name?	¿Cómo te llamas?/¿Cómo se llama usted?
My name is ...	Me llamo...
name *[of book]*	el título

narrow   *adj*

narrow	angosto(a) *[LA]*/estrecho(a)

native   *adj*

native country	el país natal/la patria
native language	la lengua materna/nativa
native born	de nacimiento
She's a native born Venezuelan.	Es venezolana de nacimiento.

native   *n*

She is a native of Lima.	Es natural de Lima./Nació en Lima./Es limeña.
I'm a native of Panama.	Soy natural de Panamá.
He speaks Spanish like a native.	Habla español como si fuera su primera lengua.
the natives (of a country)	los indígenas/los aborígenes

near   *adj & prep*

of places

I live near the park.	Vivo cerca del parque.
near here	aquí cerca

cerca de

of time

near the end of the month	hacia fines del mes
in the near future	en fecha próxima

140

other
a near relative — un pariente cercano

nearby *adv*
They live nearby. — Viven cerca/aquí cerca.

nearly *[see almost]*

neat *adj*
[room, garden, etc.] — bien cuidado(a)/arreglado(a)
[personal appearance] — pulcro(a)/esmerado(a)
neat handwriting — la escritura/letra clara

necessary *adj*
it's necessary — es necesario/preciso/hace falta
It's necessary to have a passport. — Es necesario tener un pasaporte./ Hace falta tener un pasaporte.
It's necessary for you to come alone. — Es necesario que vengas solo(a). *[Note: use of subjunctive]*
It wasn't necessary for him to do it. — No era necesario que lo hiciera.
They will do everything necessary. — Harán todo lo necesario.

need *v*
to need sth — necesitar
We need money. — Necesitamos dinero.

to demand, to require — requerir/exigir
This needs care. — Esto requiere/exige cuidado.

to need to do sth — haber de/necesitar
Do we need to be there? — ¿Hemos de asistir?/¿Necesitamos asistir?
The car needs repairing. — Hay que reparar el coche.

neighborhood *n*
[district] — el barrio
[area] — la vecindad
a neighborhood movie theater — un cine del barrio

neither (one) *adj & pron*
Neither of them has any money. — Ninguno de ellos tiene dinero.
Which of the shirts do you prefer? – Neither. — ¿Cuál de las camisas prefieres? – Ni la una ni la otra.

neither ... nor *conj*
neither ... nor — ni... ni
I neither drink nor smoke. — Ni bebo ni fumo.
She had neither the time nor the opportunity. — No tenía ni el tiempo ni la oportunidad.
Neither my brother nor my sister lives here. — Ni mi hermano ni mi hermana vive aquí.
You don't play tennis? – Neither do I./Me neither. — ¿No juegas al tenis? – Ni yo tampoco.

nerve *n*
[anatomical] — un nervio
It gets on my nerves. — Me pone los nervios en punta.
They get on my nerves. — Me fastidian terriblemente.

What nerve!   ¡Qué desvergüenza!
[courage]   el valor

nervous *adj*
apprehensive   miedoso(a)/nervioso(a)
to get nervous   ponerse nervioso(a)/sentir miedo
Don't be nervous!   ¡No sientas/tengas miedo!
It makes me nervous.   Me da miedo.

medical   nervioso(a)
a nervous breakdown   una depresión nerviosa

by nature   tímido(a)

never *adv*
never   nunca/jamás
He never eats meat.   Nunca come carne./No come nunca
carne. *[Note: If **nunca** or **jamás** follow the verb, **no** precedes it.]*

never mind
Never mind!   ¡No te molestes, olvídalo!/¡No importa, déjalo!

nevertheless *adv*
[however]   no obstante/sin embargo

new *adj*
brand-new   nuevo(a)
I have bought a new car.   He comprado un coche nuevo.
*[Note: here **nuevo** follows the noun.]*

newly acquired   nuevo(a)
What color is your new car?   ¿De qué color es tu nuevo coche?
*[Note: here **nuevo** precedes the noun.]*

other expressions
What's new?   ¿Qué hay de nuevo?
There's nothing new.   No hay nada nuevo.
It's as good as new.   Está como nuevo.

news *n*
the news   las noticias
a piece of news   una noticia
What news?   ¿Qué hay de nuevo?
a news bulletin *[radio]*   un noticiario
a newscast *[TV]*   un telediario/un noticiero
a newscaster   un(a) locutor(a) de telediario
a newspaper *[general]*   un periódico
a newspaper *[daily]*   un diario

next *adj*
of future time   próximo(a)/que viene/que entra
next week/month/year   la semana próxima/el mes próximo/el año próximo
la semana/el mes/el año que viene
next Thursday   el jueves que viene/el jueves que entra.
the next ten days   los diez días que vienen
next time   la próxima vez

of past time
the next day
On the next day they got up
early.

siguiente
el día siguiente
Al día siguiente se levantaron
temprano.

of place
He lives next door.
You must get off at the next stop.

próximo(a)/vecino(a)/de al lado
Vive en la casa vecina/de al lado.
Debes bajar en la próxima parada.

of order
He caught the next train.
Look at the next page.

próximo(a)
Tomó el próximo tren.
Mira la página siguiente.

next *adv*
[then, after that]
Next he heard a shot.
What did you do next?
Give it to him when you next
see him.
When I saw her next ...

luego/después/la próxima vez
Luego oyó un tiro.
¿Qué hiciste después?
Dáselo la próxima vez que lo
veas.
Cuando volví a verla...

next *prep*
next to
She lives next to the café.
He's sitting next to his brother.
next to nothing
We got it for next to nothing.

junto a/al lado de
Vive al lado del café.
Está sentado junto a su hermano.
casi nada
Lo adquirimos por casi nada.

nice *adj*
[likeable]
She is very nice.
[kind]
They are such nice people.
[attractive of people]
She looks very nice.
[attractive of things]

The house is very nice.
[of food]
The meals were very nice.

simpático(a)
Es muy simpática.
amable
Son personas tan amables.
guapo(a)
Es muy linda/guapa.
agradable/bonito(a)/chulo(a)
    [Mex]/regio *[LA]*/sabroso *[Ven]*
La casa es muy agradable/bonita.
rico(a)
Las comidas fueron muy ricas.

night *n*
the night
tonight
last night
the night before last
tomorrow night
in the night
at eleven o'clock at night
It's night.
at night
to work nights
to spend the night
to have a bad night
the night before
good night
to be a night owl

la noche
esta noche
anoche/ayer en la noche
anteanoche
mañana por la noche
por la noche/durante la noche
a las once de la noche
Es de noche.
de noche
trabajar de noche
pasar la noche
dormir mal/pasar una noche mala
la víspera
buenas noches
trasnochar

no *adj*

[not any] ninguno(a)/ningunos(as)
No honest man would do that. Ningún hombre honrado haría eso. *[Note: **Ninguno** shortens to **ningún** when it precedes a noun.]*

He has no money. No tiene ningún dinero. *[Note: **No** precedes the verb when **ninguno(a)** comes after.]*
No tiene dinero.

There are no tickets left. No quedan localidades. *[Note: The **ninguno** forms are frequently not used.]*

There's no problem. No hay problema.
[for emphasis] alguno(a)/algunos(as)
We have no money at all. No tenemos dinero alguno.
He made no reply. No hizo respuesta alguna.
in public notices prohibido(a)
no entry prohibida la entrada
no parking/smoking prohibido aparcar/fumar

nobody (no one) *pron*

nobody nadie
Nobody will help me. Nadie quiere ayudarme.
There was nobody in. No estaba nadie. *[Note: **No** precedes the verb when **nadie** comes after.]*

none *pron*

[not any, not one] ninguno(a)
Have you any bread? – There is none left. ¿Hay pan? – No queda ninguno.
Where are the grapes? – There are none left. ¿Dónde están las uvas? – No queda ninguna.
None of my friends is going to the party. Ninguno de mis amigos va a la fiesta.
None of the tourists came. No vino ninguno de los turistas.
none of them ninguno(a) de ellos/ellas
none of us ninguno(a) de nosotros/nosotras
none of you ninguno(a) de ustedes

nose *n*

[of person] una nariz
[of animal] un hocico
to have a good nose for tener buen olfato para

note *n*

[annotation] un apunte/una nota
to take notes sacar/tomar apuntes
[musical note/footnote] una nota
[letter] una nota/una carta
a banknote un billete
a hundred peso note un billete de cien pesos

note *v*

[to notice] notar/observar/advertir
[to note down] apuntar/anotar

nothing   *pron*
[not anything]   nada
I said nothing.   No dije nada.
Nothing interested me.   Nada me interesó./No me interesó
                                                    nada. *[Note: **No** precedes the verb when
                                                    nada comes after.]*
I have nothing to do.   No tengo nada que hacer.
nothing else   nada más
nothing much   poca cosa
nothing to write home about   nada extraordinario/nada del otro mundo

notice   *n*
[a sign]   un letrero
[a poster]   un cartel
[in a newspaper]   un anuncio
[information/warning]   un aviso
"Notice to the public"   Aviso al público
until further notice   hasta nuevo aviso
to give notice *[to quit work]*   dimitir
to give notice *[to employee]*   despedir a alguien
to dismiss sb without notice   despedir a alguien sin aviso
to give notice *[to a tenant]*   dar aviso a alguien
She gave him notice to leave.   Le dio el aviso de que se marchara.
at short notice   a corto plazo
without previous notice   sin previo aviso
a week's notice   una semana de anticipación
to take notice of someone   hacer caso a alguien
Don't take any notice of him!   ¡No le hagas caso!
to take notice of something   prestar atención a/hacer caso de algo
They took no notice of the   No prestaron atención a/no
  paintings.   hicieron caso de los cuadros.

Ø **noticia** means "an item of news;" **las noticias** means "the news."

notice   *v*
[to see/realize]   darse cuenta de
I noticed that it was raining.   Me di cuenta de que llovía.
[to take note of]   fijarse en/reparar en/notar/observar
Did you notice his shoes?   ¿Te fijaste en sus zapatos?
I didn't notice the color.   No reparé en el color.
Notice how it moves.   Observa cómo se mueve.
[to see sb/sth]   ver
She noticed you in the street.   Te vio en la calle.

now   *adv*
as expression of time
now   ahora/ya
What are you doing now?   ¿Qué haces ahora?
She's a university student now.   Ya es universitaria.
right now   ahora mismo/ahorita *[LA]*
Do it right now!   ¡Hazlo ahora mismo!
at present   actualmente/en este momento
He'll be in the office now.   En este momento estará en la oficina.
now and then/again   de vez en cuando
up to now   hasta ahora
I'm off now.   Ya me voy.

145

They're coming now.	Ya vienen.
without any sense of time	
Now!	¡A ver!
Now then!	¡Vamos a ver!

now *conj*

Now that you've arrived ...	Ahora que has llegado...

nowadays *adv*

nowadays	hoy día/hoy en día/actualmente

nowhere *adv*

[no place]	ninguna parte/por ningún lado
Where are you going? – Nowhere.	¿Adónde vas?— A ninguna parte.
They went nowhere.	No fueron a ninguna parte.
Nowhere in Spain will you see such a thing.	En ninguna parte de España verás tal cosa.
She's nowhere to be seen.	No se la encuentra por ningún lado.

nuisance *n*

of a situation or happening	una molestia/un fastidio/una incomodidad/una lata/una pesadez
What a nuisance!	¡Qué lata!/¡Qué fastidio!/¡Qué pesadez!/¡Qué macana! *[Arg]*
It's a nuisance having to get up early.	Es una molestia tener que levantarme temprano.
of a person	un(a) pesado(a)
What a nuisance you are!	¡Qué pesado(a) eres!
to make a nuisance of oneself	dar la lata

number *n*

in mathematics	un número
whole number	un número entero
even/odd number	un número par/impar
cardinal/ordinal number	un número cardinal/ordinal
digit, figure	una cifra/un número
Arabic/Roman numbers	cifras arábigas/romanas
It consists of ten numbers.	Consiste en diez cifras.
for house, telephone	un número
They live in number eight.	Viven en el número ocho.
What's your phone number?	¿Cuál es tu número de teléfono?
an amount or quantity	algunos(as)/varios(as)/un número de
a number of people	algunas/varias personas
a large number of people	buen número de personas

nuts *n*

[botanical]	frutos secos
Brazil nut	una nuez de Brasil
chestnut	una castaña
hazelnut	una avellana
peanut	un cacahuate *[Mex]*/un maní *[other LA countries]*/un cacahuete *[Sp]*
walnut	una nuez/una nuez de Castilla *[Mex]* *[Note: In Mexico* **nuez** *refers to "pecan nuts."]*

You're nuts.	Estás chalado(a)/chiflado(a). *[fam.]*
to be nuts about sb/sth	estar chalado(a)/chiflado(a) por alguien/algo
He's nuts about Teresa.	Está chalado/chiflado por Teresa.
She's nuts about music.	Está chalada/chiflada por la música.

O

object *n*
a thing   un objeto/una cosa/un artículo
a round/square object   un objeto redondo/cuadrado

aim   un objeto/un objetivo/un próposito/un intento

My object is to win.   Mi próposito es ganar.

grammar   un complemento
a direct/indirect object   un complemento directo/indirecto

object *v*
to object   hacer objeciones/oponerse/protestar
The students objected.   Los estudiantes hicieron objeciones.
I object!   ¡Yo protesto!
to object to sth   oponerse a/protestar contra
We objected to their decision.   Nos opusimos a su decisión./ Protestamos contra su decisión.

obvious *adj*
obvious   evidente/claro(a)
It's obvious.   Es evidente.
It's all very obvious.   Todo cae de su peso.

obviously *adv*
obviously   claro/evidentemente
He obviously can't do it.   Claro está que no sabe hacerlo.

occasion *n*
time   la ocasión/la vez
It was the last occasion I saw them.   Fue la última vez que los vi.
On that occasion I was late.   Esa vez/En aquella ocasión llegué tarde.
on occasion   de vez en cuando

function   un acontecimiento/una función
It will be a very important occasion.   Será un acontecimiento muy importante.

suitable occasion/opportunity   una ocasión/una oportunidad
Wait for the right occasion!   ¡Espera el momento propicio!

occasionally *adv*
occasionally   de vez en cuando/a veces

odd *adj*
strange   curioso(a)/extraño(a)/raro(a)
How odd!   ¡Qué raro!
He's an odd person.   Es una persona rara/extraña.
That's a very odd way to do it.   Es una manera muy rara de hacerlo.

of numbers   impar
an odd number   un número impar

other

I write the odd article.	Escribo algún que otro artículo.
These are odd gloves.	Éstos son guantes desparejados.
at odd moments	a ratos perdidos
odd jobs	pequeños arreglos/reparaciones
to do odd jobs around the house	hacer pequeños arreglos en toda la casa
odd jobs *[casual work]*	trabajitos

odds *n*

The odds are against it.	Es muy poco probable.
The odds are against/with you.	Tienes pocas/muchas probabilidades.

of *prep*

[in most senses] — de

a friend of mine	un amigo mío/una amiga mía
all of us	todos nosotros/todas nosotras
all of them	todos ellos/todas ellas
Some of us went to the movies.	Algunos fuimos al cine.
It's ten of six.	Son las seis menos diez.
a love of music	un amor a la música
a smell of garlic	un olor a ajo
a taste of honey	un sabor a miel
to smell of *[see smell]*	
to taste of *[see taste]*	
to think of *[see think]*	
It's very kind of you.	Eres muy amable./Es muy amable de tu parte.
of course	por supuesto/naturalmente
of no avail	inútil
It's of no avail.	Es inútil.

off *adj & adv*

power *[lights, etc.]* — apagado(a)

The lights were off.	Las luces estaban apagadas.
to turn off	apagar
Turn the gas off before you leave.	Apaga el gas antes de salir.

to be off

I'm off now.	Ya me voy.
We must be off.	Debemos marcharnos.
They're off to Brasil tomorrow.	Salen para el Brasil mañana.
Be off!	¡Fuera de aquí!
Off we go!	¡Vamos!

not to be present

to be off	estar ausente/no estar (en la oficina, etc.)
a day off	un día de descanso
to take a day off	tomarse un día de descanso

reduction, removal

twenty per cent off	un descuento del veinte por ciento
with my shoes off	sin zapatos
with her hat off	sin sombrero

to be cancelled

The match is off. *[cancelled]*	El partido está cancelado.
The match is off. *[postponed]*	El partido está aplazado.

off   *prep*

to fall off	caerse de
He fell off the roof.	Se cayó del tejado.
It fell off the desk.	Se cayó del pupitre.
She took it off the table.	Lo tomó de la mesa.
to get off *[vehicles]*	bajar (de)
They got off the train.	Bajaron del tren.
We got off at the main square.	Bajamos en la plaza mayor.
to jump off	saltar de
The cat jumped off the wall.	El gato saltó del muro.
Keep off the grass!	¡Prohibido pisar la hierba!
off the cuff	improvisado(a)
off the record	en confianza/entre nosotros(as)
off season	fuera de temporada
off color	de mal gusto
*[see also **take off**]*	

offense   *n*

to give offense	ofender
to take offense at	ofenderse por/resentirse de
[insult]	una ofensa
[crime]	un delito/un crimen
to commit an offense	cometer un delito

Ø **crimen** is a major felony, not a misdemeanor.

offer   *v*

to offer sth to sb	ofrecer algo a alguien
to offer to do sth	ofrecerse a hacer algo

office   *n*

[place of work]	una oficina
[private office]	un escritorio *[Arg & Uru]*/un despacho *[Sp]*
main office	la central
office worker	un/una oficinista
box/ticket office	la taquilla
information office	el centro de informaciones
post office	correos/la casa de correos/la oficina de correos/la central de correos *[Arg]*
tourist office	la oficina de turismo
an office block	un bloque de oficinas
[public office]	un cargo público
to hold office	ocupar un cargo

Ø **el oficio** means "office" in the sense of "trade" or "occupation."

official   *adj*

official	oficial

official   *n*

an official	un oficial/un funcionario

officially   *adv*

officially	oficialmente/de modo autorizado

often   *adv*

often	a menudo/frecuentemente/muchas veces

I often go to the beach. | Voy a menudo a la playa.
very often | muy a menudo/muchísimas veces
how often? | ¿cuántas veces?
How often did you visit her? | ¿Cuántas veces la visitaste?

oil   n

[in general] | el aceite
[geological] | el petróleo
crude oil | el petróleo bruto
vegetable oil | el aceite vegetal
oil painting | un cuadro al óleo
to check the oil [in a car] | revisar el nivel de aceite

okay (O.K.)   adj & excl
exclamation | ¡Está bien!/¡Bueno!/¡Vale!
O.K. I'm ready. | ¡Bueno! Estoy listo(a).
Shall we go? – Yes, O.K. | ¿Vamos? – Sí, vale.

as agreement | de acuerdo
Is it O.K. with you? | ¿Estás de acuerdo?
Is it O.K. with you if I go? | ¿Te importa/molesta que vaya?
It's O.K. with me. | Estoy de acuerdo.

not bad
What do you think of the hotel? – It's O.K. | ¿Qué te parece el hotel? – No está mal.

in response to an apology | no hay de qué
I'm very sorry to have troubled you. – It's O.K. | Siento mucho haberte molestado. – No hay de qué.

physical condition
Are you O.K.? | ¿Estás bien?
I feel O.K. now. | Me siento bien ahora.

old   adj
age [people] | viejo(a)/anciano(a)
an old man | un viejo/un anciano
an old woman | una vieja/una anciana
old John | el viejo Juan
older/oldest | más viejo(a)/mayor
his older/oldest daughter | su hija mayor
to get/grow old | envejecerse
How old are you? | ¿Cuántos años tienes?
I'm 15 years old. | Tengo quince años.
He's older than his wife. | Tiene más años que su esposa.
He's two years older than I. | Tiene dos años más que yo.
to get older [children] | hacerse mayor

age [things] | viejo(a)
an old house | una casa vieja
old clothes | ropa vieja/usada

old-established | viejo(a)/antiguo(a)
an old friend of mine | un(a) viejo(a) amigo(a) mío(a)

former | antiguo(a)
an old student | un antiguo estudiante
my old school | mi antiguo colegio
in the old days | antaño/en el pasado

old-fashioned   anticuado(a)/pasado(a) de moda
That skirt is old-fashioned.   Esta falda está pasada de moda.

Ø **anticuado(a)** is close to obsolete.

omelet   *n*
an omelet   una torta de huevos *[Mex]*/una tortilla *[Sp]*

Ø In Mexico and many other parts of Latin America **una tortilla** is a corn pancake.

on   *prep*
place   en/sobre/encima de
on the table   en/sobre la mesa
[on top of]   encima de
The box is on (top of) the cupboard.   La caja está encima del armario.
on the ceiling   sobre el techo
on the wall   en la pared
hanging on the wall   colgado(a) de la pared
[with sense of "in"]   en
on the street/square   en la calle/plaza
on the bus/plane/train   en el autobús/avión/tren
on the other side of the street   al otro lado de la calle
on the left/right   a la izquierda/derecha

means of transport
to get on   subir a
They got on the bus.   Subieron al autobús.
on horseback   a caballo
on foot   a pie

time
on time   a tiempo/a la hora
on Monday   el lunes *[Note: no preposition]*
I'm going to Lima on Monday.   Voy a Lima el lunes.
on Sundays   los domingos *[Note: no preposition]*
On Sundays they go to the beach.   Los domingos van a la playa.
on the next day   al día siguiente

concerning
on *[about/on the subject of]*   sobre/acerca de
a book on the history of Peru   un libro sobre la historia del Perú
What did he say on the subject   ¿Qué dijo acerca del accidente?
  of the accident?

with gerund
On seeing her, he crossed the   Al verla cruzó la calle. *[Note: The*
  street.   *infinitive is used in Spanish.]*

other
on the telephone   al teléfono
on sale   de/en venta
on business   de negocios
on vacation   de vacaciones
on the house   la casa invita
on the level   sincero(a)/en serio

verb + on
to be on *[apparatus, TV, radio]*   estar conectado(a)/puesto(a)/enchufado(a)
to be on *[light]*   estar encendido(a)
to be on *[at the movies]*   poner
"Casablanca" is on at the movies.   Ponen "Casablanca" en el cine.

to be on [at the theater]	representar
What's on at the theater?	¿Qué representan en el teatro?
to be on [a show]	estrenarse
The show is now on in New York.	Se ha estrenado el espectáculo en Nueva York.
to be on a diet	seguir un régimen
to be on duty	estar de servicio
to go on [continue]	seguir adelante
Go on as far as the park.	Sigue hasta el parque.
She went on reading.	Siguió leyendo.
to put on [clothes]	ponerse
to try on [clothes]	probarse
to spend money on	gastar dinero en
to spend time on	dedicar tiempo a
to switch/turn on [electrical apparatus, TV, radio, etc.]	encender/conectar/poner
to switch/turn on the engine	arrancar el motor
to switch/turn on the light	encender la luz
to live on	vivir con/de
I live on 500 dollars a month.	Vivo con quinientos dólares al mes.
They live on fruit.	Viven de fruta.
to congratulate sb on sth	dar la enhorabuena/felicitar a alguien por algo
to depend on	depender de

once   *adv*

once [on one occasion]	una vez
once or twice	algunas veces
once again	una vez más/otra vez
once a week	una vez por semana
at once	en seguida
at once [at the same time]	de una vez
They all spoke at once.	Todos hablaron de una vez.
all at once	de repente
He got up and left all at once.	De repente se levantó y se marchó.
once [formerly]	antes/antiguamente/en otro tiempo
The farm was prosperous once.	Antes la estancia era próspera.
Once upon a time there was...	Érase un vez.../Hubo una vez...
once in a blue moon	casi nunca/muy de tarde en tarde
once-over	un vistazo/una ojeada
He gave the hotel a once-over.	Dio/Echó un vistazo al hotel.

one   *pron*

One must insist.	Se debe insistir.
One never knows.	Nunca se sabe. [Note: **Nunca** precedes the pronoun.]
These cakes/oranges are good. – Do you want one?	Estos pastelitos/Estas naranjas son ricos(as). – ¿Quieres uno/una?
One of them will come.	Uno(a) de ellos(as) vendrá.
any one of us	cualquiera de nosotros(as)
Have you found the one you need?	¿Has encontrado el/la que necesitas?

*[See also **the one, that one, this one, which one.**]*

one another   *[see each other]*

one-way adj

a one-way ticket	un boleto de ida
[of direction]	de dirección única/de sentido único
This street is one-way.	Esta calle es de dirección única.

only adj & pron
only

	único/solo
his only son	su hijo único
They are the only two books I have left.	Son los dos únicos libros que me quedan. *[Note word order.]*
the only one(s)	el único/la única/los únicos/las únicas
I was not the only one to hear it.	No fui el único/la única en oírlo.

only adv

only	sólo/solamente/no... más que
Only my father can do it.	Sólo mi padre sabe hacerlo.
She only said that you would help me.	Dijo solamente que me ayudarías.
I only asked him for money.	No hice más que pedirle dinero.
They only have 500 pesos.	Tienen solamente quinientos pesos./No tienen más de quinientos pesos. *[Note: use of **de** when a number follows]*
You only have to ask.	No hay sino preguntar.
not only ... but also	no sólo... sino también *[Note: use of **sino**]*
Not only Juan but his wife.	No sólo Juan sino también su esposa.
If only he were here.	Ojalá estuviera aquí. *[Note: imperfect subjunctive is used after **ojalá**.]*

opening n

[a job]	una vacante
"Openings"	"Se ofrece trabajo"
"Opening for a carpenter"	"Búscase un carpintero"

operation n

[medical, military]	una operación
to carry out an operation on sb (for)	operar a alguien (de)
to have an operation (for)	ser operado(a) de/sufrir una operación (de)

opinion n

opinion	la opinión/el parecer
in my opinion	en mi opinión/a mi parecer/a mi ver
What's your opinion of ... ?	¿Qué piensas de... ?
to change one's opinion	cambiar de opinión

opportunity n

opportunity	la oportunidad/la ocasión
to have the opportunity to do sth	tener la oportunidad de hacer algo
to take the opportunity to do sth	aprovechar la ocasión para hacer algo
equal opportunities	la igualdad de oportunidades

opposite adj & n

[adjective]	opuesto(a)/de enfrente
He lives in the house opposite.	Vive en la casa de enfrente.
The museum is on the opposite bank of the river.	El museo está en la ribera opuesta del río.
the opposite page	la página opuesta/de enfrente

in the opposite direction	en sentido contrario/opuesto
[noun]	lo contrario
She always says the opposite.	Siempre dice lo contrario.

opposite *adv & prep*

I sat down opposite the boss.	Me senté enfrente del jefe.
They were sitting opposite the entrance.	Estaban sentados(as) enfrente de la entrada.
We were sitting opposite each other.	Estábamos sentados(as) uno(a) enfrente del otro/de la otra.
My office is opposite the town hall.	Mi oficina está enfrente del ayuntamiento.

or *conj*

or	o/u
What do you want, fruit or cheese?	¿Qué quieres, fruta o queso?
seven or eight	siete u ocho *[Note: **u** is used before a word starting with "o" or "ho".]*
He didn't eat or drink.	No comió ni bebió. *[Note: **ni** is used after a negative.]*

*[See also **either** and **neither**.]*

order *n*

in succession

in alphabetical/chronological/ numerical order	un orden por orden alfabético/cronológico/ numérico

peace

law and order	el orden público

command

on the orders of	una orden *[Note: feminine in this sense]*
to obey orders	por orden de cumplir las órdenes *[Note: accent in the plural]*
to be under the orders of	estar bajo el mando de

business/commercial

an order	un pedido/un encargo
to give/place an order	pedir algo/hacer un pedido de algo
made to order	hecho(a) por encargo especial/ hecho(a) a la orden
to the order of	a la orden de
banker's order	una orden bancaria

to be out of order

The elevators are out of order.	no funcionar Los ascensores no funcionan.

in order to

You will have to save a lot of money in order to buy a house in this neighborhood.	para *[+ infinitive]* Tendrás que ahorrar mucho dinero para comprar una casa en este barrio.

in order that/so that

I loaned him a thousand dollars in order for him/so that he could buy a computer.	para que *[+ subjunctive]* Le presté mil dólares para que pudiera comprar una computadora.

order *v*

to order sb to do sth	mandar/ordenar a alguien hacer algo

I ordered them to go home.	Les mandé volver a casa.
[to request]	pedir
She ordered a mixed salad.	Pidió una ensalada mixta.

other *adj & pron*
other

otro(a)/otros(as)
demás

He sold the other car.	Vendió el otro coche.
We prefer the other house.	Preferimos la otra casa.
I've read all the other books.	He leído todos los otros libros/ todos los demás libros.
She washed my other shirts.	Me lavó las otras camisas/las demás camisas.
I don't like this carpet. I want the other one.	No me gusta esta alfombra. Quiero la otra.
The others will be here soon.	Los otros/Los demás estarán aquí pronto.
one after the other	uno tras otro
Some are hungry, others are thirsty.	Unos tienen hambre, otros tienen sed.
Some man or other gave it to me.	Algún hombre me lo dio.

otherwise *conj*

[in other respects]	por otra parte/por lo demás
Otherwise the hotel was very good.	Por lo demás el hotel era muy bueno.
[if not]	si no
We must leave now, otherwise we'll miss the plane.	Tenemos que salir ahora, si no perderemos el avión.

ought *v*
ought to
You ought to go to see her.

deber
Deberías ir a verla. *[Note:conditional]*
Debieras ir a verla. *[Note: imperfect subjunctive as an alternative to the conditional]*

We ought to have bought it.

Deberíamos haberlo comprado./
Habríamos debido comprarlo. *[Note: alternative forms]*

*[see also **should**]*

our *adj*
our
our money/our house
our friends

nuestro(a)/nuestros(as)
nuestro dinero/nuestra casa
nuestros amigos/nuestras amigas

ours *pron*
[possessive]

el nuestro	la nuestra
los nuestros	las nuestras

Your garden is prettier than ours.	Tu jardín es más linda que la nuestra.
Those cases are ours.	Esas maletas son nuestras. *[Note: The definite article is omitted after the verb **ser**.]*
a friend of ours	un amigo nuestro/una amiga nuestra
some friends of ours	unos amigos nuestros/unas amigas nuestras

ourselves *[see self]*

out *adv*
to be out	estar fuera/no estar/haber salido
They're out.	Están fuera/No están/Han salido.
to come/go out	salir

out of *prep*
out of	fuera de
to be out of danger	estar fuera de peligro
to get out of bus/car/train	bajar del autobús/del coche/del tren
to go out of the house	salir de la casa
to go out of the door	salir por la puerta
She ran out of the room.	Salió corriendo de la habitación.
to jump out of the window	saltar por la ventana
to look out of the window	mirar por la ventana/asomarse a la ventana
to take sth out of a drawer	sacar algo de un cajón
He took the money out of his pocket.	Sacó el dinero de su bolsillo.
to be out of work	estar sin trabajo/estar parado(a)
seven out of ten	siete sobre diez
out of print	agotado(a)
out of the blue	inesperadamente/sin saber cómo

outdoor(s) *adj & adv*
outdoors	al aire libre/fuera de casa
to eat outdoors	comer al aire libre
an outdoor concert/restaurant	un concierto/restaurante al aire libre
Go and play outdoors!	¡Ve/¡Vayan a jugar fuera!

outside *prep*
outside (of)	fuera de/al exterior de
outside the store	fuera de la tienda
He's outside the door.	Está a la puerta.

outside *adv*
outside	fuera
to be outside	estar fuera/estar en la calle
to go outside	salir fuera/salir a la calle

over *adv*
[above]	encima/por encima
Does this go over or under?	¿Éste pasa por encima o por debajo?
[finished]	terminado/acabado
Is the game over?	¿Está terminado el partido?
As soon as the film is over ...	En cuanto termine la película...
The storm is over.	Ya pasó la tormenta.
It's all over (and done with)!	¡Ya se acabó!
She's over here/there.	Está acá/allá.
all over (the place)	por todas partes
to invite sb over	invitar a alguien a casa
Come over tonight.	Pasa a casa esta noche.
I ache all over.	Me duele todo el cuerpo/en todas partes.
to do sth over again	volver a hacer algo
Write it over again!	¡Vuelve a escribirlo!

over *prep*
place

over	encima de/por encima de
It's over your head.	Está por encima de tu cabeza.
He jumped/looked over the wall.	Saltó/Miró por encima de la tapia.
They live over the shop.	Viven por encima de la tienda.
[in contact with]	sobre
There was a sign over the door.	Había un letrero sobre la puerta.
[other]	
to cross over	atravesar/cruzar
I crossed over the street.	Atravesé/Crucé la calle.
to fall (trip) over sth	tropezar con algo
to fall over a cliff	caer por un precipicio
to fly over	sobrevolar
They will fly over the Andes.	Sobrevolarán los Andes.
all over Europe	por toda Europa
all over the world	en todo el mundo/en el mundo entero
over the counter	de venta libre/sin receta

number

past/over	más de
My mother is past eighty.	Mi madre tiene más de ochenta años.
the numbers over ten	los números superiores a diez

time

over the last few weeks	durante las últimas semanas
over the weekend	durante el fin de semana

overlook *v*

[of building]	dar a/tener vista a
The library overlooks the river.	La biblioteca da al río.
[to forget]	olvidar
I overlooked your keys.	Olvidé tus llaves.

own *adj & pron*
one's own

	propio(a)
I have my own house.	Tengo mi propia casa.
The money is all his own.	El dinero es el suyo propio.
This is all my own.	Esto es todo lo mío.

on one's own

	solo(a)
Are you on your own?	¿Estás solo(a)?
I live on my own.	Vivo solo(a).
Do it on your own!	¡Hazlo solo(a)!

own *v*
in general

	poseer/tener
He owns ten cars.	Posee/Tiene diez coches.
Do you own a computer?	¿Tienes computadora/ordenador *[Sp]*?
Who owns this dog?	¿A quién pertenece este perro?

real estate, company

	ser dueño de
He owns a large farm.	Es dueño de una estancia grande.
Who owns this publishing company?	¿Quién es dueño de esta casa editorial?

owner *n*

owner	el dueño/la dueña
	el propietario/la propietaria
His wife is the owner of the hotel.	Su esposa es propietaria del hotel.
Is the owner around?	¿Está el dueño/propietario?

P

pad *n & v*
[of paper]   un taco/un bloc
[of brake]   una zapata
to pad   acolchar

pain *n*
physical pain   el dolor/el sufrimiento
to be in pain   tener dolor/estar con dolor
to be out of pain   haber dejado de sufrir/no sufrir más
I have a pain in my arm.   Me duele el brazo.

mental pain   la pena/el dolor
It caused her great pain.   Le causó mucha pena.

nuisance
He's a pain in the neck.   Es un pesado.
It's a pain.   Es una lata.

other
to take pains to do sth   hacer grandes esfuerzos/darse mucho trabajo para hacer algo

[see also **ache**]

painful *adj*
[physically]   doloroso(a)/dolorido(a)
a painful blow/illness   un golpe doloroso
a painful illness   una enfermedad dolorosa
[difficult]   difícil/penoso(a)
a painful decision   una decisión difícil
It was very painful for me.   Me causó mucha pena.
[duty]   desagradable/nada grato(a)
It is my painful duty to tell you that ...   Tengo el deber desagradable de decirte que...

pair *n*
a pair of gloves/shoes/stockings   un par de guantes/zapatos/medias
a pair of pants   un pantalón/unos pantalones
a pair of scissors   unas tijeras
[two people, a couple]   una pareja
What a strange pair!   ¡Qué pareja tan extraña!

pancake *n*
pancake   un panqueque [LA]/una torta/una hojuela
corn/maize pancake [in Mexico]   un taco/una tortilla/una enchilada

pants *n*
pants   el pantalón/los pantalones

paper *n*
[material, general]   el papel
It's made of paper.   Es de papel.

a piece of paper	un papel/una hoja de papel
writing paper	el papel de escribir
waste paper	papeles usados
[document]	un papel/un documento
identity papers	los papeles/la documentación
exercise paper [school/college]	un ejercicio/un ensayo
examination paper	un examen/una prueba
to give a paper [academic]	leer una comunicación
written paper	un artículo
newspaper	un diario/un periódico

parents *n*

my parents	mis padres/mis papás [LA]
parent company	la casa central

Ø **los parientes** means "relatives" or "relations."

park *v trans*

to park	aparcar/estacionar(se)/parquear [LA]/atracar [Arg & Uru]/cuadrar [Per] el coche
I parked the car on the street.	Aparqué/Estacioné el coche en la calle.
Where did you park?	¿Dónde aparcaste/te estacionaste?
You can't park here.	No se puede aparcar/estacionar aquí.

parking *adj & n*

parking	el aparcamiento/estacionamiento
No parking!	¡Prohibido estacionarse/aparcar!
parking lot	un aparcamiento/un estacionamiento/ una playa de estacionamiento [LA]
parking meter	un parquímetro/un parcómetro/un contador de aparcamiento
parking place	un sitio para aparcar
to look for a parking place	buscar dónde aparcar
I couldn't find anywhere to park.	No encontré dónde aparcar.
parking ticket [fine]	una multa por estar mal aparcado

part *n*

[general]	una parte
the best/worst/funniest part is ...	lo mejor/lo peor/lo más gracioso es...
the greater part	la mayor parte
[role in theater, etc.]	un papel
to play a part	hacer/interpretar un papel
in these parts	por aquí
Are you from these parts?	¿Eres de aquí?
to take part in	tomar parte en/participar en/intervenir en
to be part of	formar parte de
spare parts [for car, etc.]	las piezas de recambio/repuesto

part *v*

[to separate]	separarse
They parted last year.	Se separaron el año pasado.
[to say good bye]	despedirse
They parted at the airport.	Se despidieron en el aeropuerto.

Ø **partir**, as well as meaning "to leave," means "to part" in the sense of "to split or break apart."

partner   n
[in marriage]   el esposo/la esposa
     el/la cónyuge
[companion]   un(a) compañero(a)
[business]   un(a) socio(a)
[in dancing, tennis, etc.]   una pareja
silent partner   un socio comanditario

party   n & v
a social event   una fiesta/una reunión [formal]
to give/have/throw a party   organizar una fiesta
to party   hacer la fiesta
a pot-luck party   una fiesta donde cada invitado(a)
     contribuye un plato

law
party [to a dispute/agreement]   una parte
a third party   una tercera persona
an interested party   un(a) interesado(a)

group   un grupo
a party of tourists   un grupo de turistas
We're a party of fifty.   Somos un grupo de cincuenta.

politics   un partido
a political party   un partido político
Democratic/Republican Party   el Partido Demócrata/Republicano
to be a member of the party   ser miembro del partido
to join the party   hacerse miembro del partido

pass   v
[general]   pasar
Pass me the sugar, please.   Pásame el azúcar por favor.
to pass an exam   aprobar en/ser aprobado(a) en un
     examen [Note: not **pasar**]
[to move past]   pasar/pasar por delante de
They are passing the White   Pasan por delante de la Casa
  House.   Blanca.
He passed her on the street.   Se cruzó con ella en la calle.
We passed each other on the way.   Nos cruzamos en el camino.
[to overtake]   pasar/adelantar a
We passed the truck at 100   Adelantamos al camión a cien
  miles an hour.   millas (a ciento sesenta kilómetros)
     por hora.
No passing!   ¡Prohibido adelantar!
[to spend time]   pasar
I spent two weeks in Quito.   Pasé quince días/dos semanas en Quito.

patron   n
[customer]   un cliente/un parroquiano
[supporter of a cause/business]   un patrocinador
[of the arts]   un mecenas
patron saint   un santo patrón/una santa patrona

Ø **un patrón/una patrona** also means "boss".

pay   n
[general]   la paga/la remuneración/la retribución

pay

[salary of professional person]	el sueldo
[wages of working person]	el salario/el sueldo
equal pay	la igualdad de retribución
pay rise	un aumento de sueldo

pay *v*

to pay	pagar
I have to pay the rent.	Tengo que pagar el alquiler.
to pay sb	pagar a alguien
You must pay the landlord.	Tienes que pagar al propietario.
to pay for sth	pagar algo *[Note: no preposition]*
They paid for the tickets.	Pagaron las entradas.
to pay back *[money]*	devolver
to pay by check	pagar con cheque
to pay by installments	pagar a plazos
to pay in advance	pagar por adelantado
to pay in cash	pagar al contado
to pay attention to	prestar atención a

peaceful *adj*

[quiet]	tranquilo(a)
[not warlike]	pacífico(a)

peas *n*

peas	los guisantes/las arvejas *[LA]*/los chícharos *[LA]*
green peas	los guisantes
chickpeas	los garbanzos/los chícharos *[LA]*
split peas	los guisantes secos

people *n*

general

	la gente
many people	mucha gente
There are many people who want to see that film.	Hay mucha gente que quiere ver esa película.
What will people say?	¿Qué dirá la gente?
There are few people around.	Hay poca gente por aquí.

countable number

	las personas
How many people are coming to the party?	¿Cuántas personas vienen a la fiesta?
There were thousands of people in the square.	Había miles de personas en la plaza.
I know several people who speak Portuguese.	Conozco a varias personas que hablan portugués.

politics

	el pueblo
the people of the United States	el pueblo de los Estados Unidos
government by the people	el gobierno del pueblo

race

	el pueblo/la nación
the Mexican people	el pueblo mexicano/la nación mexicana
the peoples of Europe	las gentes de Europa

inhabitants

	los habitantes
the people of Córdoba	los habitantes de Córdoba
All the people of the village agreed.	Todos los habitantes de la aldea se pusieron de acuerdo.

pepper n
[the spice/condiment]   la pimienta
black pepper   la pimienta negra
[the vegetable/green pepper]   el pimiento/el chile
red pepper   el pimiento rojo
sweet pepper   el pimiento morrón
red pepper/paprika   el pimentón

performance n
carrying out of duties   el ejercicio
in the performance of my duties   en el ejercicio de mi cargo

session at the movies   la sesión
continuous performance   una sesión continua
the late performance   la sesión de la noche
What time is the first performance?   ¿A qué hora es la primera sesión?

session at the theater   la función
the late performance   la función de la noche
first performance   el estreno [Note: **estreno** refers to the first ever performance of a particular play or film at a specific theater, not to the first performance of the day.]

by actor, dancer, singer   la actuación/el desempeño/la interpretación
Her performance as Carmen was magnificent.   Su interpretación del papel de Carmen fue magnífica.

by musicians   la ejecución/la interpretación
a good performance of the concerto   una buena interpretación del concierto

in sport   la actuación
The team gave a poor performance in Guadalajara.   El equipo tuvo una mala actuación en Guadalajara.

of machines   el comportamiento/el funcionamiento
[of car engine]   el rendimiento
[of car in a race]   la performance

perhaps adv
[maybe]   quizá(s)/tal vez/puede ser (que)
Perhaps he'll come tomorrow.   Quizás/Tal vez venga mañana.
Perhaps they are away.   Puede ser que estén ausentes.
Perhaps Juan did it.   Quizás lo hizo Juan. [Note: the subjunctive is used when the speaker is expressing a strong sense of doubt.]

person n
a person   una persona [Note: always feminine]
The mayor is a strange person.   El alcalde es una persona extraña.

pet n
a pet   un animal (doméstico)/un animalito de compañía/una mascota
a pet dog   un perro de casa
No pets!   ¡Animales prohibidos!
teacher's pet   el/la favorito(a) del maestro/de la maestra

phone v
to phone

to phone sb/sth
I phoned you last night.
I must phone the airport.

telefonear/llamar por teléfono/ llamar
al teléfono
telefonear a alguien/algo
Te telefoneé/llamé anoche.
Debo telefonear al aeropuerto.

phone call n
a phone call

un llamado telefónico *[LA]*/una
llamada telefónica *[Sp]*/un golpe de
teléfono *[Arg]*

photograph n & v
a photograph/a photo
to photograph/take a photograph

una fotografía/una foto
fotografiar/sacar una foto

photographer n
photographer

un(a) fotógrafo(a)

phrase n
[a saying]
[a set phrase]
[in music]
[in grammar]

un dicho/una locución/un refrán
una frase hecha
una frase
una frase

Ø **frase** can also mean "a sentence."

physical *[see checkup]*

physician n
[medical doctor]
I'm a physician.

un(a) médico(a)
Soy médico(a).

Ø **un físico** is "a physicist."

physics n
[field of study]

la física *[Note: singular]*

pick v
to choose/select
Which car did you choose?
Who is picking the team?

escoger/seleccionar
¿Qué coche escogiste?
¿Quién selecciona el equipo?

to gather
I'm going to pick some roses.
We went to pick some pears.

recoger
Voy a recoger unas rosas.
Fuimos a recoger unas peras.

pick up v
to pick up sth from the floor
[to collect]
I went to pick up my books at
the bookstore.
Go and pick up your mother at
the station!
[to learn]
She picked up a few words of
Arabic.

recoger algo del suelo
recoger
Fui a recoger mis libros en la
librería.
¡Ve a buscar a tu madre en la
estación!
aprender
Aprendió unas palabras de árabe.

[to acquire] — adquirir/comprar
We picked it up cheap. — Lo adquirimos/compramos por muy poco dinero.

[to arrest] — detener
He was picked up at the frontier. — Fue detenido en la frontera.

picture *n*
[a painting] — un cuadro/una pintura
[a drawing] — un dibujo
[a portrait] — un retrato
[a book/magazine illustration] — una ilustración
[a film] — una película
[a photograph] — una fotografía/una foto
to take pictures — sacar fotos
[on TV] — la imagen

piece *n*
[general] — un pedazo/un trozo
a piece of bread — un pedazo/trozo de pan
a piece of cake — una porción de tarta
a piece of chocolate — una porción de chocolate
a piece of paper — una hoja de papel
a piece of advice — un consejo
a piece of furniture — un mueble
a piece of information — una información
a piece of land *[for building on]* — un terreno/un solar
a piece of news — una noticia
[an extract from a book, etc.] — un trozo
a piece of luck — un poco de suerte
a piece of music — una pieza de música
a chess piece — una pieza de ajedrez
a piece of fabric/material — una pieza de tejido
a piece of crockery — una pieza
[a piece for the theater] — una pieza

pill *n*
a pill — una píldora/una pastilla

Ø **un pillo** means "a rogue;" **una pila** means "a battery."

pitch *n*
[music] — el tono
[degree] — un grado/un nivel
[slope] — una pendiente
[throw] — un lanzamiento

Ø **un pendiente** means "an earring."

pitch *v*
[to throw] — tirar/arrojar
[to set] — fijar
to pitch a tent — armar una tienda

place *n*
general — un lugar/un sitio
This is a very peaceful place. — Éste es un lugar muy tranquilo.
It was a good place to camp. — Fue un buen sitio para acampar.

plain

Any place will do.	Cualquier sitio será conveniente.
I don't see it any place.	No lo/la veo en ninguna parte.
specific place	un sitio/un local
This is the place for the new factory.	Éste es el local/sitio para la nueva fábrica.
place of business	la oficina [office]/el comercio [shop]/la fábrica [factory]
place of residence	el domicilio/la residencia
We went to their place in the country.	Fuimos a su casa en el campo.
in order	
in first/second/third place	en primer/segundo/tercer lugar
everything in its place	todo en su lugar
seat	un asiento/una plaza
The theater has only 200 places.	El teatro tiene sólo doscientos asientos.
There are no places left.	Ya no quedan plazas.
other	
to take place	tener lugar/verificarse
in place of	en lugar de/en vez de

plain *adj*
clear, obvious	claro/evidente
It was plain that ...	Era evidente que.../Estaba claro que...
of food	sencillo
I like plain cooking.	Me gusta la cocina sencilla.
simple	sencillo/llano/sin adornos
a plain dress	un vestido sencillo

plan *n*
architectural plan	un plano
He made a plan of the palace.	Trazó un plano del palacio.
schedule	un programa
today's plan	el programa de hoy
economic, political	un plan
to draw up a plan	hacer un plan
a development plan	un plan de desarrollo
personal plan	un proyecto
to make plans	hacer proyectos
I have no plans for the vacation.	No tengo proyectos para las vacaciones.
to change one's plan	cambiar de proyecto

plan *v*
to make plans	planear/idear
My wife planned the trip.	Mi esposa ideó el viaje.
What have you planned for the weekend?	¿Qué has planeado para el fin de semana?
to intend	tener intención de/pensar
I don't plan to pay for it.	No tengo intención de pagarlo.
How long do you plan to stay?	¿Cuánto tiempo piensas quedarte?

plant   n
[botanical]   una planta
[factory]   una fábrica
[equipment, machinery]   el equipo/la maquinaria/la instalación

plate   n
[for eating off]   un plato
gold/silver plate   la vajilla de oro/plata

Ø **plato** also means "a dish" on a menu; **la plata** means "silver;" **un platillo** means "a saucer."

play   v
games, sports   jugar a
Do you play golf?   ¿Juegas al golf?
We spent the evening playing chess.   Pasamos la tarde jugando al ajedrez.
[to play with sb]   jugar con
I played tennis with her.   Jugué con ella al tenis.

musical instruments   tocar a
He plays the guitar very well.   Toca muy bien a la guitarra.

a piece of music   tocar
They played my favorite piece.   Tocaron mi pieza favorita.

at a theater
What's playing at the theater   ¿Qué ponen en el teatro esta
   tonight?   noche?

please   adv
The check, please.   La cuenta, por favor.
Please tell him I've arrived.   Haga el favor de decirle que he llegado.
Pass the sugar please.   ¿Me hace el favor de pasar el azúcar?

plug   n
[electric]   un enchufe/una chavija [Mex]
[bath, wash basin, etc.]   un tapón

plus   adv, n & prep
two plus two equals four   dos más dos son cuatro
I've got 30 plus.   Tengo treinta y pico.
He cost me 50 dollars plus.   Me costó cincuenta dólares y algo más.
[besides/in addition]   además
Plus, he can't drive.   Además, no sabe manejar/conducir.
[an advantage]   una ventaja
Being able to cook well is a plus.   Saber cocinar bien es una ventaja.

P.M.
It will begin at five p.m.   Empezará a las cinco de la tarde.
The train arrived at ten p.m.   Llegó el tren a las diez de la noche.
It's four p.m.   Son las cuatro de la tarde.
It's 11.30 p.m.   Son las once y media de la noche.

point   n
general   un punto
decimal point/dot   un punto decimal/una coma

167

point

She scored 9.6 points.	Ganó 9,6 (nueve coma seis) puntos. *[Note the Spanish punctuation and means of expression.]*

in sport and games
	un punto
to win on points	ganar por puntos
They won by 50 points to ten.	Ganaron por cincuenta puntos a diez.

sharp end
	una punta
the point of a knife	la punta de un cuchillo
the point of a pen	la puntilla de una pluma
five-point star	una estrella de cinco puntas

purpose
What's the point of asking?	¿De qué sirve preguntar?
There's no point in doing it.	No vale la pena hacerlo.

place and time
point of departure	el punto de partida
point *[of the compass]*	una cuarta
at this/that point in time	en este/aquel momento
to be on the point of doing sth	estar para hacer algo

point of argument/discussion
	un punto
point at issue	el punto en cuestión
point of view	un punto de vista
from my point of view	desde mi punto de vista
to make a point	hacer una observación/establecer un punto
to be beside/off the point	no venir al caso
That's not the point.	Eso no es el caso.

characteristics
He has some good points.	Tiene algunas cualidades buenas.

matter of importance or significance
The important point is ...	Lo importante es...
This is the essential point.	Esto es lo esencial.

point *v*
to point out sth to sb	indicar/señalar algo a alguien
The guide pointed out the ruins to us.	El guía nos indicó las ruinas.
She pointed out my mistakes.	Me señaló mis errores.
I should like to point out that ...	Permíteme observar que...
to point at	señalar con el dedo
He pointed at the sign.	Señaló el letrero con el dedo.
I didn't point at you.	No te señalé con el dedo.
[to point at with a gun]	apuntar
He pointed the rifle at us.	Nos apuntó con el fusil.

poisonous *adj*
[of snakes, insects, etc.]	venenoso(a)
[drugs, fumes, substances, etc.]	tóxico(a)

police *n*
the police force	la policía
police headquarters	la jefatura de policía
police station	la comisaría/la estación de policía *[LA]*
police officer	un(a) policía/un(a) guardia/un(a) agente

police record
The police have arrested two
  men.

los antecedentes penales
La policía ha detenido a dos
  hombres. [Note: singular verb]

policy n
[political]
economic policy
foreign policy
government policy
[approach, system]
This is our policy.
insurance policy

la política
la política económica
la política exterior
la política del gobierno
el sistema
Esto es nuestro sistema.
una póliza de seguros

politics n
politics
to talk politics
to go into politics

la política [Note: singular]
hablar de política
dedicarse a la política

poor adj
[impoverished]
a poor man
a poor woman

pobre
un pobre
una mujer pobre [Note: **pobre** follows
  noun]

the poor/poor people
[unfortunate]
Poor man/woman!
Poor María!
Poor you/him/her/old thing!
Poor Teresa is ill.

los pobres
pobre
¡Pobre hombre/mujer!
¡Pobre María! [Note: **pobre** precedes noun]
¡Pobrecito(a)!
La pobre Teresa está enferma.
  [Note: use of definite article]

[bad]
I have a poor memory.
to be in poor health

malo(a)/de baja calidad
Tengo una mala memoria.
estar mal

positive adj
[opposite of negative]
a positive result
[certain, sure]
I'm positive about it.

positivo(a)
un resultado positivo
seguro(a)
Estoy seguro(a) de ello.

possibility n
possibility
[outcome]
to foresee the possibilities

una posibilidad
un resultado posible
prever los resultados posibles

possible adj
to be possible
Is it possible to talk with
  the manager?
Is it possible for your
  brother to come?
It's not possible for me to do it.
as soon as possible

ser posible
¿Es posible hablar con el
  gerente?
¿Es posible que venga tu hermano?
  [Note: subjunctive]
No me es posible hacerlo.
lo más pronto posible

possibly adv
possibly

posiblemente

I'll do it if I possibly can.
They did all they possibly could.
We'll do all we possibly can.

Lo haré si me es posible.
Hicieron todo lo que pudieron.
Haremos todo lo que podamos.
  [Note: subjunctive]

[perhaps]
Will they win? – Possibly.

quizá(s)/tal vez
¿Ganarán? – Quizás.

postpone v
[to put off]
The game has been postponed
  until Sunday.

aplazar
Se ha aplazado el partido hasta
  el domingo.

potato n
potato
potato chips

la papa [LA]/la patata [Sp]
las papas/las patatas fritas/las papas
  colochas [ES]/las papalinas [Gua]

[French fries]

las papas/patatas francesas

Ø In Latin America **una batata** means "sweet potato." Remember **el papá** means
"Dad" and **El Papa** is "the Pope."

power n
general

el poder

ability
Birds have the power of flight.
I have the power to do it.
mental powers

el poder/la facultad
Los pájaros tienen la facultad de volar.
Tengo el poder de hacerlo.
las facultades mentales

physical strength
He doesn't have the power to
  lift it.

la fuerza/la energía/el vigor
No tiene la fuerza para
  levantarlo.

nations
The USA is a world power.

la potencia
Los Estados Unidos son una potencia
  mundial.

the nuclear powers

las potencias nucleares

authority
political power
to be in power

el poder/el poderío
el poder político
estar en el poder

energy
electrical power
power cut/failure
They've cut off the power.
nuclear power
power station
nuclear power station

la fuerza/la energía/el fluido
la fuerza/energía eléctrica
un corte de corriente
Han cortado el fluido.
la energía nuclear
una central eléctrica
una central nuclear

mechanical force

la potencia/la energía/la fuerza/ el
  rendimiento

effective power
attractive/motive power
The engine is operating at
  half power.

la potencia real
la fuerza atractiva/motriz
El motor funciona a medio
  rendimiento.

cars
power brakes
power steering

los frenos asistidos
la dirección asistida

powerful *adj*
[people, organizations, etc]   poderoso(a)
a powerful president/government   un presidente/gobierno poderoso
[engines, etc.]   potente

practice *v*
to practice a profession   ejercer una profesión
to practice medicine   ejercer de médico/ejercer la
     medicina/practicar la medicina
to practice a musical instrument   hacer ejercicios en/estudiar un instrumento
to practice a sport   entrenarse en un deporte
to practice a religion   practicar una religión
to be a practicing Christian   ser un cristiano practicante
to practice one's Spanish   practicar el castellano

Ø **practicar** used with the name of a sport usually means "to take part in" or "to play;" **Practico el fútbol.** "I play soccer."

prejudice *n*/**prejudiced** *adj*
[bias in favor]   la parcialidad
[biased view]   el prejuicio
[bias against]   la mala voluntad/la prevención
racial prejudice   el prejuicio racial
to be prejudiced   tener prejuicios
She's very prejudiced.   Tiene muchos prejuicios.
to be prejudiced against sth   estar predispuesto(a) contra algo
to be prejudiced in favor of sth   estar predispuesto(a) a favor de algo

prescription *n*
prescription   una receta

Ø **receta** does not mean "receipt," for which the word is **el recibo**.

presently *adv*
[now/at the present moment]   ahora/actualmente
[soon]   dentro de poco

preservative *n*
[in food]   un producto de conservación/para
     la conservación

Ø **un preservativo** means "a condom."

pressure *n & v*
[physical, technical, meteorological]   la presión
tire pressure   la presión de los neumáticos
[influence]   la influencia/la persuasión
to be under pressure from sb   ser presionado(a) por alguien
to put pressure on sb to do sth   hacer presión sobre alguien (que haga algo)
to work under pressure   trabajar con urgencia
pressure group   el grupo de presión
[stress]   la tensión nerviosa
blood pressure   la tensión arterial
high/low blood pressure   la tensión alta/baja

pretend *v*
to pretend   fingir
to pretend to be ill   fingir estar enfermo(a)

pretty

to pretend to be asleep	fingir(se) dormido(a)
to pretend to be a reporter	darse de periodista/decirse periodista/ hacerse el/la periodista
[to claim]	pretender
I do not pretend to know.	No pretendo saber.

Ø **pretender** also means "to claim the throne," or "to have pretensions."

pretty adj

pretty	lindo(a) *[LA]*/mono(a) *[Sp]*/ bonito(a)/guapo(a)/chulo(a) *[Mex]*

Ø **mono** means "vain" in Venezuela.

prevent v

to prevent	evitar/prevenir/impedir
to prevent an accident/illness	evitar/prevenir un accidente/una enfermedad
to prevent sb from doing sth	impedir a alguien hacer algo

Ø **prevenir** also means "to warn," "to foresee."

primary adj

[first]	primario(a)
primary school	la escuela primaria
primary color	el color primario
[fundamental]	principal
the primary reason	la razón principal
of primary importance	sumamente importante

privacy n

privacy	la soledad/la intimidad
in search of privacy	en busca de soledad
desire for privacy	el deseo de estar a solas
in the privacy of one's home	en la intimidad de su casa
There is no privacy here.	Aquí no se puede estar en privado.
in the strictest privacy	en el mayor secreto

private adj

not public	privado(a)
private enterprise	la empresa privada
private life	la vida privada
personal	particular/personal
a private arrangement	un acuerdo particular
a private car	un coche particular
Private!	¡Propiedad particular!
private secretary	un(a) secretario(a) particular
my private opinion	mi opinión personal
a private citizen	un(a) particular

Ø **especial** is used to mean "particular," e.g., **una razón especial** "a particular reason."

confidential	secreto(a)/confidencial/privado(a)
a private report	un informe secreto/confidencial
private and confidential	privado y confidencial

in private	
in private	en privado/en secreto
[confidentially]	confidencialmente
The meeting was held in private.	La reunión se celebró a puerta cerrada.

The ceremony will be held in
private.

La ceremonia se celebrará en la
intimidad.

Ø **privado** in Latin America also means "mad" or "senseless."
Ø **privativo** means "exclusive."

probably adv
probably
Is she ill? – Probably.
They've probably forgotten.

probablemente
¿Está enferma? – Probablemente.
A lo mejor lo habrán olvidado.

problem n
problem
No problem!
the housing problem
a problem child

un problema [Note: masculine]
¡No hay problema!
el problema de la vivienda
un niño difícil

process n
[proceeding]
the process of the mind
the manufacturing process
data processing
in course of construction
in course of demolition
[method]

el procedimiento/el proceso
el proceso de la mente
el procedimiento de fabricación
el proceso de datos
bajo/en construcción
está siendo derribado(a)
el procedimiento/el proceso/el método/el
   sistema
el proceso técnico
el proceso

the technical process
[law]

program n
[computer, list of events]
[radio/TV show]

un programa [Note: masculine]
una emisión

progress n
[general]
to make progress
to make slow progress
[events]
to be in progress
The work is in full progress.

el progreso/los progresos
hacer progresos
avanzar despacio
la marcha/el desarrollo
estar en marcha
El trabajo está en plena marcha.

prohibit v
to prohibit
to prohibit sb from doing sth
It is forbidden to feed the
   animals.
Smoking prohibited!

prohibir
prohibir a alguien hacer algo
Se prohíbe dar de comer a los
   animales.
¡Prohibido fumar!/¡Se prohíbe fumar!

proper adj
right, suitable
at the proper time
proper shoes for the occasion
the proper word
in proper condition

en el momento oportuno
zapatos apropiados para la ocasión
la palabra exacta
en buen estado

seemly
proper behavior

la conducta correcta

public

That's not proper.
to do what is proper
[see also right]

Eso no está bien.
hacer lo que se debe

public *adj*
[general]
public holiday

público(a)
un día de fiesta/un día festivo/una fiesta legal
public school
public spirit

un instituto
el civismo

Ø **el público** not only means "the public," but also "the audience."

publish *v*
to publish
published by
My first book has just been published.
When is the magazine published?

publicar/editar
editado por
Mi primer libro acaba de salir.
¿Cuándo sale la revista?

publisher *n*
[company]
[person]
newspaper publisher

una casa editorial
un editor
el propietario de un periódico

purple *adj*
purple

púrpura *[inv]*/purpúreo(a)/morado(a) *[Sp]*

purpose *n*
[intention]
My purpose in doing this ...
on purpose
[sense of purpose]

el propósito/la intención/el objeto
Mi propósito al hacer esto...
a propósito
la resolución

purse *n*
a purse

un bolso *[LA]*/una bolsa *[Sp]*

put *v*
[to place]
to put away
to put back
to put down (on ground)
to put in
to put off *[postpone]*
to put on *[clothes]*
to put on *[shoes]*
to put on *[light, appliances]*
to put on *[play]*
to put on weight
to put out *[light, fire]*
to put through *[phone]*
to put sb up
Can you put me up for the night?
to put up with sb or sth
I can't put up with her any more.
I can't put up with (it) any more.

poner/colocar/meter
devolver a su lugar
devolver a su lugar
poner en tierra/en el suelo
meter/introducir
aplazar
ponerse
ponerse/calzarse
encender/poner
representar/poner en escena
engordar/echar carnes
apagar
poner con
hospedar/alojar a alguien
¿Me puedes dar una habitación para esta noche?
aguantar
No la aguanto más.
No aguanto más.

174

Q

qualification *n*
[of a person]
He doesn't have the
    qualifications for the job.
[paper qualifications]
What are your qualifications?
[for membership]
Do you have the qualifications
    for membership?

la capacidad/la aptitud
No tiene las aptitudes para el
    puesto.
los títulos
¿Qué títulos tienes?
el requisito
¿Tienes los requisitos para ser
    miembro?

qualified *adj*
Are you qualified for that job?
a qualified engineer
in a qualified sense
to be qualified to vote

¿Tienes los requisitos para ese puesto?
un ingeniero titulado
en un sentido limitado
estar capacitado(a) para votar

qualify *v*
to qualify [academically]
He qualified as a lawyer.
to qualify for the finals

obtener el título de...
Obtuvo el título de abogado.
satisfacer los requisitos/clasificarse
    para los exámenes finales

quality *n & adj*
[nature, kind]
of good quality
a quality jacket
[characteristic, e.g. moral]
They have some good qualities.

la calidad
de buena calidad
una chaqueta de calidad
la cualidad
Tienen unas buenas cualidades.

quantity *n*
quantity

la cantidad

quarter *n*
[fraction]
a quarter of a kilo of flour
the first quarter of the moon
a quarter [coin]
a quarter of an hour
a quarter after/past four
a quarter of/to four
[division of academic year]
[of town]
the old quarter

un cuarto/una cuarta parte
un cuarto de kilo de harina
el primer cuarto de la luna
una moneda de 25 centavos
un cuarto de hora
las cuatro y cuarto
las cuatro menos cuarto
el trimestre
el barrio
el barrio viejo

question *n*
to ask sb a question
I asked him many questions.
[matter, subject]
the Cuban question
The question is, ...

hacer una pregunta a alguien
Le hice muchas preguntas.
el asunto/la cuestión/el problema
el problema cubano
El caso es, ...

175

question

It's a question of knowing whom to ask.
Se trata de saber a quién preguntar.

It's not a question of money.
No se trata de dinero/No es cuestión de dinero.

That's not the question.
No se trata de eso.

It's out of the question.
Es imposible.

without question
sin duda/indudablemente

question v

to question sb
hacer preguntas a alguien

The police questioned me.
Los guardias me interrogaron.

[to doubt]
cuestionar/dudar de

Do you question his motives?
¿Dudas de sus motivos?

questionable adj

questionable
cuestionable/dudoso(a)/discutible

It's questionable whether they are right.
Es dudoso si tengan razón. *[Note: use of subjunctive]*

quick adj

[fast]
rápido(a)/veloz/ligero(a)

a quick reflex
un reflejo rápido

be quick!
¡date prisa!

to be quick about sth
hacer algo rápidamente

a quick temper
un genio vivo

[clever]
agudo(a)/ágil/listo(a) *[Note: **Listo** is used with **ser** when it means "clever," and with **estar** when it means "ready."]*

[early]
pronto(a)

a quick reply
una pronta contestación

quickly adv

[fast]
de prisa/rápidamente

[soon]
pronto

as quickly as possible
lo más pronto posible

quiet adj

[silent]
silencioso(a)/callado(a)

[of a person by nature]
callado(a)/reservado(a)

a quiet place
un lugar tranquilo

to keep quiet
callarse

Be quiet!
¡Cállate!/¡Silencio!

quit v

to resign from

I've quit my job.
He abandonado mi puesto./He dimitido.

to stop
dejar de hacer algo

Why don't you quit doing that?
¿Por qué no dejas de hacer eso?

Quit saying that!
¡Deja de decir eso/hablar así!

I quit!
¡Me rajo!

¡Quit fooling!
¡Déjate de tonterías!

quite adv

completely
totalmente/completamente

This is completely new.	Esto es completamente nuevo.
We quite understand.	Lo comprendemos perfectamente.
She is quite right.	Está en lo cierto.
Quite so!	¡Así es!/¡Efectivamente!
He's quite a hero.	Es realmente un héroe/todo un héroe.

rather	bastante
He is quite rich.	Es bastante rico.
quite a few	bastantes
There were quite a few books.	Había bastantes libros.
quite a while	un buen rato/bastante tiempo

quiz *n*

[in school]	una prueba/un examen
a quiz show	un concurso de televisión/un concurso radiofónico
to quiz sb about sth	interrogar a alguien sobre algo
They quizzed him about the theft.	Le interrogaron sobre el robo.

quotation *n*

[passage or sentence cited]	la cita/la citación
[financial]	la cotización
today's quotation	la cotización del día
[business estimate]	un presupuesto
They gave us a quotation.	Nos dieron un presupuesto.
quotation marks	las comillas
in quotation marks	entre comillas
to open/close quotation marks	abrir/cerrar las comillas

quote *v*

to cite exactly	citar
to quote (from) Lorca	citar a Lorca
You can quote me.	Puede Ud. mencionar mi nombre.
Don't quote me!	¡No me menciones!
You must quote the number of the invoice.	Debes expresar el número de la factura.

to name a price	estimar un precio
They quoted a very high price.	El precio que estimaron fue muy alto.
This is the best price I can quote you.	Éste es mi mejor precio.

financially	
The dollar is quoted at X pesos.	La cotización del dólar está a X pesos.
It is not quoted on the stock exchange.	No se cotiza en la Bolsa.
What is today's price?	¿A cuánto está la cotización del día?

R

race *n*

[sporting]	una carrera
horse race	una carrera de caballos
long-distance race	una carrera de fondo
relay race	una carrera de relevos
to run a race	tomar parte en una carrera
human race	la raza humana/el género humano

radio *n*

radio [waves]	la radio
radio [set]	el radio [most of LA]/la radio [Sp]

Ø **el radio** also means "radius" in geometry.

raise *n & v*

to raise one's hands	levantar las manos
to raise the flag	alzar la bandera
to raise prices	aumentar los precios/el sueldo
to raise sb's salary	aumentar el sueldo a alguien
to raise funds	reunir fondos
raise in salary	un aumento de sueldo

rank *n & v*

[line]	una fila
[military position]	una graduación
[status]	la posición/la categoría
ranking	una clasificación
to rank	figurar/estar
to outrank	ser de categoría superior a

rare *adj*

rare	poco frecuente/poco común
a rare visitor	un visitante poco frecuente
This bird is rare in Cuba.	Este pájaro es poco común en Cuba.

Ø **raro** means "odd," "strange."

rate *n*

[price]	un precio/una tasa
[at hotel, etc.]	la tarifa
rate for the job	el sueldo justo
rate of exchange	el cambio/el tipo de cambio
rate of interest	el tipo de interés
postage rate	la tarifa
birth rate	el índice de natalidad
at any rate	de todas formas/de todos modos

rather *adv*

with an adjective	algo/bastante/un poco
I'm rather glad.	Estoy bastante contento(a).
He's rather strange.	Es algo raro.

to indicate preference
I would rather go to Mexico.
She would rather the red ones.

Preferiría/Me gustaría más ir a México.
Preferiría los rojos.

to correct a statement
These are his books, or rather
  his fiancée's.

Éstos son sus libros, o mejor
  dicho los de su novia.

reach n
to be within reach
to be within arm's reach
to be out of reach
within easy reach of the hotel
It's within easy reach by car.

estar al alcance de
estar al alcance de la mano
estar fuera del alcance
a corta distancia del hotel
Es fácilmente accesible en coche.

reach v
We reached Cancún on Saturday.
You can reach me by phone.
Your letter didn't reach me
  until yesterday.
to reach one's goal

Llegamos a Cancún el sábado.
Puedes telefonearme/llamarme.
Tu carta no llegó a mis manos
  antes de ayer.
llegar a la meta/realizar una ambición

reading n
reading
I like reading.
I have a lot of reading to do.

la lectura
Me gusta leer.
Tengo mucho que leer.

ready adj
to be ready
Are you ready?
to get ready to leave
to get sth ready

estar listo(a)/preparado(a)
¿Estás listo(a)?
prepararse para salir
preparar algo

Ø **listo** means "clever" when used with **ser**.

real adj
real
She's a real friend.
the real world
It's the real McCoy.

real/verdadero(a)/auténtico(a)
Es una verdadera amiga.
el mundo real
Es lo auténtico.

Ø **real** also means "royal."

realize v
[to comprehend, learn]
I didn't realize he was here.
Didn't you realize that?
They realized the danger.
[to convert into money]
to realize one's assets
to realize an ambition
My ambitions were realized.

darse cuenta de/hacerse cargo de
No me di cuenta de que estaba aquí.
¿No te diste cuenta de eso?
Se dieron cuenta del peligro.
realizar
realizar sus bienes
realizar una ambición
Mis ambiciones se realizaron/se
  hicieron realidad.

really adv
really
I don't really know.
The play was really good.

de verdad/realmente/en realidad
En realidad no lo sé.
La comedia fue verdaderamente buena.

Really?	¿De veras?/¿De verdad?
Not really?	¿Lo dices en serio?

reason *n*

[faculty]	la razón
to lose one's reason	perder la razón
[motive]	la razón/el motivo/la causa
the reason for my visit	el motivo de mi visita
for this reason	por esta razón/por esto
the reason why	el por qué/la razón por qué
We have reason to believe that ...	Tenemos motivo para creer que...
It stands to reason.	Es evidente.

receipt *n*

a receipt	un recibo
on receipt of the goods	al recibo de/al recibir los géneros
I acknowledge receipt of your letter.	Acuso recibo de su carta.
receipts *[money received]*	los ingresos

Ø **una receta** means "recipe" or "prescription."

receiver *n*

[addressee of letter, etc.]	un(a) destinatario(a)
radio receiver	un receptor
telephone receiver	el auricular
to pick up/hang up the receiver	descolgar/colgar el auricular

recipe *n*

[in cooking]	la receta

Ø **receta** also means "prescription."

record *n*

[music]	un disco
to make a record	grabar un disco
to play a record	tocar un disco
record player	un tocadiscos
[sport]	un récord/una marca
world record	el récord/la marca mundial
to beat the record	batir el récord/superar la marca
a record time	un tiempo récord
an academic/professional record	un expediente académico/ profesional

record *v*

to record *[music, voice]*	grabar
to record on tape	grabar en cinta

Ø **recordar** normally means "to remember" or "to remind," but is also found in Latin America with the meaning "to record."

recover *v intrans*

to recover from an illness	recuperarse/reponerse/restablecerse de una enfermedad
I have completely recovered.	Me he curado del todo.
He is recovering slowly from the operation.	Está reponiéndose poco a poco de la operación.

Shares have recovered. | Las acciones han vuelto a subir.

recover *v trans*
to recover one's health | recobrar la salud/reponerse
to recover consciousness | recobrar el conocimiento/volver en sí
to recover one's appetite/strength | recobrar el apetito/las fuerzas
to recover lost/stolen property | recuperar un objeto perdido/los géneros robados

red *adj*
red | rojo(a)/colorado(a)
red-haired | pelirrojo(a)
redhead | una pelirroja
red wine | el vino tinto

refer *v*
to refer to | referirse a/mencionar/hacer referencia a
What are you referring to? | ¿A qué te refieres?
He referred to your absence. | Se refirió a tu ausencia.
I won't refer to it again. | No volveré a mencionarlo.
Refer to page nine. | Véase la página nueve.

regard(s) *n*
[attention, care] | la atención
without regard to | sin hacer caso de/sin considerar
having regard to | en atención a/considerando/teniendo en cuenta

[esteem] | el respeto/la consideración/la estimación
to have a high regard for sb | respetar mucho a alguien/tener a alguien en gran estima

I have a high regard for them. | Les tengo en gran estima.
to show no regard for others | no tener ninguna consideración con los demás

[greetings] | recuerdos
Please give my regards to your wife. | Recuerdos a tu esposa/Saluda de mi parte a tu esposa.
with regard to/as regards | en cuanto a/por lo que se refiere a/con respecto a

register *v*
[instruments] | marcar/indicar
The thermometer registered 12 degrees. | El termómetro marcó doce grados.
to register for a course/class | matricularse en una asignatura/una clase

to register at a hotel | firmar el registro en un hotel
to register mail | recomendar *[LA]*/certificar una carta
a registered letter | una carta recomendada *[LA]*/certificada *[Sp]*

to register luggage | facturar el equipaje
registered trademark | una marca registrada
to register for the draft | ingresar/ingresarse *[Mex]*

Ø **registrar** normally means "to search" in the police sense of searching luggage, premises, etc.

registration n

registration number *[car]*	la matrícula
registration *[for a course,etc.]*	el registro/la inscripción/la matrícula
registration fee	los derechos de matrícula

regular adj

[habitual, regular, usual]	asiduo(a)/habitual/acostumbrado(a)
the regular customers	los clientes habituales
the regular staff	los empleados permanentes
the regulars *[bar/café/club]*	los asiduos/las asiduas
regular bus/train service	un servicio regular de autobuses/trenes
regular job	un empleo fijo/seguro/permanente
I arrived at my regular time.	Llegué a mi hora acostumbrada.
This is my regular work.	Éste es mi trabajo acostumbrado.
[normal/ordinary]	normal/corriente
regular gas	la gasolina normal
a regular day	un día corriente
regular size	de tamaño regular/medio

Ø **regular** often means "so-so."

relation/relationship n

[link, connection]	la relación/la conexión
the relation between the government and the unions	la relación entre el gobierno y los sindicatos
It bears no relation to the facts.	No tiene nada que ver con los hechos.
[relationship between people]	la relación/las relaciones
to have a good relationship with sb	tener buenas relaciones con alguien
to break a relationship with sb	romper con alguien
business/diplomatic/political relations	las relaciones comerciales/ diplomáticas/políticas
to break off/establish relations	romper/establecer relaciones
family relationship	el parentesco
What is his relationship to your family?	¿Qué parentesco hay entre él y tu familia?
*[family member: see **relative**]*	

relative n

my relatives	mis parientes
They're relatives of mine.	Son parientes míos.

Ø **parientes** does not mean "parents," which is rendered by **padres.**

relax v

[to rest]	descansar
I relaxed by swimming every evening.	Descansé nadando todas las tardes.
[to calm down]	calmarse
Relax!	¡Cálmate!/¡No te apures!

rely v

to rely on	confiar en/contar con/fiarse de
You can't rely on the weather.	No puede fiarse del tiempo.
I am relying on you.	Cuento contigo./Confío en ti.
I am relying on you to do it.	Cuento contigo para hacerlo./ Confío en que lo hagas.

remain *v*
[to stay]	quedar(se)/permanecer
I remained in bed for a week.	(Me) Quedé en cama una semana.
She remained standing/sitting.	Permaneció de pie/sentada.
[to survive]	quedar
Many people remained in the village.	Quedó mucha gente en la aldea.
[to be left over]	sobrar
Very little bread remained.	Sobró muy poco pan.

remark *n & v*
[comment]	una observación
to make a remark	hacer una observación
He made some remarks on her behavior.	Hizo unas observaciones sobre su conducta.
She remarked to us that it was cold.	Nos observó que hacía frío.

Ø **remarcar** is an anglicism which is found in Latin America.

remember *v*
to remember	acordarse de/recordar
Do you remember his name?	¿Te acuerdas de su nombre?
I don't remember the color.	No recuerdo el color.
He remembered to phone his wife.	Se acordó de telefonear a su esposa.
Did you remember to buy the wine?	¿Recordaste comprar el vino?

Ø **acordarse de** and **recordar** are interchangeable for "to remember."

remind *v*
This reminds me of the summer.	Esto me recuerda el verano.
Your brother reminds me of the president.	Tu hermano me recuerda al presidente.
He reminded us that it was getting dark.	Nos recordó que anochecía.
to remind sb to do sth	recordar a alguien que haga algo
Remind me to go to the bank.	Recuérdame que vaya al banco. *[Note: subjunctive]*
That reminds me ...!	¡Y a propósito...!

Ø **acordarse de** cannot be used in place of **recordar** with the meaning of "to remind."

rent *n & v*
to rent *[car, house, etc.]*	alquilar/rentar *[LA]*
the rent	el alquiler/la renta *[LA]*
to pay the rent	pagar el alquiler/la renta
House/Appartment to rent	Se alquila casa/apartamento
	Se renta casa/apartamento

Ø **la renta** also means "income" (from property, dividends, etc.) and is not used for "rent" in Spain.

rental *n*
car rental	el alquiler del coche
[income from rents]	la renta

repair(s)   n

repairs *[car]* — las reparaciones/las composturas *[Mex]*
Closed for repairs! — ¡Cerrado por reformas!
The house is in good repair. — La casa está en buen estado.

report   n

[account] — un relato/una relación
[official] — un informe
newspaper report — un reportaje/una crónica
school report — un boletín
weather report — un boletín meteorológico

representative   n

[elected] — un diputado/un representante
[salesperson] — un viajante/un representante comercial

require   v

to demand — exigir
The officials require that you fill out this form. — Los oficiales exigen que rellenes este formulario. *[Note: subjunctive]*

to need — necesitar
I require 100 dollars. — Necesito cien dólares.

required   adj

[necessary] — necesario(a)
the required qualifications — los requisitos necesarios
a required course *[college/school]* — un curso obligatorio
within the required time — dentro del plazo prescrito

resign   v

to resign *[from a job]* — dimitir
to resign oneself to — resignarse a

resort   n

holiday resort — una estación/un punto de veraneo
seaside resort — una estación balnearia/una playa
ski resort — una estación de esquiar
summer resort — una estación veraniega
winter resort — una estación de invierno
tourist resort — un centro de turismo
as a last resort — en último caso

Ø **un resorte** means "a coiled spring."

resort   v

to resort to bribery — recurrir al soborno

rest   n & v

the remainder — el resto/lo demás/los demás
the rest of the students — los demás estudiantes
Where are the rest? — ¿Dónde están los demás?
the rest of the day/time — el resto del día/tiempo
Tell me the rest! — ¡Cuéntame lo demás!

relaxation — el descanso/el reposo

to rest/have a rest	descansar
May he/she rest in peace.	Descanse en paz.

Ø **restar** means "to subtract," "to deduct."

restrooms n
ladies' room	el baño para señoras/damas
men's room	el baño para caballeros
[public]	el baño/los servicios

resumé n
[summary]	un resumen
[news summary]	un resumen de noticias
[CV]	un currículum vitae

resume v
to resume	continuar/comenzar de nuevo

retire v/retirement n
to retire from a job	jubilarse
to retire from the armed forces	retirarse
I'm retired.	Soy jubilado(a).
[act of retirement]	la jubilación
[state of retirement]	el retiro
to retire for the night	ir a acostarse

return v intrans
[to come back, go back]	volver/regresar
to return home	volver a casa

return v trans
[to give/send/take back]	devolver
Have you returned the books?	¿Has devuelto los libros?
Return to sender.	Devuélvase al remitente.
[to pay back]	devolver/reembolsar
I returned the money to him.	Le reembolsé el dinero.

reverse adj, n & v
[direction]	contrario(a)/opuesto(a)
They went in the reverse direction.	Fueron en sentido contrario.
to reverse/drive in reverse	dar marcha atrás
to reverse the car	dar marcha atrás al coche
[order]	inverso(a)/invertido(a)
in reverse order	en orden inverso
[opposite]	contrario(a)
It's quite the reverse.	Es todo lo contrario.
to reverse one's decision	revocar su decisión

review n & v
review [of play, film, show]	una reseña
to review a play/film	reseñar una comedia/una película
review [journal]	una revista
[to reconsider]	reconsiderar
They reviewed their policy.	Reconsideraron su política.
[to take stock of]	examinar/estudiar

185

Let's review the situation.
to review for an exam

Estudiemos la situación.
repasar los libros para un examen

rich *adj*
[people]
[food]
[color]
to get rich
the rich

rico(a)
sabroso(a)
vivo(a)/brillante
enriquecerse
los ricos

ride *n & v*
[on horse]
[in car, on bicycle]
to go for a ride
to go for a ride in a car
It's a short ride.
He gave me a ride home.
to ride a horse
to ride a bicycle
Can you ride a bicycle?

una cabalgata/un paseo a caballo
un paseo en coche/en bicicleta
pasearse a caballo
dar un paseo en coche
Es poco camino/poca distancia.
Me llevó a casa en coche.
montar a caballo
ir en bicicleta
¿Sabes montar en bicicleta?

rider *n*
horse-rider
[cyclist]
[motor cyclist]

un jinete/una jineta
un(a) ciclista
un(a) motociclista

right *adj, adv & n*
appropriate, suitable

the right time
the right man for the job
to say the right thing
She was wearing the right
  clothes.
I thought it right to ask him.

apropiado(a)/propio(a)/indicado(a)/
  conveniente/lo que conviene
la hora apropiada
el hombre más indicado para el cargo
decir lo que conviene
Llevaba la ropa apropiada.

Me pareció conveniente preguntarle.

correct
the right answer
the right answer [math]
the right word
Do you have the right time?
Is this the right road for Jalisco?
My watch is right.
to be right
I'm right.
You're quite right.
That's right.

correcto(a)/exacto(a)/verdadero(a)
la respuesta correcta
la solución correcta
la palabra exacta/apropiada
¿Tienes la hora exacta?
¿Es ésta el camino de Jalisco?
Mi reloj va bien.
tener razón
Tengo razón.
Estás en lo cierto.
Sí, eso es./¡Justo!

opposite of left
on/to the right
your right hand
the right(-hand) drawer
the right-hand lane
to keep to the right
the right-hand side
right turn
to turn right

derecho(a)
a la derecha
tu mano derecha
el cajón de derecha
el carril de derecha
circular por la derecha
la derecha
una vuelta a la derecha
torcer a la derecha

to be on the right *[politics]*	ser de derechas
a right-winger	un(a) derechista

moral, just — bueno(a)

right conduct	la buena conducta
to know right from wrong	saber lo que está bien y lo que está mal.
to do the right thing	hacer bien
civil rights	los derechos civiles
equal rights	la igualdad de derechos
women's rights	los derechos de la mujer
You have no right to do that.	No tienes el derecho de hacer eso.

all right

I'm all right.	Estoy bien.
All right? *[agreed]*	¿De acuerdo?/¿Vale?
[see also okay]	

other

right here	aquí mismo
right now	ahora mismo
to come right	arreglarse/salir bien
It'll all come right in the end.	Todo se arreglará/saldrá bien.
to go right on	seguir adelante
Right on!	¡Vale!/¡Justo!

ring   *n*

[jewelry]	un anillo/una sortija
engagement ring	una alianza/un anillo de compromiso/ un anillo de pedida/un anillo de comprometida/una sortija de pedida
wedding ring	una alianza/un anillo de boda
boxing ring	un ring/un cuadrilátero
bull ring	una plaza de toros
circus ring	una pista
the rings of Saturn	los anillos de Saturno

ring   *v*

[to telephone]	telefonear/llamar (por teléfono)
to ring the bell *[electric]*	tocar el timbre
Ring the bell!	¡Toca el timbre!
[of bells]	sonar
The bells are ringing.	Suenan las campanas.

river   *n*

river	un río
down/up river	río abajo/río arriba

road   *n*

[general]	un camino
the road to Mérida	el camino de Mérida
[main road]	una carretera
the road between Lima and the coast	la carretera entre Lima y la costa
[in town]	una calle
road sign	una señal de carretera

robe   *n*

bathrobe/dressing gown	un batín *[man's]*/una bata *[woman's]*

[judge's]	una toga/un traje talar
[priest's]	una sotana

room *n*
in a house/apartment

un cuarto/una habitación/una pieza *[LA]*/un ambiente *[Arg]*

bathroom	un cuarto de baño
bedroom	una recámara *[LA]*/un dormitorio/ una alcoba/un cuarto/una habitación
Julia is working in her room.	Julia está trabajando en su cuarto/habitación.
dining room	un comedor
living room	un cuarto de estar/una sala de estar/un salón/un living *[Sp]*

in hotels

hotel room	una habitación
double room	una habitación para dos personas
single room	una habitación individual
ladies' room	el lavabo/servicio de señoras
men's room	el lavabo/servicio de caballeros

in public building una sala

waiting room	una sala de espera
classroom	un aula *[fem]*
conference/lecture room	una sala de conferencias

space un espacio/un sitio

Is there room?	¿Hay sitio?
Is there room for this?	¿Cabe esto?
There's room for eight in his car.	Caben ocho en su coche.
Is there room for me?	¿Quepo yo?
There's plenty of room.	Queda mucho espacio libre.

round *[see around]*

rubber *n*
[material] el caucho *[LA]*/la goma *[Sp]*

It's made of rubber.	Es de goma.

rude *adj*
[offensive] grosero(a)/ descortés(-esa)/ofensivo(a)/ mal educado(a)

You were very rude to her.	Estuviste muy descortés con ella.
He's a very rude person.	Es una persona muy mal educada.
a rude gesture	un gesto grosero
a rude remark	una grosería
to make rude remarks	decir groserías
a rude word	una palabrota

Ø **rudo(a)** means "rough" or "rude" when referring to wood.

ruin *v*
[financial/health/life/reputation] arruinar

The strike ruined the firm.	La huelga arruinó la empresa.
The climate ruined his health.	El clima arruinó su salud.
[to spoil events, objects]	estropear
The rain ruined the picnic.	La lluvia estropeó la merienda.

My garden was ruined by the storm.	Mi jardín fue estropeado por la tormenta.
His father was ruined.	Su padre fue arruinado.
The city was ruined after the earthquake.	La ciudad quedó en ruinas después del terremoto.

run *v*

[people, animals]	correr
to run downstairs/upstairs	bajar/subir la escalera corriendo
to run in/out	entrar/salir corriendo
[machinery]	marchar/andar/funcionar
The car is running smoothly.	El coche marcha bien.
It runs on gas.	Funciona con gasolina.
The engine was running.	El motor estaba en marcha.
I'll run you to the airport.	Te llevaré al aeropuerto.
The buses do not run on Sundays.	Los autobuses no circulan los domingos./No hay servicio de autobuses los domingos.
The trains run every hour.	Los trenes salen cada hora.
to run a car	tener un coche
to run a temperature	tener una fiebre
to run a business	dirigir una empresa
to run for office	presentarse como/ser candidato(a) para un puesto
to run away	escaparse/huir
to run out of *[commodity]*	agotarse/acabarse
We've run out of money/bread.	Se nos ha acabado el dinero/el pan.
They ran out of gas.	Se quedaron sin gasolina.

S

's/s'
[possessive]

| | [Note: Spanish has no equivalent of the English apostrophe s; **de** is used to denote possession] |

José's house — la casa de José
the boys' father — el padre de los chicos
the dog's owner — el dueño del perro
My car is bigger than my boss's. — Mi coche es más grande que el de mi jefe.
His tickets are more expensive than his friends'. — Sus localidades son más caras que las de sus amigos.

sad *adj*
[unhappy] — triste
[deplorable] — lamentable

safe *adj*
from danger — salvo(a)/fuera de peligro/ileso(a)
You'll be safe here. — Aquí estarás fuera de peligro.
safe and sound — sano(a) y salvo(a)
All the passengers were safe. — Todos los pasajeros salieron ilesos.
safely — a buen puerto/sin accidente
We arrived home safely. — Llegamos a casa a buen puerto/sin accidente.

secure, not dangerous — seguro(a)/sin peligro/a salvo
a safe beach — una playa sin peligro
This bridge is not very safe. — Este puente no es muy seguro.
These toys are safe. — Estos juguetes no son peligrosos.

sensible — prudente
a safe driver — un conductor prudente
at a safe distance — a una distancia prudente

saint *n*
a saint — un santo/una santa
Saint John — San Juan [Note: **Santo** shortens to **San** before a male saint's name unless it begins with **Do** or **To**.]
Saint Dominic/Saint Thomas — Santo Domingo/Santo Tomás
Saint Mary — Santa María

Ø **el santo** also means "saint's day" which in the Spanish-speaking world is often of greater significance than one's birthday.

sale *n*
sale — una venta
for sale — se vende
House for sale — Se vende (una) casa
to put a house up for sale — ofrecer una casa en venta
on sale — de rebaja
on sale in all book stores — de venta en todas las librerías

annual/summer sale, etc.	un saldo/unas rebajas
clearance sale	una liquidación
public sale/auction	una subasta
Sale! *[in shop windows, etc.]*	¡Grandes rebajas!
sale price *[retail]*	el precio de venta
reduced price	el precio de saldo

salt *n*

salt	la sal

Ø **un salto** means "a jump."

same   *adj & pron*

same	mismo(a)/igual
It's the same man.	Es el mismo hombre. *[Note: position of adjective]*
at the same time	al mismo tiempo
It's all the same.	Es lo mismo.
It's all the same to me.	Me es igual.
It's the same old story.	Es lo de siempre.
The same to you!	¡Igualmente!
Same again? *[drinks, etc.]*	¿Igual que antes?/¿Lo de antes?

save   *v*

from danger, death, destruction — salvar/rescatar/impedir

to save sb's life	salvar la vida a alguien
The dog saved my life.	El perro me salvó la vida.
The firefighters saved the old mission.	Los bomberos salvaron la misión vieja.
He saved the woman from drowning.	Salvó a la mujer que se estaba ahogando.
They saved me from falling.	Impidieron que cayera yo.

to store — guardar/reservar

We saved some bread and fruit.	Guardamos pan y fruta.
Save me a seat, please.	Guárdame un asiento, por favor.

to collect — coleccionar

Do you save stamps?	¿Coleccionas estampillas/sellos?

money — ahorrar

He has saved a lot of money.	Ha ahorrado mucho dinero.
I am saving up for my vacation.	Ahorro dinero para mis vacaciones.
She's saving up for a car.	Ahorra dinero para comprar un coche.
savings account	una cuenta de ahorros

time — ahorrar

He saved time by buying his ticket in advance.	Ahorró tiempo sacando su boleto con anticipación.

sport — parar

The goalkeeper saved the penalty.	El portero paró el penalty.

say   *v*

to say	decir
How do you say "help" in Spanish?	¿Cómo se dice "help" en castellano?
They say it's very popular.	Dicen que es muy popular. *[Note: **que** may not be omitted.]*
It is said to be impossible.	Se dice que es imposible.

No sooner said than done! ¡Dicho y hecho!

scary adj
[frightening] espantoso(a)/pavoroso(a)
[easily frightened] asustadizo(a)
It's a scary place. Es un sitio espantoso.
a scary movie una película de miedo

schedule n
[list] una lista
[of events] un programa
My schedule includes the cathedral Mi programa de visitas incluye la catedral.
[work to be done] un plan
a tight schedule un plan riguroso
The work is behind schedule. El trabajo sufre retraso/está atrasado.
The work is on schedule. El trabajo no sufre retraso.
[timetable] un horario
The plane is behind schedule. El avión sufre un retraso.
The train arrived on schedule. El tren llegó sin retraso.

schedule v
[meeting, visit, etc.] fijar la hora de
The game is scheduled for five El partido está previsto para las
 o'clock. cinco.
[transportation] establecer el horario de
[work] proyectar/redactar el plan de
I am scheduled to leave at ten. Según el programa saldré a las diez./
 Se ha fijado mi salida para las diez.

school n
[general] una escuela
primary school una escuela primaria
high/secondary school una escuela secundaria/un
 instituto (de segunda enseñanza)
junior high school un colegio de bachillerato elemental
to go to school ir a la escuela/al colegio *[Note: use of
 definite article]*
[college or university] una universidad
[department of university] un departamento/una facultad
to finish school acabar sus estudios

scientist n
scientist un(a) científico(a)/un(a) cientista *[LA]*

season n
[of the year] la estación
[sport, social] la temporada
soccer season la temporada de fútbol

seat n
[chair] un asiento/una silla
[in buses, planes, etc.] un asiento/una plaza
[in theater, movies, etc.] una localidad
[ticket for theater, etc.] una localidad/una entrada
I want two seats for tomorrow. Quiero dos localidades para mañana.
There are no seats left. No quedan entradas.

This seat is taken.	Este asiento está ocupado.
Have/Take a seat!	¡Siéntate!

second *adj*

second-hand	de segunda mano/usado(a)
second-hand clothes	ropa usada
second-hand book/car	un libro/coche de segunda mano

secretary *n*

[in an office]	un(a) secretario(a)
[in government]	un ministro

seed *n*

[for sowing]	una semilla/una simiente
[within fruit]	una pepita
to sow seeds	sembrar de semillas

seem *v*

to seem	parecer
How does it seem to you?	¿Qué te parece?
He seems very nice.	Parece muy amable.
So it seems.	Así parece.
It seems that they want to stay.	Parece que quieren quedarse.
It does not seem that he is coming.	No parece que venga. *[Note: use of subjunctive]*
It seems to me he's lying.	Me parece que dice mentiras.

self *pron*

in a reflexive verb

myself	me
yourself	te
himself/herself/itself/yourself/oneself	se
ourselves	nos
themselves/yourselves	se
to cut oneself	cortarse
Have you hurt yourself?	¿Te has hecho daño?
I helped/served myself.	Me serví.

in an imperative

Look at yourself in the mirror!	¡Mírate en el espejo!
Don't deceive yourself.	¡No te engañes!

emphatic

I myself	yo mismo(a)
you yourself	tú mismo(a)/usted mismo(a)
he himself/she herself	él mismo/ella misma
we ourselves	nosotros(as) mismos(as)
they themselves	ellos mismos/ellas mismas
you yourselves	ustedes mismos(as)
I'll go myself.	Iré yo mismo(a).
One must do it oneself.	Se debe hacerlo sí mismo.

(all) by oneself

I can't do it by myself.	No puedo hacerlo solo(a).
We went by ourselves.	Fuimos nosotros solos.

self-service *n*

self-service restaurant/store	un autoservicio

senior adj & n

senior citizen	un(a) jubilado(a)
a senior [at university]	un(a) estudiante de último año
senior year	el último año de estudios
He is my senior. [age]	Tiene más años que yo./Es más viejo que yo.
He is my senior. [rank]	Tiene categoría superior a la mía.

sense n

the five senses	los cinco sentidos
[hearing]	el oído
[sight]	la vista
[smell]	el olfato
[taste]	el gusto
[touch]	el tacto
common sense	el sentido común
sense of humor	el sentido del humor
It doesn't make sense.	No tiene sentido.
[feeling]	una sensación
a sense of grief/pleasure	una sensación de dolor/placer

sensible adj

[having good sense]	sensato(a)/prudente
She's a very sensible person.	Es una persona muy sensata.
[reasonable]	razonable/prudente/lógico(a)
The most sensible thing to do would be ...	Lo más razonable sería...
[of clothes]	práctico(a)
He was wearing sensible shoes.	Llevaba zapatos prácticos.

Ø **sensible** means "sensitive."

sensitive adj

sensitive	sensible
My sister is very sensitive.	Mi hermana es muy sensible.
He is sensitive to the cold.	Es sensible al frío.
[easily offended]	susceptible
They are sensitive to criticism.	Son susceptibles a la crítica.

Ø **sensitivo(a)** means "sentient" or "aware."

sentence n

[grammar]	una frase/una oración
[in law]	una sentencia
to pass sentence	pronunciar sentencia

serious adj

[general]	serio(a)
His father is very serious.	Su padre es muy serio.
It was a serious decision.	Fue una decisión seria.
Are you serious (about it)?	¿Lo dices en serio?
I am serious.	Hablo en serio.
[of illness/injury]	grave
Our goalkeeper suffered a serious injury.	Nuestro portero sufrió una lesión grave.
to be seriously ill/injured	estar gravemente enfermo(a)/ lesionado(a)

servant *n*
[domestic] un(a) criado(a)
civil servant un(a) funcionario(a)

several *adj & pron*
several varios(as)/algunos(as)/diversos(as)
There are several people in Hay varias personas en la
  the swimming pool.   alberca/piscina.
Several of them attended. Algunos(as) de ellos/ellas asistieron.
Several of us are going. Algunos(as) de nosotros(as) vamos.

share *n*
[of something] una parte/una porción
in equal shares por partes iguales
He paid his share of the cost. Pagó su parte del coste.
[financial] una acción

share *v*
[to divide] partir/dividir
I shared the cake with them. Dividí el pastel con ellos/ellas.
[to share out] repartir/distribuir
The money was shared among us. Repartieron el dinero entre nosotros.
[to have/hold in common] compartir
We had to share a room. Tuvimos que compartir una habitación.
I have sth to share with you. Tengo algo que decirte.

she *pron*
She's working in Panama. Trabaja en Panamá.
She will come, but not her Ella sí vendrá pero su hija no.
  daughter.   *[Note: Ella, like all the other subject
  pronouns, is usually omitted; it is used for
  emphasis and clarification.]*

Ø **ella** can also mean "her" following a preposition, e.g., "It's for her," is translated by **Es
para ella.**

shoot *v*
[an arrow/bullet/gun] disparar
to shoot at sb tirar a alguien/pegar un tiro a
  alguien/disparar contra alguien

They shot at me. Dispararon contra mí.
Don't shoot! ¡No dispare! *[usted form]*
[to kill] pegar un tiro/matar a tiros a alguien
He shot his brother. Pegó un tiro/Mató a tiros a su hermano.
[to wound] herir
He shot a motorist. Hirió a un motorista.
A policeman was shot. [killed] Un guardia fue matado a tiros.
A policeman was shot. [wounded] Un guardia fue/quedó herido.
[to execute] fusilar
He was shot by the soldiers. Fue fusilado por los soldados.
to shoot a film rodar una película/filmar

shop *n*
a store una tienda
a department store un almacén
a workshop un taller

shopping n & v

shopping	las compras
to go shopping	hacer las compras/ir de compras/ir de tiendas
shop window	una vidriera/una vitrina *[LA]*/un escaparate *[Sp]*

short adj

[length, distance]	corto(a)
a short distance	una distancia corta
shortwave radio	un radio de onda corta
[message]	breve
[person]	bajo(a)
a short man/woman	un hombre bajo/una mujer baja
[time]	corto(a)/breve/de poca duración
a short visit	una visita de poca duración
for a short time	por poco tiempo
to be short of	estar falto(a) de/faltar/no tener

shorts n

shorts	un pantalón corto

should v

	*[**deber** in the conditional or imperfect subjunctive]*
You should do it.	Deberías hacerlo.*[conditional]*
	Debieras hacerlo. *[imperfect subjunctive]*
I should have helped her.	Debería haberla ayudado./Debiera haberla ayudado/Habría debido ayudarla./ Hubiera debido ayudarla. *[Note: alternative forms]*

*[see also **ought**]*

show n

[exhibition]	una exposición
dog show	una exposición canina
[entertainment]	una función/un espectáculo
The last show starts at 10.	La última función empieza a las diez.
to go to a show	ir al teatro/ir a un espectáculo
TV show	una emisión/un programa

show v

to show sth to sb	enseñar/mostrar algo a alguien
I showed him the letter.	Le enseñé la carta.
to show sb how to do sth	enseñar/mostrar a alguien a hacer algo
to show in	hacer pasar
Show her in.	Que pase./Hágala pasar. *[**usted** form]*

shower n

shower	la regadera *[LA]*/la ducha *[Sp]*

Ø In Spain **la regadera** means "watering can."

sick adj

ill	enfermo(a)
to be sick	estar enfermo(a) *[Note: **estar** is used]*
to feel sick	sentirse mal
to get sick	caer enfermo(a)/enfermarse

to get seasick/travel sick	marearse

disgusted

to sicken	dar asco a
It makes me sick.	Me da asco./Me repugna.

tired of

to be sick (and tired) of	estar harto(a) de
I'm sick (and tired) of rice.	Estoy harto(a) de arroz.
I'm sick (and tired) of telling you.	Estoy harto(a) de decírtelo.

side n

side	un lado
by the side of	al lado de
by the side of the lake/river	a la orilla del lago/río
by the side of the road	al borde del camino
by/at the seaside	a orillas del mar
on this side	por este lado
on the other side	por otro lado
on both sides	por ambos lados
on one side ... on the other ...	por una parte... por otra...

sidewalk n

sidewalk	una acera/una banqueta [Mex]/ una vereda [Arg]

sign n
with the hand

to make a (rude) sign to sb	hacer una señal (grosera) a alguien

indication

It's a good sign.	Es buena señal.
It's a sign of rain.	Es indicio de lluvia.
There's no sign of it.	No se lo ve en ninguna parte.

una señal/una seña

una señal/un indicio

public sign

[notice, placard]	una señal
	un letrero
neon sign	un letrero de neón
road sign	una señal de carretera
shop sign	un rótulo

written symbol

signs of the zodiac	un signo/un símbolo
	los signos del zodiaco

silence n/silent adj

Silence!	¡Silencio!/¡Cállate!
to be silent	callarse/guardar silencio [more polite]
silent	silencioso(a)
silent [people only]	callado(a)
a silent film	una película muda

simple adj

[of things]	simple
It's a simple formality.	Es un trámite simple.
[simple-minded, stupid]	simple
Her brother is simple.	Su hermano es simple.
[uncomplicated, plain]	sencillo(a)
They are simple people.	Son personas sencillas.
to live a simple life	llevar una vida sencilla

since *conj & prep*

time

He's been in London since yesterday.

It hasn't rained since we've been here.

I haven't seen them since they arrived.

desde *[prep]*/desde que *[conj]*

Está en Londres desde ayer. *[Note: present tense]*

No ha llovido desde que estamos aquí. *[Note: present tense]*

No los he visto desde su llegada/ desde que llegaron.

reason

Since they have no money, they cannot go to the concert.

puesto que/ya que

Puesto que no tienen dinero, no pueden ir al concierto.

sincerely *[see yours sincerely]*

single *adj*

[unmarried]

a single man/woman

a single bed/room

a single ticket

a single coat of paint

[only one]

There was a single tree in the square.

There wasn't a single flower in his garden.

soltero(a)

un soltero/una soltera

una cama/habitación individual

un boleto sencillo/de ida

una simple capa de pintura

solo(a)/único(a)

Había un árbol único en la plaza.

No había ni una sola flor en su jardín.

sit/sitting *v*

to sit down

Sit down!

to be sitting down/seated

She's sitting down. *[action]*

She's sitting down. *[state]*

to sit up *[from lying position]*

He sat up in bed.

sentarse

¡Siéntate!/¡Siéntese!/¡Siéntense!

estar sentado(a)

Está sentándose./Se está sentando.

Está sentada.

incorporarse/pararse *[LA]*

Se incorporó en la cama.

size *n*

[general]

What size is it?

It's the size of an egg.

[clothes]

What size do you wear?

What size shirt do you wear?

I wear a size 10.

[shoes, gloves]

What size shoes do you wear?

I wear a size 10.

el tamaño/las dimensiones

¿De qué tamaño es?/¿Cómo es de grande?/¿Qué dimensiones tiene?

Es del tamaño de un huevo.

la talla

¿Cuál es tu/su talla?

¿Qué talla de camisa es la tuya/ la de usted?

Mi talla es el 10.

el número

¿Qué número calzas/calza usted?

Uso/Calzo el número 10.

skirt *n*

skirt

la falda/la pollera *[Arg, Bol, Chi, Uru]*

sleep *v* /asleep *adj* /sleepy *adj*

to sleep

to go to sleep

to be asleep

My wife is asleep.

dormir

dormirse

estar durmiendo/estar dormido(a)

Mi esposa está durmiendo/dormida.

[to spend the night]	pasar la noche/acostarse
He's sleeping at his uncle's.	Pasa la noche en casa de su tío.
to be sleepy	tener sueño
to get sleepy	empezar a tener sueño

slip   n

[half slip]	una combinación de medio cuerpo
[full slip]	una combinación

Ø **un slip** means "briefs" (men's or women's) in Spain, and in Latin America "swimming trunks."

slow   adj

slow	lento(a)
It's slow work.	Es un trabajo lento.
They're slow workers.	Trabajan despacio.
a slow train	un tren correo/un ómnibus
Your clock is slow.	Tu reloj se atrasa.
My watch is five minutes slow.	Mi reloj se atrasa cinco minutos./lleva cinco minutos de retraso.
to be slow to do sth/in doing	tardar en hacer algo
They are very slow to reply.	Tardan mucho en contestar.

small   adj

small	chico(a) [LA]/pequeño(a)
a small house	una casa chica/pequeña
	una casita [Note: The suffix **ito** or **ita** is often used to convey the idea of smallness.]

smart   adj

elegant — elegante
a smart dress	un vestido elegante
She looks very smart.	Está muy elegante./¡Qué elegante está!

fashionable — de moda
She always wears smart shoes.	Siempre lleva zapatos de moda.
It's a smart restaurant.	Es un restaurante de moda.

bright, intelligent — inteligente/listo(a)/vivo(a)
He's a smart guy.	Es un tío inteligente/listo.

quick, prompt — pronto(a)/rápido(a)
Smart work by the policeman prevented the attack.	Una pronta acción de parte del guardia evitó el atentado.

smell   n & v

[odor]	un olor
a nice smell	un olor agradable
a bad smell	un mal olor/un hedor
sense of smell	el olfato
to have a keen sense of smell	tener buen olfato
to smell	oler
It smells nice.	Huele bien
It smelled bad.	Olía mal.
This rose doesn't smell.	Esta rosa no tiene olor.
to smell of	oler a
It smells of garlic.	Huele a ajo.

smoke n & v

smoke	el humo
to smoke (glass, bacon)	ahumar
to smoke (tobacco)	fumar

snack n

to have a snack	tomar un bocadillo/comer algo
snacks [appetizers]	las botanas [Mex]/los antojetos [Per]/ los ingredientes [Arg]/los pasapalos [Ven]/ las tapas [Sp]/los aperitivos [Note: These are the traditional snacks served in bars such as chips, nuts, olives, shrimp, etc.]
snackbar	una cafetería

Ø **un aperitivo** also means a pre-dinner drink.

so adv

so	tan
He is so ill.	Está tan enfermo.
I am so cold/hot.	Tengo tanto frío/calor.
He's so hungry/thirsty.	Tiene tanta hambre/sed.
so much	tanto(a)
They have so much money.	Tienen tanto dinero.
so many	tantos(as)
We have so many friends.	Tenemos tantos(as) amigos(as).
I think so.	Creo que sí./Lo creo.
I don't think so.	Creo que no./No lo creo.
I hope so/not.	Espero que sí/no.
I told you so!	¡Ya te lo dije!
So what?	¿Y qué?
[thus, therefore]	así
and so on	y así sucesivamente

so conj

[as a result]	por (lo) tanto
The box office was closed so I couldn't buy tickets.	La taquilla estaba cerrada y por lo tanto no podía comprar localidades.
so that [purpose]	para que [+ subjunctive]
I gave her the money so that she should pay for the meal.	Le di el dinero para que pagara la comida.
so that [result]	de modo que [+ indicative]
The taxi was late so that we missed the train.	El taxi llegó tarde de modo que perdimos el tren.

solid adj

[general]	sólido(a)
a solid state	un estado sólido
[of gold, silver, oak, etc.]	macizo(a)
The statue is solid silver.	La estatua es de plata maciza.
a solid meal	una comida fuerte/sustanciosa
solid ground	la tierra firme
I have solid grounds for thinking that he is lying.	Tengo buenos motivos para creer que dice mentiras/miente.

some adj

some	algún/alguna [singular] algunos(as) [plural] unos(as)/unos(as) cuantos(as)

Some woman told me.	Alguna mujer me lo dijo.
I'll go to Japan some day.	Algún día iré al Japón.
There were some people in the street.	Había algunas personas en la calle.
I saw them some days ago.	Los vi hace unos días.

a quantity

un poco de/algo de *[singular]*
algunos(as) *[plural]*

Do you have some chocolate?	¿Tienes (un poco de) chocolate?
Paco has some rice and flour.	Paco tiene (un poco de) arroz y harina.
There are some cherries on the table.	Hay (algunas) cerezas en la mesa. *[Note: The Spanish for "some" is frequently omitted when referring to quantity.]*

other expressions

some distance away	a cierta distancia
for some reason or other	por alguna que otra razón
some other time	otro día
I spent some three hours there.	Pasé unas tres horas allí.

some *pron*

There's no sugar left. I'll go and buy some.	No queda azúcar. Voy a comprar un poco.
I have some grapes. Do you want some?	Tengo uvas. ¿Quieres unas?
Some of my friends live here.	Algunos de mis amigos viven aquí.

somebody/someone *pron*

somebody	alguien
somebody else	algún otro/otra persona

somehow *adv*

You must do it somehow (or other).	Debes hacerlo de algún modo/de un modo u otro.
Somehow I don't believe you.	Por alguna que otra razón no te creo.

someplace *[see somewhere]*

something *pron*

something	algo/alguna cosa
I have something to tell you.	Tengo algo que decirte.
Do you want something to eat?	¿Quieres algo que comer? *[Note: use of que]*
something else	otra cosa

sometimes *adv*

sometimes	algunas veces/a veces/de vez en cuando

somewhere *adv*

somewhere	en alguna parte/a alguna parte
I left my umbrella somewhere.	Dejé mi paraguas en alguna parte.
He's gone somewhere.	Ha ido a alguna parte.
somewhere else	en otra parte/a otra parte
It must be somewhere else.	Debe estar en otra parte.
She went somewhere else.	Fue a otra parte.

soon _adv_

soon	pronto/dentro de poco
They'll be back soon.	Volverán pronto/dentro de poco.
See you soon!	¡Hasta pronto!
soon afterwards	poco después
[early]	temprano
too soon	demasiado temprano/pronto
the sooner the better	cuanto antes, mejor
sooner or later	tarde o temprano
as soon as	en cuanto/tan pronto como/así que
He will come as soon as he can.	Vendrá en cuanto pueda. _[Note: subjunctive when future time implied]_
I came back to New York as soon as I finished school.	Volví a Nueva York en cuanto terminé mis estudios. _[Note: indicative where action already completed.]_
as soon as possible	cuanto antes/lo antes posible/lo más pronto posible

Ø **pronto** means "ready" in Argentina and Uruguay.

sorry _adj_

[Pardon me?]	¿Perdón?/¿Mande? _[Mex]_
[Excuse me!]	¡Disculpe!/¡Discúlpeme, por favor! _[**usted** forms]_
I am very sorry.	Lo siento mucho.
I'm sorry I'm late.	Siento/Lamento llegar tarde.
I'm sorry you're ill.	Siento/Lamento que estés enfermo(a). _[Note: subjunctive]_
I feel sorry for them.	Les compadezco./Les tengo lástima./ Tengo pena por ellos./Me dan lástima.

south _n & adj_

the south	el sur
south(ern)	del sur/meridional
South America	la América del Sur/Sudamérica
South American	sudamericano(a)

space _n_

[general]	el espacio
blank space	un espacio en blanco
outer space	el espacio/el espacio exterior/interplanetario
to clear/leave a space for	hacer/dejar un sitio para
[see also **room**]	

Spanish _adj_

Spanish	español(a) _[Note: small 'e']_

Spanish _n_

language	el castellano/el español _[Note: small 'c' or 'e']_
Do you speak Spanish?	¿Hablas castellano/español?
Say it in Spanish, please.	Dilo en castellano/español, por favor.
Spanish is not a difficult language.	El castellano/español no es un idioma difícil. _[Note: use of definite article with name of a language except after **hablar** and **en**]_

Ø **castellano** means "Castilian" but is used all over the Spanish-speaking world for the Spanish language.

people

the Spanish/Spaniards	los españoles
He's Spanish/a Spaniard.	Es español.
She's Spanish/a Spaniard.	Es española. *[Note: omission of the indefinite article]*

spare *adj*

spare time	el tiempo libre/desocupado
spare parts *[for car, etc.]*	las piezas de recambio/repuesto
spare tire/wheel	un neumático/una llanta/una rueda de repuesto
[left over]	sobrante
I have some spare potatoes.	Tengo unas papas sobrantes.
[available]	disponible
Do you have any spare rooms?	¿Tienen unas habitaciones disponibles?

spare *v*

[do without]	prescindir de
Can you spare her today?	¿Puedes prescindir de ella hoy?
to spare time	conceder/dedicar tiempo
I can spare you five minutes.	Puedo concederte cinco minutos.
Can you spare me a moment?	¿Tienes un momento?
I can't spare the time.	No tengo tiempo.
I can't spare enough time.	No puedo dedicar bastante tiempo.
time to spare	tiempo de sobra
to spare money	dar dinero
I can only spare you 50 pesos.	Puedo darte sólo cincuenta pesos.
to spare sb's life	perdonar la vida a alguien

speak *v*

on telephone

Who's speaking?	¿De parte de quién?/¿Quién habla?
Speaking.	Al habla.
May I speak with ... ?	¿Se puede hablar con... ?

spell *v*/**spelling** *n*

to spell	escribir/deletrear
How do you spell it?	¿Cómo se escribe?
You have spelled it wrong.	Lo has escrito mal.
Can you spell it for me?	¿Quieres deletreármelo?

spend *v*

to spend money	gastar dinero
He spent a lot of money on his car.	Gastó mucho dinero en su coche.
to spend time	pasar tiempo
We spent two years in Chile.	Pasamos dos años en Chile.
to spend time on	dedicar tiempo a
He spends very little time on his garden.	Dedica muy poco tiempo a su jardín.

spoil *[see ruin]*

sport *n*

to play a sport	practicar un deporte *[Note: not jugar]*
sportsman/woman	un/una deportista

stage   *n*
[*platform*]   una plataforma
[*in theater*]   un escenario/una escena
to go on the stage   hacerse actor/actriz
[*of journey*]   una etapa
in/by stages   por etapas
at this stage of the journey   en esta etapa del viaje

stair(s)   *n*
[*a step*]   un peldaño/un escalón
staircase   una escalera
to go up/down the stairs   subir/bajar la escalera
moving stairs   una escalera móvil/mecánica
spiral staircase   una escalera de caracol

stamp   *n*
postage stamp   una estampilla *[LA]*/un timbre
     [Mex]/un sello *[Sp]*

stand   *v*
to stand up   levantarse
[*to get to one's feet*]   ponerse de pie/pararse *[LA]*
to be standing   estar
He was standing by the door.   Estaba cerca de la puerta.
[*to be on one's feet*]   estar de pie/estar parado(a)
My son is the one who is standing.   Mi hijo es el que está de pie.
[*to tolerate*]   soportar/aguantar
I can't stand it any more!   ¡No aguanto más!/¡No puedo más!

starting from   *prep*
a partir del lunes   starting from Monday

stay   *v*
[*to remain*]   quedar(se)/permanecer
I stayed in/at home.   Me quedé en casa.
We stayed in bed.   Guardamos cama.
They stayed here for a week.   Se quedaron aquí una semana.
She stayed silent.   Quedó callada.
[*to lodge*]   hospedarse/alojarse
to stay at a hotel   hospedarse/alojarse en un hotel
to stay with friends   hospedarse/alojarse con amigos
She's staying with friends for
  a few days.   Pasa unos días con amigos.
Where are you staying?   ¿Dónde vives?

other
to stay out   quedarse fuera
She stayed out till midnight.   No volvió a casa hasta medianoche.
to stay up   velar/no acostarse
to stay up late   acostarse tarde
to stay up all night   trasnochar

step   *n*
footstep   un paso
step by step   paso a paso
[*stair*]   un peldaño/un escalón/una grada

| to take a step forward/back | dar un paso adelante/hacia atrás |

family relations

stepbrother/stepsister	un hermanastro/una hermanastra
stepchild	un hijastro/una hijastra
stepfather/stepmother	un padrastro/una madrastra
stepson/stepdaughter	un hijastro/una hijastra

still adj

[motionless]	inmóvil/quieto(a)
Keep/Sit/Stand still!	¡Estáte quieto(a)!
She lay still.	Permaneció inmóvil.
[quiet]	tranquilo(a)/silencioso(a)
Everything was still and quiet.	Todo estaba tranquilo.

still adv

still	todavía/aún
They are still in New York.	Están todavía en Nueva York.
He still hasn't arrived.	No ha llegado todavía.
I still remember her.	Todavía la recuerdo./La recuerdo aún.

Ø **aun**, without an accent, means "even."

stomach n

| the stomach | el estómago/el vientre |
| I have a stomach ache. | Tengo dolor de estómago. |

Ø **estómago** is the general word for "stomach;" **vientre** really means "belly," "bowels," or "womb."

stop v

to stop sth/sb	parar/detener algo/ a alguien
He stopped the car.	Paró el coche.
Stop the car!	¡Para el coche!
We stopped a passer-by.	Paramos a un transeúnte.
[to come to a halt]	pararse/detenerse
The car stopped.	El coche se paró.
My watch has stopped.	Mi reloj se ha parado.
to stop doing sth	dejar de hacer algo
The lawyer stopped talking.	El abogado dejó de hablar.
Has it stopped raining?	¿Ha dejado de llover?/¿Ha cesado la lluvia?
[to prevent sb from doing sth]	impedir a alguien hacer algo
He stopped us from working.	Nos impidió trabajar.
[to forbid sb from doing sth]	prohibir a alguien hacer algo
Her mother stopped her from going to the party.	Su madre le prohibió ir a la fiesta.

store n

[a shop]	una tienda
a department store	un (gran) almacén
grocery store	una pulpería [LA]/(una tienda de) abarrotes [Mex]/una tienda de ultramarinos [Sp]/una bodega [Car]

storm n

| a storm | una tormenta/una tempestad |

Ø **un tormento** means "torture," "torment."

stove   *n*
[for heating]   una estufa
[for cooking]   un hornillo/una cocina
an electric/gas cooker   una cocina eléctrica/de gas

straight   *adj*
straight   derecho(a)/recto(a)
a straight line   una línea recta
straight hair   el pelo lacio/liso

straight   *adv*
Go straight ahead!   ¡Ve todo seguido!/¡Sigue todo
                                         derecho!/¡Sigue adelante!
The airport is straight ahead.   El aeropuerto se encuentra todo
                                         seguido.

strange   *adj*/**stranger**   *n*
strange   extraño(a)/raro(a)/curioso(a)
a stranger   un(a) desconocido(a)

Ø **extranjero(a)** means "foreign" or "foreigner."

street   *n*
main street   la calle mayor/principal
down/up the street   calle abajo/arriba

stress   *n & v*
[strain, tension]   la tensión
to be under stress   sufrir una tensión nerviosa
[to emphasize]   subrayar
He stressed its importance.   Subrayó su importancia.
to stress a syllable   acentuar una sílaba

student   *n*
[at elementary or high school]   un(a) alumno(a)
[at college or university]   un(a) estudiante

study   *v*
to study   estudiar
to study for an exam   prepararse para un examen

subject   *n*
[citizen of a country]   un(a) súbdito(a)
[grammar]   un sujeto
[theme, topic]   un tema/una materia/un asunto/una
                                         cuestión
[school/university subject]   una asignatura
on the subject of   a propósito de
to change the subject   cambiar de tema/conversación/
                                         volver la hoja

succeed   *v*
[to be successful of a person]   tener éxito
They didn't succeed.   No tuvieron éxito.
to succeed in doing sth   lograr/conseguir hacer algo
I didn't succeed in seeing her.   No logré verla.

[of plans]	salir bien
His plans succeeded.	Sus proyectos salieron bien.
[to a throne, title, etc.]	suceder
He succeeded to the throne of Spain.	Sucedió al trono de España.

success *n*/successful *adj*

success	el éxito
successful	exitoso
to be (very) successful	tener (mucho) éxito
a succesful business	una empresa próspera

Ø **éxito** does not mean "exit," which translates as **la salida**.

such *adj & adv*

with a noun	tal
such a house	tal casa
such people	tales personas

with an adjective	tan
such a pretty house	una casa tan linda
such interesting people	unas personas tan interesantes
such a long time ago	hace tanto tiempo

sue *v*

to sue sb for damages	demandar a uno por daños y perjuicios
to sue for divorce	presentar demanda de divorcio/ solicitar el divorcio

suggest *v*/suggestion *n*

to suggest	sugerir
to suggest to sb that ...	sugerir/proponer a alguien que...
I suggest you go alone.	Sugiero/Propongo que vayas solo(a). *[Note: use of subjunctive]*

[to advise]	aconsejar/indicar
What are you suggesting?	¿Qué es lo que insinúas/ pretendes?
suggestion	una sugerencia
an immoral suggestion	una idea inmoral
There is no suggestion of treason.	No hay indicio de traición/Nada indica la traición.

suit *n*

[man's]	un traje/un flux *[Ven]*
[woman's]	un conjunto
[cards]	un palo
[legal]	un pleito/un litigio/un proceso
to bring a suit against sb for sth	entablar una demanda contra alguien por algo

suit *v*

to suit *[arrangements, etc.]*	convenir/gustar
Does Friday suit you?	¿Le conviene el viernes?
to suit *[clothes, colors]*	sentar a/ir bien a
That dress suits you.	Ese vestido te sienta/va bien.
Those colors do not suit her.	Esos colores no le sientan bien.

suitable *adj*

suitable	adecuado(a)/apropiado(a)/conveniente

You must wear suitable clothes.   Debes llevar ropa apropiada.
Tomorrow is quite suitable.   Mañana me conviene muy bien.
This film is not suitable for children.   Esta película no es apta para menores.

suitcase   n
a suitcase   una maleta/una valija *[Arg]*

supply   v
to supply sth   facilitar/proporcionar
They supplied us with the   Nos facilitaron los repuestos/los
    spare parts/facts/information.   datos/la información.

support   v
physically   apoyar/sostener
Six columns support the roof.   Seis columnas sostienen el tejado./El
    tejado descansa sobre seis columnas.

financially   mantener/sustentar
He has to support two families.   Tiene que mantener dos familias.
I cannot support myself.   No puedo mantenerme.

to favor   apoyar
Which party/proposal/team do   ¿Qué partido/propuesta/equipo
    you support?   apoyas?
I support *[I'm a fan of]* the Mets.   Soy hincha de los "Mets."

suppose   v
to suppose   suponer
I suppose so/not.   Supongo que sí/no.
to be supposed to   deber
He is supposed to meet them at   Debe recibirlos en el
    the airport.   aeropuerto.
You're supposed to be in bed.   Deberías estar en la cama.
They're supposed to be in Peru.   Dicen que están en el Perú.

suspect   v
to suspect   sospechar
I suspect you of having stolen it.   Sospecho que lo has robado.
I suspected as much!   ¡Ya me lo figuraba!

suspicious   adj
causing suspicion   sospechoso(a)
Her behavior was suspicious.   Su conducta fue sospechosa.

feeling suspicion   receloso(a)
I'm suspicious about that.   Me recelo de eso./Tengo sospechas
    acerca de eso.

swear   v/swearword   n
to swear an oath   prestar juramento/jurar
to be sworn in   prestar juramento
[to curse]   jurar/blasfemar
a swearword   un taco/una palabrota

sweet   adj
[naturally sweet]   dulce
These grapes are sweet.   Estas uvas son dulces.
[sweetened]   azucarado(a)

a sweetened drink	una bebida azucarada
My coffee is too sweet.	Mi café tiene demasiado azúcar.
[good-natured]	amable/dulce
That's very sweet of you!	¡Eres muy amable!

Ø **el dulce** means "brown sugar" in Central America, Colombia, and Venezuela. Elsewhere **el azúcar negro** is used.

swim *v*
to swim	nadar
to swim across a lake/river	pasar un lago/río a nado
to swim *[as a sport]*	practicar la natación

swimming pool *n*
una alberca *[LA]*/una piscina *[Sp]*

Ø **una alberca** would mean "cistern" to a Spaniard.

to switch off *v*
[electrical apparatus, TV, radio, etc.]	apagar
to switch off the engine	apagar el motor
to switch off the light	apagar la luz

to switch on *v*
[electrical apparatus, TV, radio, etc.]	encender/conectar/poner
to switch on the engine	poner en marcha el motor
to switch on the light	encender la luz

sympathetic *adj*
[showing pity]	compasivo(a)/compadecido(a)
to be sympathetic to sb	compadecerse de alguien/estar compasivo(a) con alguien
[kind]	amable/benévolo(a)

Ø **simpático** means "nice," "good-natured."

sympathize *v*
[in someone's troubles]	compadecerse/condolerse/sentirlo por
I sympathize with the victims.	Me compadezco con las víctimas./Lo siento por las víctimas.
[on a bereavement]	dar el pésame
I sympathize with you on your son's death.	Te doy el pésame por la muerte de tu hijo.
[to understand]	comprender/entender
I sympathize with your point of view, but ...	Comprendo tu punto de vista, pero...

Ø **simpatizar** means "to get along very well with somebody."

sympathy *n*
[pity, compassion]	la compasión/la condolencia
[kindness]	la amabilidad/la benevolencia
[on a bereavement]	el pésame
to express sympathy	dar el pésame

Ø **la simpatía** means "liking," "affection."

T

table *n*

table	una mesa
table [Math]	una tabla
to set the table	poner la mesa

Ø **una tabla** also means "plank," "board."

tablet *n*
[medical]   un comprimido/una tableta

take *v*
in general   tomar/llevar
to take the bus/train, etc.   tomar el tren/el autobús, etc.

to take sb somewhere   llevar a alguien a un sitio/ acompañar
         a alguien a un sitio

A taxi took me to the station.   Un taxi me llevó a la estación.
He took us to the hospital.   Nos acompañó al hospital.

to take sth somewhere   llevar algo a un sitio
I took my suit to the dry cleaner's.   Llevé el traje a la tintorería.

to take sth from sb   quitar algo a alguien
They took his wallet from him.   Le quitaron su cartera.

other
to take a photograph	sacar una foto(grafía)
to take a walk	dar un paseo
to take a drive/ride	dar un paseo en coche
to take a trip	hacer un viaje
to take an exam	hacer un examen/presentarse a un examen
to take a seat	sentarse
to take after	parecerse a

take in *v*
to take sth in	entrar algo a un sitio
Take the cases in!	¡Entra las maletas!
to take in a garment	achicar una prenda
[a person]	hacer pasar
I took him into the kitchen.	Le hizo pasar a la cocina.

take off *v*
to take off [objects]	quitar/sacar
I took the book off the shelf.	Saqué el libro del estante.
He took off the lid.	Quitó la tapa.
to take off [clothes]	quitarse
You must take off your hat.	Debes quitarte el sombrero.
to take off [aircraft]	despegar
The plane took off for Havana.	El avión despegó para La Habana.

take out *v*
He took some money out of his
     pocket.   Sacó dinero de su bolsillo.
I took out the garbage.   Boté/Saqué la basura.

They take the children/dog out
  every day.

Llevan de paseo a los niños/al
  perro todos los días.

take place *v*
to take place
The game took place yesterday.

tener lugar
El partido tuvo lugar ayer.

take up/down *v*
to take up/down
I'll take the suitcases up/down.

subir/bajar
Voy a subir/bajar las maletas.

take time *v*
Take your time!
to take time to do sth

He'll take a long time to do that.

¡No hay prisa!/¡Hazlo con calma!
tardar en hacer algo/demorarse en
  hacer algo *[LA]*
Tardará mucho en hacer eso.

tall
tall
My brother is very tall.
He's six feet tall.
How tall are you?
How tall is the tower?

The tower is 20 meters tall.

alto(a)
Mi hermano es muy alto.
Mide seis pies.
¿Cuánto mides?
¿Cuántos metros de alto/altura tiene la
  torre?
La torre tiene 20 metros de alto/altura.

tape *n & v*
[general, sewing, sport]
Scotch tape
recording tape

cassette tape
tape measure
to tape record
tape recorder
tape recording

una cinta
la cinta adhesiva
una cinta de grabación/una cinta
  magnetofónica
una casete
una cinta métrica
grabar en cinta
un magnetofón/un magnetófono
una grabación en cinta

taste *v*
to taste
Would you like to taste the wine?
It tastes nice.
to taste of/like
It tastes of/like raspberries.

probar
¿Quieres probar el vino?
Está bueno(a)/rico(a)/sabroso(a).
saber a
Sabe a frambuesas.

taste *n*
[flavor]
a taste of honey
[style, manners]
She has good taste.
She has good taste in clothes.
in good taste

un sabor
un sabor a miel
el buen gusto
Tiene buen gusto.
Tiene gusto para vestir.
de buen gusto

teach *v*
to teach
to teach sb to do sth
He taught me to play the piano.

enseñar
enseñar a alguien a hacer algo
Me enseñó a tocar el piano.

211

teacher

I teach English.	Enseño inglés./Soy profesor(a) de inglés.

teacher *n*
*[general, high school,
   college, university]* — un(a) profesor(a)
[primary school] — un(a) maestro(a)

telephone   *[see phone]*

television   *n*

to be on television	estar en la televisión
to watch television	mirar/ver la televisión *[Note: use of definite article]*
What's on television?	¿Qué ponen en la televisión?
TV *[familiar]*	la tele
color television	la televisión en colores
TV channel	el canal de televisión
TV program	una emisión
TV remote control	el telemando
TV screen	la pantalla
TV set	un televisor/un aparato de televisión
to switch off the TV	apagar la televisión
to switch on the TV	prender *[LA]*/encender la televisión

tell   *v*

[general]	decir
to tell the truth	decir la verdad
to tell sb to do sth	decir a alguien que haga algo/ mandar a alguien hacer algo
Tell him to set the table.	Dile que ponga la mesa./Mándale poner la mesa.
to tell sb a story	contar una historia a alguien

temperature   *n*

temperature	la temperatura
The temperature yesterday was 50 degrees.	Registró ayer una temperatura de cincuenta grados.
[medical]	una fiebre/una calentura
to have/run a temperature	tener calentura
I've got a temperature of 102.	Tengo calentura de treinta y nueve grados centígrados. ·

Ø **tener calentura** means "to be in heat" in Chile, so it is advisable there to use **tener fiebre**.

tend   *v*

to tend to	tender a/inclinarse a/tener tendencia a
She tends to travel a lot.	Se inclina a viajar mucho.

test   *n*

[scientific]	una prueba/un ensayo
[school, college]	un examen/un test
a driving test	un examen de conducción
[medical]	una prueba/un análisis
a blood test	un análisis de sangre
I had a blood test.	Me hicieron un análisis de sangre.

212

an eye test	un examen para graduar la vista
[see also **exam***]*	

than *conj*

He speaks Spanish better than you.	Habla castellano mejor que tú.
They have more money than us.	Tienen más dinero que nosotros.
[see also **more***]*	

thank *v*

to thank sb for sth	agradecer algo a alguien/ dar las gracias a alguien por algo
I thanked her for the present.	Le agradecí el regalo./Le di las gracias por el regalo.
I thanked them for coming.	Les agradecí el haber venido./ Les di las gracias por haber venido.
Thanks/Thank you.	Gracias.
Thank you very much.	Muchas gracias.
Thank goodness!	¡Menos mal!

that *conj*

[introducing a clause]	que
He said (that) he would come.	Dijo que vendría.
I think (that) it's raining.	Creo que está lloviendo.
I hope you are right.	Espero que tengas razón.

Ø Although the conjunction "that" is frequently omitted in English, you may not omit **que** in Spanish.

that *dem pron & adj*

adjective

masculine	feminine
ese	esa
aquel	aquella

I like that picture.	Me gusta ese cuadro.
My wife prefers that picture (over there).	Mi esposa prefiere aquel cuadro.
He likes that house.	Le gusta esa casa.
We prefer that house (over there).	Preferimos aquella casa. *[Note:* **aquel**/**aquella** *refer to things that are further away.]*

pronoun

masculine	feminine	neuter
ése	ésa	eso
aquél	aquélla	aquello

Which car do you like most? That one or that one (over there)?	¿Qué coche le gusta más? ¿Ése o aquél?
Which shirt do you prefer? That one or that one (over there)?	¿Qué camisa prefieres? Ésa o aquélla? *[Note: There is an accent on the pronouns.]*
I don't understand that.	No entiendo eso. *[Note: The neuter forms* **eso** *and* **aquello** *refer not to concrete objects or people but to whole concepts or ideas.]*

Ø **aquél/aquélla** are used to translate "the former," as in **Aquél fue a España, éste fue a México.** "The former went to Spain, the latter went to Mexico."

213

that

that   *rel pron*

| | que *[subject and object]* |
| | lo que *[neuter]* |

the box that is on the table	la caja que está en la mesa
the film (that) I saw	la película que vi
all (that) I want	todo lo que quiero
[with prepositions]	que/el cual/la cual/los cuales/las
	cuales/el que/la que/los que/las que

It's the garden (that) there	Es el jardín en el cual/en el que
is a palm tree in.	hay una palmera.
That's the table (that) I put	Ésa es la mesa sobre la cual/la
the money on.	que puse el dinero.
Are they the binoculars (that)	¿Son los anteojos por los cuales/
he was looking through?	los que miraba?
I'm talking about the houses	Hablo de las casas detrás de las
(that) there was a lake behind.	cuales/las que había un lago.

Ø Although the pronoun "that" is frequently omitted in English, you may not omit **que, el cual, la cual, los cuales, las cuales, el que, la que, los que, las que** in Spanish.

the   *art*

| | el *[masc sing]* | la *[fem sing]* |
| | los *[masc pl]* | las *[fem pl]* |

He gave a tip to the waiter.	Dio una propina al mesero. *[Note:*
	a + el = al]
the months of the year	los meses del año *[Note: de + el = del]*

the one/the ones/those   *dem pron*

| | el que/la que/los que/las que |

Which book? – The one (that is)	¿Qué libro – El que está en el
on the shelf.	estante.
Which tie? – The one (that) I	¿Qué corbata? – La que compré
bought yesterday.	ayer.
Which horses? – The ones (that	¿Qué caballos? – Los que están
are) in the corral.	en el corral.
Which rings? – The ones (that)	¿Qué sortijas? – Las que nos
she showed us.	mostró.
It's the one I was talking about.	Es el/la de que hablaba.

their   *adj*

[singular: masc & fem]	su
[plural: masc & fem]	sus
Have you seen their house?	¿Has visto su casa?
They invited their relatives	Invitaron a sus parientes y a sus
and friends.	amigos. *[Note: adjective repeated.]*

Ø As **su** can also mean "his," "her," "its," and "your," you can add **de ellos/de ellas** after the noun if the meaning is not entirely clear, e.g., **su casa de ellos/ellas** "their house."

theirs   *pron*

[singular]	el suyo/la suya
[plural]	los suyos/las suyas
Is this your car? – No, it's theirs.	¿Es éste su coche? – No, es suyo. *[Note: The*
	*definite article is omitted after the verb **ser**.]*
I don't like your house. I	No me gusta tu casa. Prefiero
prefer theirs.	la suya.

214

Ø As **suyo/a/os/as** could also mean "his," "hers," or "yours," you can replace them with **de ellos/de ellas** if there is any chance of confusion, e.g., "It's theirs". **Es de ellos/de ellas**.

them *pron*

[direct object: masculine]	los/les [Note: **Los** is far more common than **les** in Latin America; **les** is frequently used in Spain.]
[direct object: feminine]	las
[indirect object] to them	les
[disjunctive]	ellos/ellas/sí
Do you know them?	¿Los/Les/Las conoces?
Did you lend them the car?	¿Les prestaste el coche?
Yes, I lent it to them.	Sí, se lo presté. [Note: When **les** is followed by **lo, la, los** or **las** it changes to **se**.]
	Sí, se lo presté a ellos/ellas. [Note: As **se** has so many possible meanings you can add **a ellos/a ellas** after the verb to stress that here it means "to them."]
Do you remember them?	¿Te acuerdas de ellos/ellas?
They looked around them.	Miraron alrededor de sí. [Note: **Sí** is used instead of **ellos** or **ellas** as it refers to the same person as the subject of the verb.]
They took the money with them.	Llevaron el dinero consigo. [Note: the special form of **sí** used after **con**.]

themselves *[see self]*

then *adv*
at that time

	entonces/por entonces/en ese momento/en aquella época
until then	hasta entonces
since then	desde entonces
I didn't go to bed then.	No me acosté entonces.
He was working in Lima then.	En aquella época trabajaba en Lima.
Then it began to rain.	En ese momento comenzó a llover.

next, afterwards

	luego/después
Then he had lunch and then he went back to the office.	Luego comió y después volvió a la oficina.

then *conj*

Well then, let's go.	Pues bien, vamos.
Well in that case, I'll stay.	Pues, en ese caso, quedaré.
What do you want then?	Pues, ¿qué quieres?/¿Qué quieres entonces?

there *adv*

there	allí/allá/ahí
There it is.	Allí está.
They're going there tomorrow.	Van allí mañana.
It's down/over there.	Está allá.
It's there, in front of you.	Está ahí, delante de ti.
right there	allí mismo
there is/are	hay
There is nobody on the beach.	No hay nadie en la playa.
There are no tomatoes.	No hay jitomates.

these

| there was/were | había |
| there will be | habrá |

these *dem pron & adj*
adjective

	masculine	feminine
	estos	estas

| I like these hats. | Me gustan estos sombreros. |
| He's going to buy these ties. | Va a comprar estas corbatas. |

pronoun

	masculine	feminine
	éstos	éstas

Which shoes do you like most? — ¿Qué zapatos te gustan más? –
  – I like these (ones).   Me gustan éstos.
Which boots do you prefer? ¿Qué botas prefieres? – Prefiero
  – I prefer these (ones)   éstas. *[Note: There is an accent on*
    ***éstos/éstas** when they are pronouns.]*

Ø **éstos/éstas** are used to translate "the latter," as in **Aquéllos fueron a España,
éstos fueron a México.** "The former went to Spain, the latter went to Mexico."

they *pron*

they	ellos/ellas
They are strangers.	Son forasteros.
They cannot come, but their	Ellos no pueden venir, pero sus
friends can.	amigos sí. *[Note: **Ellos/Ellas** like all the other subject pronouns, are usually omitted; they are used for emphasis and clarification.]*

Ø **Ellos/Ellas** can also mean "them" following a preposition, e.g., "It's for them" is
translated by **Es para ellos/ellas.**

thin *adj*

| thin | flaco(a) *[LA]*/delgado(a) |
| to get thin | adelgazar |

thing *n*
general

| What a strange thing! | una cosa |
| | ¡Qué cosa tan rara! |

object

a thing of value	una cosa/un objeto/un artículo
[belongings, possessions]	un objeto de valor
They have some lovely things.	las cosas
	Tienen unas cosas bellas.
Where shall I put my things?	¿Dónde pongo mis cosas?

matter, circumstance

It's quite an important thing.	una cosa/un asunto/lo + adjective
the main/most important thing	Es un asunto bastante importante.
the best/worst thing	lo más importante/lo esencial
How are things?	lo mejor/peor
	¿Qué tal?

think *v*
general

| He thinks a lot. | pensar |
| | Piensa mucho. |

to think of doing sth

| I'm thinking of going to Spain. | pensar hacer algo |
| | Pienso ir a España. |

to think about sth/sb

pensar en algo/alguien

What are you thinking about?	¿En qué piensas?
I'm thinking about the vacation.	Pienso en las vacaciones.
She's thinking about her son.	Piensa en su hijo.
to have an opinion about	pensar de/parecer
What did you think of the film?	¿Qué pensaste de la película?/
	¿Qué te pareció la película?
I thought it was very good.	Pensé que fue muy buena./Me
	pareció muy buena.
to believe	creer
Do you think he'll come?	¿Crees que vendrá?
I think so./I don't think so.	Creo que sí./Creo que no.

third *adj*

the third turning on the right	la tercera bocacalle a la derecha
the third world	el tercer mundo *[Note: **Tercero***
	*becomes **tercer** before a noun.]*
a third	una tercera parte/un tercio
He only won a third of the votes.	Sólo ganó un tercio de los votos.
third party insurance	el seguro contra tercera persona

thirst *n* /**thirsty** *adj*

thirst	la sed
to be very thirsty	tener mucha sed
to get thirsty	empezar a tener sed

this *dem pron & adj*
adjective

	masculine	feminine
	este	esta
I like this book.	Me gusta este libro.	
He's going to buy this house.	Va a comprar esta casa.	

pronoun

	masculine	feminine	neuter
	éste	ésta	eso
Which car do you like most?	¿Qué coche te gusta más? – Me		
– I like this one.	gusta éste.		
Which skirt do you prefer?	¿Qué falda prefieres? – Prefiero ésta.		
– I prefer this one.	*[Note: There is an accent on **éste**/*		
	***ésta** when they are pronouns.]*		
I don't understand this.	No entiendo esto. *[Note: The neuter*		
	*form **esto** refers not to concrete objects or*		
	people but to whole concepts or ideas.]		

Ø **éste/ésta** are used to translate "the latter," as in **Aquél fue a España, éste fue a México.** "The former went to Spain, the latter went to Mexico."

those *dem pron & adj*
adjective

	masculine	feminine
	esos	esas
	aquellos	aquellas
I like those gloves.	Me gustan esos guantes.	
My wife prefers those gloves	Mi esposa prefiere aquellos	
(over there).	guantes.	
He likes those flowers.	Le gustan esas flores.	
We prefer those flowers (over	Preferimos aquellas flores.	
there).	*[Note: **aquellos/aquellas** refer*	
	to things that are further away.]	

pronoun

masculine	feminine
ésos	ésas
aquéllos	aquéllas

Which lemons do you want?
Those (ones) or those over there?

¿Qué limones quieres? ¿Ésos o aquéllos?

Which oranges are you buying?
Those (ones) or those over there?

¿Qué naranjas compras? ¿Ésas o aquéllas? *[Note: There is an accent on the pronouns.]*

Ø **aquéllos/aquéllas** are used to translate "the former," as in **Aquéllos fueron a España, éstos fueron a México.** "The former went to Spain, the latter went to Mexico."

thousand   *n*
a/one thousand dollars
ten thousand pesos

mil dólares *[Note: no article]*
diez mil pesos

thousands   *n*
There are thousands of them.

Hay miles de ellos.

through   *prep*
place
They ran through the fields.
I got in through the front door.

por/a través de/de un lado a otro de
Corrieron por los campos.
Entré por la puerta principal.

time
(from) Monday through Friday
all through January
all through the night

hasta/durante
desde el lunes hasta el viernes
durante enero
durante la noche entera *[Note: **por la noche** means "in the night".]*

means
Through not knowing the rules, he lost the game.
She got the job through her sister.
Through her I learned that you were getting married.

por/por medio de/debido a/gracias a
Por no saber las reglas, perdió el partido.
Consiguió el puesto debido a/ gracias a su hermana.
Por ella supe que iban a casarse.

other
I'm through. *[finished]*
She's through with him.

He terminado.
Ha roto con él.

throughout   *prep*
place
throughout the State
throughout Venezuela

por todo/por todas partes de
por todo el Estado
por todas partes de Venezuela

time
throughout the year
throughout my life

durante todo/en todo
durante todo el año
durante/en toda mi vida

ticket   *n*
[travel]
[theater, movies, show, game]
[plane/boat]
a one-way ticket
a round-trip ticket

un boleto *[LA]*/un billete *[Sp]*
una entrada/una localidad
un pasaje *[LA]*/un billete *[Sp]*
un boleto/billete de ida
un boleto de ida y regreso/un billete de ida y vuelta

season ticket *[rail]*	un boleto de abono
season ticket *[theater, sport]*	un abono de temporada
ticket office/window *[rail]*	una boletería *[LA]*/una taquilla
	[Sp]/un despacho de billetes
complimentary ticket	una entrada de favor
parking ticket	una multa (por aparcamiento indebido)

tidy *adj*

The house is not very tidy.	La casa no está muy ordenada.
He's a very tidy person.	Es una persona muy ordenada.
She has very tidy hair.	Tiene el pelo bien arreglado.
[clean]	limpio(a)

tidy *v*

to tidy sth	arreglar/poner en orden/limpiar algo
to tidy one's hair	arreglarse el pelo
to tidy away one's things	poner sus cosas en su sitio/
	devolver sus cosas a su lugar
to tidy up	arreglar las cosas/ponerlo todo en orden

till *[see until]*

time *n*

in general

	el tiempo
to find/have time for	tener tiempo para
to have plenty of time	tener tiempo de sobra
Time flies.	El tiempo vuela.
on time	a/con tiempo
full-time	de plena dedicación/de jornada completa
part-time	de media jornada/de dedicación parcial
to have a good time	pasarlo bien/divertirse
Have a good time!	¡Que lo pases bien!

by the clock

	la hora
What time is it?/What's the time?	¿Qué hora es?
It's time to leave.	Ya es hora de salir.
at this time of day	a esta hora

occasion

	la vez
this time	esta vez
the first/last/next time	la primera/última/próxima vez
for the first/last time	por primera/última vez
at times	a veces
each/every time	cada vez
many times	muchas veces
several times	varias/algunas veces
sometimes	unas veces
from time to time	de vez en cuando

historical period

	la época/los tiempos
at the time of the Incas	en la época/en los tiempos de los incas
At that time we lived in Italy.	En esta época vivimos en Italia.

period of time

	el período/el plazo/el tiempo/el rato
a long time	mucho tiempo
a long time ago	hace mucho tiempo
a short time	poco tiempo/un rato
a short time ago	hace poco

in a short time	en breve
spare time	ratos libres/horas libres
extra time *[sport]*	la prórroga
point of time	un momento
at the present time	en este momento/en la actualidad/ actualmente
any time	en cualquier momento
at the/that time	por entonces/en aquel entonces
at the same time	al mismo tiempo/a la vez
season	la estación
at this time of the year	en esta estación del año

tin *n*

[metal]	el estaño
It's made of tin.	Es de estaño.
tinplate	la hojalata

tip *n*

[a gratuity]	una propina
[advice]	un consejo/un aviso
[horse racing]	una información/un pronóstico

tire *n*

a tire	una llanta *[LA]*/un caucho *[Ven]*/una goma *[Arg & Uru]*/un neumático *[Sp]*/una cubierta *[Sp]*

tired *adj*

to be tired	estar cansado(a)
to tire/get tired	cansarse
to be tired of *[fed up]*	estar harto(a) de
I'm tired of watching TV.	Estoy harto(a) de mirar la televisión.

to *prep*
direction, destination

	a
He went to Africa/Spain/Lima.	Fue a Africa/España/Lima.
She went to the market/the hairdresser's.	Fue al mercado/a la peluquería.
	[Note: a + el = al]
They went to Marta's.	Fueron a casa de Marta.
the road to Guadalajara	la carretera de Guadalajara
the train to Mérida	el tren de Mérida/con destino Mérida

in order to

	para
I need some money to pay her.	Necesito dinero para pagarle.

with an infinitive

To see is to believe.	Ver es creer.
I want to buy a car.	Quiero comprar un coche.
They went to see her.	Fueron a verla.
He forgot to pay the bill.	Se olvidó de pagar la cuenta.

other

to be kind to sb	ser amable con alguien
How kind of them to take it!	¡Qué amables han sido en llevarlo!

today *adv*

today	hoy
[at the present time]	hoy día/hoy en día

a week/fortnight today	de hoy en ocho/quince días

together *adv*

They worked together.	Trabajaban juntos.
All together now!	¡Todos juntos!/¡Todos a la vez!
We were all together in the bar.	Estábamos todos reunidos en el bar.
a get-together	una reunión/una fiesta

toilet *n*

[at home]	el baño/el excusado/el retrete
[public]	los servicios/los baños

tomato *n*

tomato	un jitomate [Mex]/un tomate

too *adv*

also, in addition   también

You too? – Yes, me too.	¿Tú también? – Sí, yo también. *[Note: The subject pronouns are used.]*

too, too much   demasiado

This coffee is too cold.	Este café está demasiado frío.
You drink too much.	Bebes demasiado.

top *n*

[of list, table, page]	la cabeza
[of tree]	la copa
[surface]	la superficie
[of bottle]	el tapón/la tapa
at the top of page eight	a la cabeza de la página ocho
at the top of the hill	en la cumbre/cima de la colina
at the top of the stairs/tree	en lo alto de la escalera/del árbol
from top to bottom	de arriba abajo
at top speed	a toda velocidad

topic *n*/**topical** *adj*

topic of conversation	un asunto
essay topic	el tema
a topical issue	un asunto actual/corriente/de interés actual

tour *n & v*

[of country, region]	un viaje/un viaje de turismo/una excursión
[of building, exhibition]	una visita
conducted tour	una excursión con guía/una visita en grupo
package tour	un viaje con todo incluido
[by actors, musicians, sports teams]	una gira
to tour/make a tour of	viajar por/recorrer/visitar
They are touring Costa Rica.	Viajan por/Recorren Costa Rica.
We toured the factory/palace.	Visitamos la fábrica/el palacio.
The team is on a tour of Mexico.	El equipo está de gira en México.
My friends are on tour.	Mis amigos están de viaje.
We're touring.	Hacemos viajes de turismo.
The Tour of France [cycling]	La Vuelta a Francia
a tour of duty	un turno de servicio

221

toward(s) *prep*
place, time
towards Toledo
towards three o'clock

hacia
hacia Toledo
hacia las tres

feelings
My feelings towards her have
  changed.

con/para con
Mis sentimientos para con ella
  han cambiado.

town *n*
[large town, city]
[small, country town]
to go to town
I live in town.
She's out of town.
Let's go downtown.

una ciudad
un pueblo/una población
ir a la ciudad
Vivo en la ciudad.
Está fuera/de viaje.
Vamos al centro.

trade *n*
[calling, occupation]
He's a plumber by trade.
[business]
[industry]
foreign trade
[craft]

el oficio
Es de oficio plomero/fontanero.
el negocio
la industria
el comercio exterior
la artesanía

traffic *n*
[transportation]
The traffic is heavy/light.
rush-hour traffic
two-way traffic
one-way traffic

traffic circle
traffic jam
traffic lights
traffic sign
[drugs]
drug traffic

el tráfico/la circulación/el tránsito *[LA]*
Hay muchos/pocos coches.
la circulación de la hora punta
la doble circulación
la dirección única/el sentido único/una
  mano *[Arg]*/el tránsito *[Chi]*/una vía *[Col]*
una glorieta/un cruce giratorio/un redondel
un embotellamiento/un atasco
las luces de tráfico/el semáforo
una señal de tráfico
el tráfico
el tráfico de narcóticos

train *v intrans*
to train for *[sport]*
I'm training for the Olympics.
to train for a profession

entrenarse para
Me entreno para los Juegos Olímpicos.
seguir un curso de formación
  profesional/cursar sus estudios

train *v trans*
to train an athlete
to train an animal
to train sb for a job/
  profession

entrenar a un(a) atleta
amaestrar un animal
preparar a alguien para un puesto
  /una profesión

training *n*
[sports]
physical training
to be in training
[professional]

el entrenamiento/la preparación
la gimnasia/la cultura física
estar entrenado(a)/en forma
la formación

transfer v
[to a new position/place]
The company transferred to Bogotá.
I was transferred to Quito.
[to a new course]
[transportation]
The passengers must transfer
  in Córdoba.
Martín has been transferred to
  Real Madrid.

trasladarse
La empresa se trasladó a Bogotá.
Me trasladaron a Quito.
cambiar a otra asignatura
transbordar/hacer transbordo
Los pasajeros deben transbordar/
  hacer transbordo en Córdoba.
Martín se ha traspasado al Real
  Madrid.

Ø **trasladarse** is used in many parts of Latin America to mean "to move house."

translate v
to translate from Spanish to
  English
Translate into German.

traducir del castellano al inglés

Traduce al alemán.

transportation n
[in general]
public transportation
means of transportation

el transporte
los transportes colectivos/públicos
el medio de transporte

Ø **la transportación** exists but is not used a great deal.

trash *[see garbage]*

tray n
a tray

un charol *[Mex]*/una bandeja *[Sp]*

treat n & v
to pay for sb
He's treating us to dinner.
It's my treat.

convidar/invitar
Nos ha convidado a cenar.
Invito yo.

medical
to treat patients
He is being treated for 'flu.

atender/tratar a enfermos(as)
Le tratan para la gripe.

personal relations
They treated me very well.

tratar a alguien
Me trataron muy bien.

Ø **tratar de** means "to try to."

trip n
a business trip
to take a trip
[see also tour]

un viaje de negocios
hacer un viaje

trouble n
difficulty, problem
What's the trouble?
to get into trouble
to be in trouble with the police.
The plane has engine trouble.

la dificultad/el inconveniente
¿Qué pasa?/¿Pasa algo?
meterse en un lío
tener dificultades con la policía.
El avión tiene una avería del motor.

bother
It's no trouble.
It's not worth the trouble.

la molestia/la dificultad/el esfuerzo
No es molestia./No cuesta nada.
No vale la pena.

to take the trouble to do sth	tomarse/darse la molestia de hacer algo

medical

to have heart trouble	tener una enfermedad cardíaca

trouble *v*

I'm sorry to have to trouble you.	Lamento tener que molestarte.
Please don't trouble yourself!	¡No te molestes!/¡No se moleste!
	¡No te preocupes!/¡No se preocupe!

trunk *n*

[case]	un baúl [Col]/una cajuela [Mex]/ una maletera [Per]/ una maleta
[of car]	un portaequipaje(s)/un maletero
[of tree]	un tronco
[of elephant]	una trompa

try *v*

[make an effort]	esforzarse/hacer un esfuerzo
She tried very hard.	Hizo grandes esfuerzos.
[to attempt]	tratar/intentar
to try to do sth	tratar de/intentar/probar hacer algo
He'll try to help us.	Tratará de/Intentará ayudarnos.
[to taste]	probar
Would you like to try the wine?	¿Quiere usted probar el vino?
to try on [clothes]	probarse
I would like to try on the jacket.	Quisiera probarme la chaqueta.

tuition *n*

tuition fees	la matrícula

turn *n*

a turn to the left/right	una vuelta a la izquierda/derecha
Turn to the left.	Da una vuelta a la izquierda.
No right turn!	¡Prohibido girar a la derecha!
Whose turn is it?	¿A quién le toca?
It's my turn.	Me toca a mí.
by/in turns	por turnos/sucesivamente

Ø **el turno** means "turn of duty," "shift," e.g., **el turno de noche** means "the night shift."

turn on/off *v*

to turn on [electrical apparatus, TV, radio, etc.]	encender/conectar/poner
to turn on the engine	arrancar el motor/poner en marcha el motor
to turn on the light	encender la luz

turn round *v*

[car]	dar la vuelta (a un coche)
You must turn (the car) round here.	Tienes que dar la vuelta (al coche) aquí.
[person]	darse vuelta [LA]/voltearse [LA]/ volverse [Sp]
I turned round to see what was happening.	Me di la vuelta para ver lo que pasaba.

turnpike *n*

turnpike	una autopista de peaje

twenty one   *adj*

twenty one

He's twenty one.

How many girls are there? –
  Twenty one.

veintiun(o)/veintiuna

Tiene veintiún años. *[Note:*
  Veintiuno *becomes* **veintiún,** *with an*
  accent added on the **u,** *before a masculine*
  noun.]
¿Cuántas chicas hay? – Veintiuna.

twice   *adv*

twice

twice a day/week/month/year

dos veces

dos veces el día/la semana/el mes
  /el año

type   *n*

[kind]

people of that type

[character]

What a strange type he is!

[in printing]

bold/italic type

un tipo

gente de ese tipo

un tipo/un sujeto/un tío

¡Qué tío tan raro es!

un tipo/una letra/un carácter

las letras negritas/cursivas

type   *v*

to type

typing

typist

escribir a máquina/mecanografiar

la mecanografía

un(a) mecanógrafo(a)

typo   *n*

[printing error]

[spelling error]

[typing error]

una errata/un error de imprenta/
  un gazapo *[fam]*
un error de ortografía
un error de mecanografía

U

U-boat *n*
a U-boat

un submarino alemán

ugly *adj*
[physical]
[figurative]
[dangerous]
an ugly situation
[unpleasant]
an ugly guy
to be in an ugly mood

feo(a)
peligroso(a)/feo(a)
peligroso(a)
una situación peligrosa
lamentable
un tipo de cuidado
estar de un humor de perros

un-
[negative prefix]

*[There are several different equivalents
   in Spanish for the prefix **un-**.]*

unable
unoccupied
unnatural
unkind
unambitious
unaccompanied
un-American

incapaz
desocupado(a)
no natural
nada amistoso(a)
poco ambicioso(a)
sin compañía
antiamericano(a)

uncomfortable *adj*
[physical discomfort]
These clothes are
   uncomfortable.
I was very uncomfortable in
   that bed.
[ill at ease]
He looked very uncomfortable
   during the interview.
They made life uncomfortable
   for her.

incómodo(a)
Esta ropa es incómoda.

Me encontré muy incómodo(a) en
   esa cama.
inquieto(a)/molesto(a)
Pareció muy inquieto durante la
   entrevista.
Le crearon dificultades a ella.

under *prep*
[stationary]
He was sitting under the tree.
[involving motion]
We went under a bridge.
[under the rule of]
under the Aztecs
[less than]
the numbers under thirty
I finished it in under two
   hours
[according to]
under Article 5 of the
   Constitution
under my contract

bajo/debajo de
Estaba sentado debajo del árbol.
por debajo de
Pasamos por debajo de un puente.
bajo
bajo los aztecas
menos de/inferior a
los números menos de/inferior a treinta
Tardé menos de dos horas en
   acabarlo.
conforme a/según
conforme al Artículo 5 de la
   Constitución
según mi contrato

underneath *adv*

underneath

It's underneath.

They went underneath.

debajo

Está debajo.

Fueron por debajo.

unfortunate *adj*

person

They are most unfortunate.

How unfortunate you were!

desgraciado(a)/desdichado(a)

Son muy desgraciados(as).

¡Qué mala suerte tuviste!

event

an unfortunate event

funesto(a)/desgraciado(a)

un suceso desgraciado

regrettable

It's unfortunate that he
  cannot pay them.

Es de lamentar que no pueda
  pagarles. *[Note: subjunctive]*

comment, manner

I made an unfortunate remark.

infeliz/inoportuno(a)

Hice una observación inoportuna.

unfortunately *adv*

unfortunately

por desgracia

unless *conj*

unless

a menos que *[+ subjunctive]*

si no *[+ indicative]*

We will play tennis tonight
  unless it rains.

Unless you tell him, he won't
  know anything.

Jugaremos al tenis esta noche a
  menos que llueva.

Si no se lo dices, no sabrá nada.

unlike *prep*

unlike

Unlike the others she's going
  to the theater.

a diferencia de

A diferencia de los otros ella
  va al teatro.

until *conj*

until

hasta que *[+ subjunctive with future
  time; + indicative with past time]*

hasta *[+ infinitive]*

I'll wait until she arrives.

I waited until she arrived.

I walked for ten miles until I
  reached the river.

Esperaré hasta que llegue.

Esperé hasta que llegó.

Caminé diez millas hasta llegar
  al río. *[Note: **Hasta** and the infinitive are
  used because the subject of both clauses is
  the same.]*

until *prep*

until

She waited until five o'clock.

hasta

Esperó hasta las cinco.

up *adv & prep*

up

What was he doing up there?

His house is further up the street.

arriba/por arriba

¿Qué estaba haciendo allá arriba?

Su casa está más allá en la calle.

verb + **up**

to be up

to come/go up

estar levantado(a)

subir

upset

to get up [from bed, a seat]	levantarse (de)/pararse [LA]
to get up [to stand]	ponerse de pie
to lift sb/sth up	levantar a alguien/algo
I went up the street.	Subí la calle.
He ran up the street.	Corrió calle arriba.
She ran up the stairs.	Subió las escaleras corriendo.
to run up bills	contraer deudas
to take/bring sth up	subir
Bring the suitcases up, please.	Haga el favor de subir las maletas.
It's up to you.	Te toca a ti.

upset adj
[physically]	trastornado(a)
She has an upset stomach.	Tiene el estómago trastornado.
He's feeling a little upset.	Siente indispuesto.
[mentally]	trastornado(a)/apurado(a)
Her mother was very upset.	Su madre estaba muy apurada.
He is easily upset.	Se apura por cualquier cosa.
[angry at]	enfadado(a)/disgustado(a) por
I was upset at his behavior.	Estaba enfadado(a) por su conducta.

upstairs adv
to go upstairs	ir arriba/subir la escalera
We sleep upstairs.	Dormimos en el piso superior.
the apartment upstairs	el apartamento de arriba

us pron
[direct object]	nos
[indirect object] to us	nos
[disjunctive, object of prepositions]	nosotros/nosotras
He saw us on the beach.	Nos vio en la playa.
They gave the clothes to us.	Nos dieron la ropa.
Give it to us!	¡Dánoslo!
Don't give them to us!	¡No nos los des!
These are for us.	Éstos son para nosotros/nosotras.

U.S. [United States] n
| the United States (US) | (los) Estados Unidos ([los] EE. UU.) |

use n
directions for use	el modo de empleo
to make use of sth	servirse de/utilizar algo
What use is that machine?	¿De qué sirve ese aparato?
Is that any use?	¿Sirve para algo?
It's no use.	No sirve para nada./Es inútil.
What's the use?	¿Para qué?
What's the use of doing that?	¿De qué sirve hacer eso?
Can I be of use?	¿Puedo ayudar?/¿Puedo servirle en algo?

use v
to use	usar/emplear/servirse de/utilizar
I used a knife to open it.	Empleé un cuchillo para abrirlo.
What word do you use in Greek?	¿Qué palabra usas en griego?
What's it used for?	¿Para qué sirve?
It's used for building.	Sirve para construir.

I could use a drink!	¡Qué sed tengo!/¡Me gustaría tomar algo!
I could use a holiday!	¡Qué bien me vendrían unas vacaciones!
A handkerchief was used as a bandage.	Se utilizó un pañuelo como venda. /Un pañuelo sirvió de venda.

used *v*

[to express regular actions in the past]	*[Use either the imperfect tense or the imperfect of the verb **soler** followed by the infinitive.]*
When I lived in Madrid I used to spend Sundays in the country.	Cuando vivía en Madrid, pasaba/ solía pasar los domingos en el campo.
They never used to arrive before ten.	Nunca llegaban/solían llegar antes de las diez.

used *adj*

accustomed to — acostumbrado(a) a

She's still not used to this climate.	Todavía no está acostumbrado(a) a este clima.
to get used to sth	acostumbrarse a algo
You must get used to his way of doing it.	Debes acostumbrarte a su modo de hacerlo.

second-hand — de segunda mano/de ocasión/ usado(a)

He sells used cars.	Vende coches de segunda mano.

Ø **usado(a)** often means "worn" or "worn out."

used up — agotado(a)

Their provisions are used up.	Sus provisiones están agotadas.

usual *adj*

usual	acostumbrado(a)/habitual
He went out at the usual time.	Salió a la hora acostumbrada.
as usual	como siempre/como de costumbre
What will you have? The usual? *[a drink, food]*	¿Qué vas a tomar? ¿Lo de siempre?

usually *adv*

usually	por lo general
He usually has a beer.	Por lo general toma una cerveza./ Suele tomar una cerveza. *[Note: the verb **soler** can also be used.]*

utility *n*

a public utility	una empresa de servicio público

V

vacancy *n*
[in hotel]
Do you have any vacancies?

"No vacancies"
We have no vacancies for May.

[see also **openings.***]*

un cuarto/una habitación vacante
¿Hay algún cuarto vacante?/¿Tiene algo disponible?
"Completo"
Para mayo no hay nada disponible. /En mayo todo está lleno.

vacation *n*
vacation
to be on vacation
to take a vacation
to spend the summer vacation

las vacaciones *[Note: usually plural]*
estar de vacaciones/pasar las vacaciones
tomarse unas vacaciones
veranear

vain *adj*
[useless, fruitless]
in vain
My efforts were in vain.
[conceited]
Her sister is so vain.

vano(a)/inútil
en vano
Mis esfuerzos resultaron inútiles.
vanidoso(a)/presumido(a)
Su hermana es tan vanidosa.

valid *adj*
valid
It is a valid argument.
I have a valid ticket.
Your ticket is no longer valid.
[of laws]
That law is still valid.

válido(a)/valedero(a)
Es un argumento válido.
Tengo un boleto valedero.
Tu boleto ha caducado ya/ya no vale.
vigente
Esa ley es todavía vigente.

valuable *adj*
Is it valuable?
valuables

¿Vale mucho?/¿Tiene valor?
los objetos de valor

various *adj*
[different]
for various reasons
in various ways
[several]
Various prisoners have escaped.

diferentes/distintos(as)/diversos(as)
por diversas razones
de diversos modos
algunos(as)/varios(as)
Varios presos se han escapado.

verge *n & v*
[border, edge]
on the verge of
to be on the verge of doing sth
She was on the verge of tears.
to verge
He is verging to the left.

el borde/el margen
al borde de
estar a punto de hacer algo
Estaba a punto de echarse a llorar.
orientarse/inclinarse
Se orienta/inclina a la izquierda.

verse *n*
[poetry]

las poesías/los versos

He writes verse.	Escribe versos.
a verse of a poem	una estrofa
a line of verse	un verso

very *adv*
[with an adjective]	muy
very pleasant	muy agradable
[with a noun]	mucho(a)
It's very hot.	Hace mucho calor.
very much	muchísimo(a)
very many	muchísimos(as) *[Note: Do not use **muy** with **mucho**.]*

vessel *n*
[ship]	una nave
[receptacle]	una vasija/un recipiente
blood vessel	un vaso sanguíneo

vested *adj*
vested	concedido(a)
a vested interest	un derecho adquirido/un interés personal
to have vested interests in a company	tener intereses en una empresa

video *n & v*
a video camera	una videocámara
a videocassette	un casete de vídeo/un videocasete
a videorecorder (VCR)	un vídeo/una videograbadora
a videorecording *[act]*	una videograbación
a videorecording *[object]*	un videograma
a videotape	una cinta de vídeo/una videocinta

visitor *n*
a visitor	un(a) visitante/una visita
[tourist, excursionist]	un(a) turista/un(a) excursionista
*[see also **guest**]*	

vivid *adj*
[color, light]	intenso(a)
[imagination, impression, memory]	vivo(a)
[description]	gráfico(a)/enérgico(a)/pintoresco(a)

vulgar *adj*
[common]	común/corriente
[lacking refinement]	vulgar/ordinario(a)
[rude]	grosero(a)
a vulgar joke	un chiste verde
Don't be vulgar!	¡No seas grosero(a)!

W

wage *n*
[of worker]   el salario
[of employee]   el sueldo
wage earner   un asalariado

wage *v*
to wage a campaign   emprender/proseguir una campaña
to wage war   hacer guerra

wait *v*
to wait   esperar/aguardar
Wait a moment!   ¡Espera un momento!
to wait for   esperar *[Note: no preposition to translate "for"]*

I am waiting for the bus.   Estoy esperando el autobús.
I've been waiting for my wife Hace diez minutos que espero a
  for ten minutes.   mi esposa.
We'll wait until she returns. Esperaremos hasta que vuelva.
                    [Note: subjunctive]

to wait up   velar/no acostarse
to wait at table   servir a la mesa
to wait on sb   servir a alguien

waiter/waitress *n*
a waiter   un garzón *[Arg & Uru]*/un mesero *[Col & Mex]*/un mesonero *[Ven]*/un mozo *[Bol & Per]*/un camarero*[Sp]*

a waitress   una garzona *[Arg & Uru]*/una mesera *[Col & Mex]*/una mesonera *[Ven]*/una moza *[Bol & Per]*/una camarera *[Sp]*

walk *n & v*
in general   caminar/andar
I was walking by the river. Caminaba a orillas del río.
She walks very slowly.   Camina muy despacio.
Can your child walk?   ¿Sabe andar tu niño?
He has had an accident and Ha sufrido un accidente y ya no
  cannot walk yet.   puede andar.

to go for a walk   ir de paseo/dar un paseo
I went for a walk through the park. Fui de paseo por el parque.
Do you want to take a walk? ¿Quieres dar un paseo/una vuelta?

as opposed to driving or riding ir a pie/andar
I prefer to walk to the office. Prefiero ir a pie a la oficina.
Let's walk.   Vamos a pie.

wall *n*
[exterior wall]   un muro
the walls of the house   los muros de la casa
[inside wall]   una pared

There are pictures on the wall.	Hay cuadros en la pared.
[garden wall]	una tapia
[city wall]	una muralla
the old walls of Valencia	las antiguas murallas de Valencia

want *v*

to want	querer/desear
I want two seats.	Quiero dos plazas.
He wants to go to Madrid.	Quiere ir a Madrid.
He wants us to go to Madrid.	Quiere que vayamos a Madrid.
	[Note: use of subjunctive]

Ø **querer** also means "to love," e.g., **Quiere a su esposa.** "He loves his wife."

warm *adj*
liquids, things

	caliente
The water is quite warm.	El agua está bastante caliente.
They need warm clothes.	Necesitan ropa caliente.
[lukewarm]	tibio(a)

climate

	cálido(a)
a warm climate	un clima cálido
[season, day]	caluroso(a)/de calor
a warm day/summer	un día/verano caluroso

of people

to be warm	tener calor
I'm very warm.	Tengo mucho calor.
to give sb a warm welcome	dispensar a alguien un recibimiento/ una bienvenida caluroso(a)
warm-hearted	afectuoso(a)

of weather

to be warm	hacer calor
It's very warm here in the summer.	Hace mucho calor aquí en el verano.

warmly *adv*

[affectionately]	afectuosamente/cariñosamente
[cordially]	calurosamente
[enthusiastically]	con entusiasmo

wash *v*

to wash sb/sth	lavar algo/a alguien
I must wash this shirt.	Debo lavar esta camisa.
She was washing the child's face.	Lavaba la cara al niño.
to wash (oneself)/have a wash	lavarse
I wash before breakfast.	Me lavo antes del desayuno.
She was washing her face.	Se lavaba la cara.
to wash the dishes	fregar los platos/lavar los platos [Arg & Uru]
the washing [dirty clothes]	la ropa sucia/la ropa para lavar
the washing [clean]	el tendido/la colada
a washing machine	una lavadora
a dishwasher	un lavaplatos

Ø **fregar** has obscene connotations in Argentina and Uruguay, so in those countries use **lavar** with **los platos**.

washbasin *n*

washbasin	un lavabo/un lavamanos [Bol, Ecu, Per]

waste *n & v*

It's a waste of effort.	Es un esfuerzo inútil/una pérdida de energía.
It's a waste of time.	Es tiempo perdido/una pérdida de tiempo.
[litter]	los desperdicios
Waste! *[sign on garbage cans]*	¡Desperdicios!
to waste food	desperdiciar la comida
to waste money *[to spend on unnecessary things]*	gastar dinero
[to squander money]	desperdiciar/malgastar dinero
to waste time	perder/desperdiciar el tiempo
a wastebasket	un cesto de los papeles/una papelera

watch *v*

to watch a film/TV program	ver una película/un programa
I didn't watch that program.	No vi ese programa.
to watch closely	mirar/observar/contemplar
He doesn't play; he prefers to watch.	No juega; prefiere mirar.
to watch over *[look after]*	cuidar/vigilar
I have to watch over the children.	Tengo que cuidar a los niños.
to watch over *[sick person]*	velar
Watch out!	¡Cuidado!/¡Ojo!

way *n*
road, route

You will have to ask the way.	Tendrás que preguntar por el camino.
Which is the way to the station, please?	¿Por favor, qué camino tomo para ir a la estación?
I showed them the way to the church.	Les indiqué el camino a la iglesia.
on the way to Santiago	camino de Santiago
to go out of one's way	desviarse del camino
the way in/out	la entrada/salida
"No way through"	"Cerrado el paso"
to go the wrong way	equivocarse de camino
to make one's way to	dirigirse a
She made her way to the hotel.	Se dirigió al hotel.

distance

a long way off	a gran distancia/a lo lejos/muy lejos
a short way off	a poca distancia/no muy lejos
Mérida is a long way from here.	Mérida está muy lejos de aquí.

direction

This way, please.	Por aquí, por favor.
Which way are you going?	¿Por dónde vas?
one-way *[street, road]*	dirección única/sentido único/una mano *[Arg]*/tránsito *[Chi]*/una vía *[Col]*

manner

in this/that way	la manera/el modo de esta/esa manera de este/ese modo
Do it this way!	¡Hazlo de esta manera/de este modo!
way of life	el estilo de vida
You can do it any way you like.	Puedes hacerlo de cualquier modo que te guste. *[Note: subjunctive]*

other
by the way — a propósito

we *pron*
we — nosotros *[masc]*/nosotras *[fem]*
we men — nosotros los hombres
we women — nosotras las mujeres
They have no money; we have plenty. — Ellos no tienen dinero; nosotros tenemos mucho. *[Note: **nosotros/nosotras**, like all the other subject pronouns, are usually omitted; they are used for emphasis and clarification.]*

weather *n*
What's the weather like? — ¿Qué tiempo hace?
The weather is fine/bad. — Hace buen/mal tiempo.
The weather is hot/cold. — Hace calor/frío.
a weather forecast — un parte/boletín/pronóstico meteorológico
a weather report — un boletín meteorológico

wedding *n*
a wedding — una boda/un casamiento/unas bodas
silver/golden wedding — las bodas de plata/oro
a wedding cake — una tarta/un pastel de boda
the wedding day — el día de boda
a wedding dress — un traje de novia
a wedding present — un regalo de boda
a wedding ring — un anillo de boda
to have a church/civil wedding — casarse por la iglesia/por lo civil
to have a quiet wedding — casarse en la intimidad/en privado

week *n*
a week — una semana/ocho días
two weeks — dos semanas/quince días
a week today — de hoy en ocho días
the weekend — el fin de semana

weigh *v*/**weight** *n*
to weigh — pesar
What/How much do you weigh? — ¿Cuánto pesas?
It weighs 100 kilos. — Pesa cien kilos.
to lose weight — adelgazar
to put on weight — engordar/hacerse más gordo(a)

welcome *adj*
Welcome on board! *[plane]* — ¡Bienvenidos a bordo!
Welcome to Chile! — ¡Bienvenido(a)(os)(as) a Chile!
You're always welcome here. — Estás en tu casa./Está en su casa.
You're welcome. *[response to "thank you"]* — De nada./No hay de qué.
You're welcome to use my car. — Mi coche está a tu disposición.
He's welcome to come with us. — Puede acompañarnos.

welcome *n & v*
a welcome — una bienvenida

Welcome to Tijuana *[sign]*	Bienvenida a Tijuana
to welcome sb	dar la bienvenida a alguien
[to meet]	recibir
He welcomed us at the airport.	Nos recibió en el aeropuerto.
They gave me a warm welcome.	Me dispensaron una calurosa acogida.

well *adv*
successfully

	bien
They did it very well.	Lo hicieron muy bien.
He was always well dressed.	Siempre iba bien vestido.

concessive

Well, I'm not sure.	Pues, no estoy seguro(a).
well now	ahora bien
well then	pues bien
Well?	¿Y entonces?
Well then?	¿Y qué?
Well, I'll explain.	Bueno, te lo explicaré.

health

to be well	estar bien
to feel well	sentirse bien
I'm very well.	Estoy muy bien.
to get well	reponerse

what *inter adj*

What time is it?	¿Qué hora es?
What's the weather like?	¿Qué tiempo hace?
What records did you buy?	¿Qué discos compraste?
*[see also **which**]*	

what *exclam*

What/What a(n) ... !	¡Qué...!
What a character he is!	¡Qué tipo es!
What a fool you are!	¡Qué tonto(a) eres!
What a pity!	¡Qué lástima!
What!	¡Cómo!

what *inter pron*

What happened?	¿Qué pasó/sucedió?
What do you want?	¿Qué quieres?
What are you thinking about?	¿En qué piensas?
What did you dream about?	¿Con qué soñaste?
What are you afraid of?	¿De qué tienes miedo?
What else?	¿Qué más?
What is it?/What's this?	¿Qué es?/¿Qué es esto?
What are they?	¿Qué son?
What's it made of?	¿De qué es?
What is it like?	¿Cómo es?
What is your name?	¿Cómo te llamas?/¿Cómo se llama?
What? *[I beg your pardon.]*	¿Cómo?
Do you know what happened?	¿Sabes qué/lo que pasó?
Don't you know what he said?	¿No sabes qué/lo que dijo?

What is/are ... ?

What is your address?	¿Cuál es tu/su dirección?/¿Cuáles son tus/sus señas?

What is your address here in Quito?	¿Cuál es tu/su domicilio aquí en Quito?
What is your phone number?	¿Cuál es tu/su número de teléfono?
What is your first name?	¿Cuál es tu/su nombre de pila?
What is your surname?	¿Cuál es tu/su apellido?
What are your favorite films?	¿Cuáles son tus/sus películas preferidas?

what   *rel pron*
[that which]

	lo que
That's not what I want.	Eso no es lo que quiero.
What I like most is chess.	Lo que me gusta más es el ajedrez.

whatever   *adj*

whatever	cualquier *[sing]*/cualesquier *[pl]*
I'll wear whatever clothes I like.	Voy a ponerme cualquier ropa que me guste. *[Note: subjunctive]*
He'll pay for whatever books I need.	Pagará cualesquier libros que necesite. *[Note: subjunctive]*

whatever   *pron*

Do whatever you like!	¡Haz todo lo que quieras!
Whatever it may be.	Sea lo que sea.
Whatever happens.	Pase lo que pase.
Whatever he says.	Diga lo que diga.
Whatever you see.	Cualquier cosa que veas.
	[Note: subjunctive in the above examples]
Whatever I have is yours.	Todo lo que tengo es tuyo.

when   *adv & conj*

when	cuando
When it's sunny I go to the beach.	Cuando hace sol voy a la playa.
I'll go to bed when I'm tired.	Me acostaré cuando tenga sueño. *[Note: use of subjunctive when future time is referred to]*
When will you buy a new car?	¿Cuándo comprarás un coche nuevo? *[Note: accent on **cuándo** when it is a question]*
I asked him when he would go.	Le pregunté cuándo iría.

whenever   *adv & conj*

Come whenever you like.	Ven cuando quieras. *[Note: subjunctive]*
Whenever that may be.	Cuando quiera que sea. *[Note: subjunctive]*
I visit them whenever I can.	Les visito cuando puedo.
Whenever he visited us he used to give me candy.	Cuando nos visitaba me daba caramelos.

where *adv*
interrogative

	¿dónde?
Where are you?	¿Dónde estás?
Where are you going?	¿Adónde vas?
Where are you from?	¿De dónde eres?
Where does the bus leave from?	¿De dónde sale el autobús?

wherever

relative

I go where I like.	Voy donde quiera. *[Note: subjunctive]*
That's the house where my father was born.	Ésa es la casa donde nació mi padre.

Ø Note the accent on **dónde** as an interrogative.

wherever *adv*

Wherever I go my dog comes with me.	Dondequiera que vaya mi perro me acompaña. *[Note: subjunctive]*
Wherever they are you must find them.	Dondequiera que estén debes encontrarlos. *[Note: subjunctive]*

whether *conj*

I asked him whether he could help us.	Le pregunté si podría ayudarnos.
Do you know whether the bus has left yet?	¿Sabes si el autobús ya ha salido?
I doubt whether she speaks Russian.	Dudo que hable ruso. *[Note: subjunctive after **dudar que**]*

which *inter adj*

Which newspaper do you want?	¿Qué periódico quieres?
Which shoes did you buy?	¿Qué zapatos compraste?
*[see also **what**]*	

which (one) *inter pron*

which one/which ones	cuál/cuáles
Which one do you prefer?	¿Cuál prefieres?
Which ones did you sell?	¿Cuáles vendiste?

which *rel pron*

	que *[subject and object]* lo que *[neuter]*
The cat which killed the bird is mine.	El gato que mató al pájaro es mío.
The car (which) he drives is Italian.	El coche que conduce es italiano.
He went to visit his aunt, which pleased her greatly.	Fue a visitar a su tía, lo que le gustó muchísimo.
[with prepositions]	que/el cual/la cual/los cuales/las cuales/el que/la que/los que/las que
Those are the shops I was thinking about.	Ésas son las tiendas en las que pensaba.

Ø Although the pronoun "which" is frequently omitted in English, you may not omit **que, el cual, la cual, los cuales, las cuales, el que, la que, los que, las que** in Spanish.
Ø Most English speakers make little or no distinction between "that" and "which." Fortunately the Spanish forms cover both.
See also **that** *[rel pron]*.

whichever *adj & pron*

You can have whichever hat you like.	Puedes tener cualquier sombrero que te guste. *[Note: subjunctive]*
Give her whichever of the books she wants.	Dale cualquier de los libros que quiera. *[Note: subjunctive]*

while *conj*
time

While I was in Spain, my dog died.

I'll do it while you are at the office.

mientras

Mientras estaba en España, murió el perro.

Lo haré mientras estés en la oficina. *[Note: subjunctive when future is referred to]*

whereas

She is studying French while her brother is studying physics.

mientras (que)

Ella estudia el francés mientras (que) su hermano estudia física.

concessive
[although]

While I think it is difficult I insist you do it.

aunque

Aunque pienso que es difícil, insisto en que lo hagas.

who/whom *inter pron*

Who?

Whom?

Who told you that?

Who are coming to the party?

Who(m) did you see?

Who(m) was he talking about?

¿Quién? *[sing]* ¿Quiénes? *[pl]*

¿A quién *[sing]* ¿A quiénes? *[pl]*

¿Quién te lo dijo eso?

¿Quiénes vienen a la fiesta?

¿A quién(es) viste?

¿De quién(es) hablaba?

who/whom *rel pron*

que *[subject]*

a quien/a quienes *[object]*

the man who was here yesterday

the man (whom) I saw

the women (whom) she met

[after a preposition]

the man (whom) you were afraid of

the actress (whom) I was thinking of

el hombre que estaba aquí ayer

el hombre a quien vi

las mujeres a quienes encontró

quien/quienes

el hombre de quien tenías miedo

la actriz en quien pensaba

Ø Although "whom" may be omitted in English, the Spanish equivalent cannot be.

he/she/those who

he/she who

He/she who wants to can go in.

el que/la que

El/la que quiera puede entrar.
[Note: Subjunctive is used if the reference is to an indefinite person or persons.]

those who

Those who have arrived early will receive a prize.

los que/las que

Los/las que han llegado temprano recibirán un premio.

whoever/whomever *pron*

Whoever he/she is

Whoever finds them can keep them.

Quienquiera que sea *[Note: subjunctive]*

Quienquiera que los encuentre puede quedarse con ellos.
[Note: subjunctive]

You can tell who(m)ever you like.

Whoever told you is lying.

Puedes decírtelo a cualquiera.

Quien/El que te lo dijo dice mentiras.

whole *adj & pron*

the whole world

Tell me the whole truth.

el mundo entero

Dime toda la verdad.

whose

I toured the whole of Caracas.	Recorrí todo Caracas.
They heard the whole thing.	Lo oyeron todo.
We bought the whole lot.	Compramos todo.

Ø **todo el mundo** means "everybody."

whose   *inter adj & pron*
Whose ... ?	¿De quién/quiénes... ?
Whose is this knife?	¿De quién es este cuchillo?
Whose money is this?	¿De quién es este dinero?

whose   *rel pron*
whose	cuyo(a)/cuyos(as)
the man whose son is in prison	el hombre cuyo hijo está en la cárcel
the man whose wife is ill	el hombre cuya esposa está enferma
the tourists whose cases were lost	los turistas cuyas maletas se perdieron
the ladies whose husbands are away	las señoras cuyos esposos están fuera

why   *adv & conj*
Why did you do that?	¿Por qué lo hiciste?
I don't know why she left.	No sé por qué se marchó.
That's why I cannot pay you.	Por eso no puedo pagarte./Ésa es la razón por la que no puedo pagarte. *[Note: not por qué]*

wife   *n*
wife	la esposa/la mujer *[Sp]*

willing   *adj*
to be willing	querer/querer hacerlo/estar dispuesto(a)
Are they willing to help her?	¿Quieren ayudarla?/¿Están dispuestos(as) a ayudarla?
No, they're not willing.	No, no quieren.

window   *n*
a window	una ventana
a shop window	una vidriera *[LA]*/una luna *[Per]* /un escaparate *[Sp]*
[of a car]	una ventanilla

wish   *n & v*
a wish	un deseo
to make a wish	pensar un deseo
to wish sb a happy birthday/ a happy Christmas/a happy new year/a good journey	desear a alguien un feliz cumpleaños/ unas felices Pascuas/un feliz año nuevo/un buen viaje

to want
I wish to see the manager.	Deseo/Quiero ver al gerente.
I wish I were there.	Ojalá estuviera allí.
I wish you could come.	Ojalá pudieras venir. *[Note: use of imperfect subjunctive after ojalá]*

with   *prep*
in general   con

with me/you	conmigo/contigo
with him(self)/her(self)	consigo
*[see under **him** and **her**]*	
with you(rself)/you(rselves)	consigo
*[see under **you**]*	
[with "no"]	sin
with no difficulty	sin dificultad

other

the man with the beard	el hombre de la barba
You cannot enter the mosque with your shoes on.	No puedes entrar en la mezquita llevando puestos los zapatos.
with all speed	a toda prisa
with a single blow	de un solo golpe
to be covered with mud/snow	estar cubierto(a) de lodo/nieve
to be filled with water	estar lleno(a) de agua
to be in love with sb	estar enamorado(a) de alguien
to be pleased/satisfied with sth	estar contento(a)/satisfecho(a) de
It's pouring with rain.	Está lloviendo a cántaros.
to jump with joy	saltar de alegría
to tremble with fear	temblar de miedo
to be "with it"	estar al tanto/estar al día
to be "with it" *[clothes]*	estar de moda

within *prep*

within the city	dentro de la ciudad
within a radius of five miles	en un radio de ocho kilómetros
within 20 meters of the camp	a unos veinte metros del campamento
within a week	dentro de una semana/antes de terminar la semana

without *prep*

without	sin
without a car/any money	sin coche/dinero *[Note: no article]*
without any problems	sin problema

word *n*

[in general]	la palabra
word for word	palabra por palabra
words of a song	la letra
in other words	en otros términos/es decir
without a word	sin decir palabra
What is the word for ... in Spanish?	¿Cómo se dice... en castellano?

work *n*

[task to be done]	el trabajo
I have a lot of work to do.	Tengo mucho trabajo que hacer.
[employment, job]	el trabajo/el empleo/la ocupación
I don't like my work.	No me gusta mi trabajo.
to be at work	estar en la oficina/la fábrica/la tienda, etc.
to have work	tener trabajo/un empleo
to be out of work	estar desempleado(a)/estar parado(a)/no tener trabajo
a work permit	un permiso de trabajo
[art/literary/music]	una obra

work

the works of Cervantes	las obras de Cervantes
roadworks	las obras de carretera
[see also job]	

work *v*
people

	trabajar
My brother works nights.	Mi hermano trabaja de noche.
to work the land	cultivar la tierra

things

The elevator doesn't work.	El ascensor no funciona.

worker *n*
[general]

	un(a) trabajador(a)
He's a hard worker.	Es muy trabajador.
the workers *[political]*	los obreros
manual/blue-collar worker	un(a) obrero(a)
a skilled worker	un(a) obrero(a) cualificado(a)
clerical/white-collar/shop worker	un(a) empleado(a)

worn out *adj*
[things]

	gastado(a)/estropeado(a)
His boots are worn out.	Sus botas están estropeadas.
[people]	agotado(a)/rendido(a)
I'm worn out.	Estoy rendido(a)./No puedo más.

worry *v*

to worry	preocuparse por/inquietarse por
Don't worry about that!	¡No te preocupes por eso!
She is very worried about her exams.	Está muy preocupada por sus exámenes.
This problem is worrying me.	Este problema me inquieta.

worse/worst *adj*

worse	peor
the worst	el/la peor
The red one is worse than the white.	El rojo es peor que el blanco.
The green is the worst.	El verde es el peor.
This is the worst film I've seen.	Ésta es la peor película que haya visto. *[Note: subjunctive]*
the worst thing is	lo peor es

worse/worst *adv*

I play worse than my sister.	Juego peor que mi hermana.
My brother plays the worst.	Mi hermano juega peor./Es mi hermano que juega peor.
How do you feel now? – Worse.	¿Cómo te sientes ahora? – Peor.

worth *adj*

to be worth	valer
How much is it worth?	¿Cuánto vale?
It isn't worth anything.	No vale nada.
Is it worth studying Latin?	¿Vale la pena estudiar el latín?
It isn't worth it/the trouble.	No vale la pena.

would *v*
conditional
[conditional and imperfect subjunctive tenses]

My father said he would do it.	Mi padre dijo que lo haría.

242

I would like to go to the Philippines.	Querría/Quisiera ir a las Filipinas. *[Note: The imperfect subjunctive can be used instead of the conditional tense; this is especially the case with **querer**.]*
I would do it if I could.	Lo haría si pudiera. *[Note: Imperfect subjunctive is used after **si** in unfulfilled conditions.]*
I would have done it if I could.	Lo habría hecho si hubiera podido.

habitual action in the past
[imperfect tense]

When I was in New York I would go to the theater every week.	Cuando estaba en Nueva York iba al teatro todas las semanas.

polite requests

I would like to reserve a table, please.	Quisiera reservar una mesa, por favor.
I would like a coffee, please.	Me gustaría tomar un café, por favor.

wrong   *adj & adv*
morally wrong

It's wrong to kill.	malo(a)
He was wrong to do that.	Matar es un crimen.
[unfair]	Hizo mal en hacer eso.
	injusto(a)

incorrect or mistaken

to be wrong	equivocarse/estar equivocado(a)/ no tener razón
You're wrong. *[making a mistake]*	Te equivocas.
You're wrong. *[made a mistake]*	Te has equivocado./Estás equivocado(a).
to get sth wrong	equivocarse de algo
I took the wrong way.	Me equivoqué de camino.
She went to the wrong office.	Se equivocó de oficina.
You're doing it wrong.	No se hace así.
The answer is wrong.	La respuesta es incorrecta/inexacta.

trouble

Is something wrong?	¿Pasa algo?
What's wrong with you?	¿Qué te pasa?
to be wrong *[machinery]*	no andar bien
Something's wrong with my watch.	Mi reloj no anda bien.
to go wrong *[machinery]*	andar fallando
It's been going wrong for days.	Hace unos días que anda fallando.

X

x-ray *n*
X-rays	los rayos X
an X-ray	una radiografía
to X-ray	radiografiar

Y

year   n

a year	un año
twice a year	dos veces al año
last year	el año pasado
next year [in present time]	el año que viene
next year [in past time]	el año siguiente
He's five years old.	Tiene cinco años.
for (many) years	durante (muchos) años
Happy New Year!	¡Feliz Año Nuevo!
New Year's Day	el día del Año Nuevo
New Year's Eve	la noche vieja
the fiscal/school year	el año económico/escolar

yellow   adj

[color]	amarillo(a)
[coward]	(un) cobarde

yet   adv & conj

time

	todavía/aún
not yet	todavía no
It hasn't started yet.	Todavía no ha comenzado.
yet again	otra vez más

however

	sin embargo
He was tired, yet he couldn't sleep.	Estaba cansado; sin embargo no podía dormir.

you   pron

subject

[familiar singular]	tú
	vos [mainly Argentina & Uruguay]
[familiar plural]	vosotros/vosotras [Spain only]
	ustedes (Uds.)
[formal singular]	usted (Ud.)
[formal plural]	ustedes (Uds.)
	[Note: like the other subject pronouns, all the above are usually omitted; they are used for emphasis and clarification.]
Is that you?	¿Eres tú?/¿Sos vos?/¿Es usted?/ ¿Son ustedes?/¿Sois vosotros(as)?

object

[familiar singular]	te [direct & indirect; also used in Argentina, Uruguay and Costa Rica for people addressed as **vos**.]
[familiar plural]	os [Spain only]
	los/las [direct] les [indirect]
[formal singular]	lo/la [direct]
	le [indirect]

your

[formal plural]	los/las *[direct]*
	les *[indirect]*
I can't hear you.	No te/lo/la/los/las/os oigo.

disjunctive

[familiar singular]	ti
	vos *[mainly Argentina & Uruguay]*
[familiar plural]	vosotros/vosotras *[Spain only]*
	ustedes (Uds.)
[formal singular]	usted (Ud.)
[formal plural]	ustedes (Uds.)
This is for you.	Esto es para ti/vos/usted/ustedes /vosotros(as).

reflexive

[familiar singular]	te
	vos *[mainly Argentina & Uruguay]*
[familiar plural]	os *[Spain only]*
	se
[formal singular & plural]	se
At what time do you get up?	¿A qué hora te levantas/se levanta(n)/os levantáis?

your *adj*

[familiar singular]	tu/tus *[also used when addressing people with **vos**.]*
[familiar plural]	vuestro/s, vuestra/s *[Spain only]*
	su/sus
[formal singular & plural]	su/sus
your house	tu/su/vuestra casa
your parents	tus/sus/vuestros padres

yours *pron*

[familiar singular]	el tuyo/la tuya
	los tuyos/las tuyas
[familiar plural]	el vuestro/la vuestra
	los vuestros/las vuestras *[Spain only]*
	el suyo/la suya
	los suyos/las suyas
[formal singular & plural]	el suyo/la suya
	los suyos/las suyas
Is that his luggage? – it's yours.	No, ¿Es ése su equipaje? – No, es tuyo/suyo/vuestro. *[Note: The definite article is omitted after the verb **ser**.]*
I can't find my keys. Will you lend me yours?	No encuentro mis llaves. ¿Quieres prestarme las tuyas?/¿Quiere(n) prestarme las suyas?

Ø As **suyo/a/os/as** could also mean "his," "hers," or "theirs," you can replace them with **de usted/de ustedes** if there is any chance of confusion: e.g., "It's yours". **Es de usted/de ustedes.**

yours sincerely
in a business letter

Le saluda atentamente/Atentamente /Su seguro servidor

in a personal letter	Cordialmente/Con un cordial saludo/Un abrazo

youth   *n*
[stage of one's life]	la juventud
[young person]	el/la joven
youth hostel	un albergue de juventud

yucky   *adj*
yucky	asqueroso(a)

Z

zip *n*
zip code   el código postal

zipper *n*
a zipper   un cierre/una cremallera

zoom *n & v*
[noise]   un zumbido
[lens]   un objetivo zoom
to zoom by   pasar volando